95021 760

0687

# NEW CENTURY BIBLE

*General Editors*

## RONALD E. CLEMENTS

M.A., B.D., PH.D. (Old Testament)

## MATTHEW BLACK

D.D., D.LITT., F.B.A. (New Testament)

# I Peter

# NEW CENTURY BIBLE

*Based on the Revised Standard Version*

# I Peter

*Edited by*

## ERNEST BEST

**M.A., B.D., Ph.D.**

*Professor of Biblical Criticism,*
*University of Glasgow*

the Attic Press, Inc.

GREENWOOD, S. C.

OLIPHANTS

MARSHALL, MORGAN & SCOTT
I BATH STREET
ECIV 9LB

© Marshall, Morgan & Scott 1971
Reprinted 1977

ISBN 0 551 00610 2
Made and printed in Great Britain by
Butler & Tanner Ltd, Frome and London
771013/L20

# CONTENTS

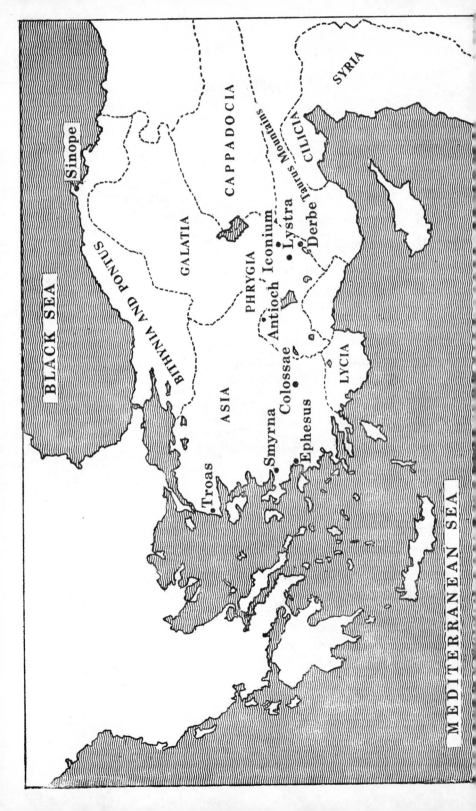

# PREFACE

Within the past twenty years several important commentaries on 1 Peter have appeared, notably those of Selwyn, Beare, Schelkle, Spicq, and Preisker's edition of Windisch; the primitive Christian oral tradition has also been closely investigated. All this has contributed to a better understanding of 1 Peter. I acknowledge my vast debt to all this scholarship but in view of the purpose of the present series of commentaries I have not thought it necessary to compile lists of those scholars who accept or reject each possible interpretation of the text; such lists would only serve as a hindrance to those who do not know their way around the field of New Testament scholarship, and those who do, know where to obtain these lists from the major commentaries. I have also sought to avoid unnecessary reference to literature in languages other than English. The commentary of J. N. D. Kelly (*The Epistles of Peter and Jude*, London, 1969) unfortunately appeared after my manuscript had gone to the publisher and I was unable to profit from his many insights. It will be seen that on many questions of introduction we are not far apart, though I would have greater doubts as to Petrine authorship.

My thanks are due to Principal M. Black for the invitation to write this volume, to Professor R. McL. Wilson for many helpful suggestions, to my wife who assisted with typing and proof-reading, to Mr David R. Drain and the Reverend Earl S. Johnson for proof-reading, and to the Research Fund of the Faculties of Arts and Divinity in the University of St Andrews for a grant towards the cost of the final typing of the manuscript.

# ABBREVIATIONS

| | |
|---|---|
| RV | Revised Version |
| RSV | Revised Standard Version |
| S.B.T. | Studies in Biblical Theology |
| *T.D.N.T.* | *Theological Dictionary of the New Testament* (a translation by G. W. Bromiley of *T.W.N.T.*) |
| *T.W.N.T.* | *Theologisches Wörterbuch zum Neuen Testament* (ed. G. Kittel and G. Friedrich) |
| *Z.N.W.* | *Zeitschrift für die neutestamentliche Wissenschaft* |
| CD | The Damascus Rule |
| IQH | The Hymns |
| IQM | The War Rule |
| IQpHab. | Commentary on Habakkuk |
| IQpNah. | Commentary on Nahum |
| IQS | The Community Rule |
| IQSa | The Messianic Rule |
| 4QFlor. | A Midrash on the Last Days |
| 4QpIsa[d] | Commentary on Isaiah |

(English titles as in G. Vermes,
*The Dead Sea Scrolls in English*, London, 1962)

(For the names of commentators see Bibliography)

# BIBLIOGRAPHY

Beare, F.W.,     *The First Epistle of Peter* (2nd edn.) Oxford, 1958.

Bennett, W.H.,     *The General Epistles* (Century Bible) Edinburgh, 1901.

Bigg, C.,     *St. Peter and St. Jude* (I.C.C.) (2nd edn.) Edinburgh, 1910.

Boismard, M.-E.,     *Quatre Hymnes baptismales dans la première Épître de Pierre* (Lectio Divina 30) Paris, 1961.

Cranfield, C.E.B.,     *I and II Peter and Jude* (Torch) London, 1960.

Guthrie, D.,     *New Testament Introduction: Hebrews to Revelation* (2nd edn.) London, 1964

Hart, J.H.A.,     *The First Epistle General of Peter* (The Expositor's Greek Testament V) London, n.d.

Hort, F.J.A.,     *The First Epistle of St. Peter (I.1–II.17)* London, 1898.

Knopf, R.,     *Die Briefe Petri und Judä* (Meyer 7th edn.) Göttingen, 1912.

Leaney, A.R.C.,     *The Letters of Peter and Jude* (Cambridge Bible Commentary) Cambridge, 1967.

Moffatt, J.,     *The General Epistles: Peter, James and Judas* (Moffatt) London, 1928.

Preisker  —  see Windisch.

Reicke, Bo,     *The Epistles of James, Peter and Jude* (Anchor) New York, 1964.

Schelkle, K.H.,     *Die Petrusbriefe: Der Judasbrief* (Herders Theologischer Kommentar zum NT) Freiburg-Basel-Wien, 1964 (2nd edition).

Schlatter, A.,     *Die Briefe des Petrus, Judas, Jakobus. Der Brief an die Hebräer* (Erläuterungen zum NT) Stuttgart, 1950.

Schneider, J.,     *Die Kirchenbriefe* (Das NT Deutsch) 9th edn. Göttingen, 1961.

Schweizer, E.,     *Der erste Petrusbrief* (Zurcher BibelKommentare) 2nd edn. Zürich 1949.

Selwyn, E.G.,     *The First Epistle of St. Peter* London, 1946.

Soden, H. von,     *Die Briefe des Petrus, Jakobus, Judas* (Hand-Commentar zum NT) 2nd edn. Freiburg and Leipzig 1893.

Spicq, C.,     *Les Épitres de Saint Pierre* (Sources Bibliques) Paris 1966.

Stibbs  —  see Walls

Walls, A.F. and Stibbs, A.M.,     *The First Epistle General of Peter* (Tyndale) London, 1959.

Wand, J.W.C.,     *The General Epistles of St. Peter and St. Jude* (Westminster) London, 1934.

Windisch, H.,     *Die Katholischen Briefe* (Handbuch zum NT) 3rd edn. by H. Preisker, Tübingen, 1951.

Wohlenberg, G.,     *Der erste und zweite Petrusbrief und der Judasbrief* (Kommentar zum NT) 2nd edn. Leipzig, 1915.

# INTRODUCTION
## to
## I Peter

# I. PURPOSE OF THE LETTER

1 Peter is a genuine letter, not a sermon or essay, written in the manner of the ancient world (see on 1:1f; 5:12–14); but there are many kinds of letters ranging all the way from the extremely personal writings of two good friends to the epistle designed for publication. The more intimate and personal the letter the greater will be the detail which specially refers to the sender and recipients; 1 Peter is not of this type; the letters of Paul approximate more nearly to it. 1 Peter is addressed to a wide circle of Gentile readers (see pp. 19f) spread over a large area (see pp. 3f); it was therefore impossible for the writer either to greet individuals by name or to refer to the difficulties peculiar to any one Christian community; like a bishop writing to the churches of his diocese he can only deal with the most general of problems, and even these only in a very general way. But though the letter is of such a nature there are many points which remain obscure to us in it; the condition of the church and the world in the first century was something writer and readers knew fully and casual references would be picked up easily by them while we are left in doubt. This is one factor which makes interpretation difficult.

At the conclusion the writer tells us his aim: he has written briefly 'exhorting and declaring that this is the true grace of God' in which his readers are to 'stand fast' (5:12). They know this grace manifested in the new life which they enjoy through the resurrection of Jesus Christ (1:3–5), in the ransom that was paid for them in his death (1:18–21), in the life they experience as members of God's people (2:4–10), in the example of Jesus in his sufferings (2:21–5), in the forgiveness of sins in baptism (3:18–22), in gifts of ministry to the church (4:10f). This same grace of God enables them to purify their lives as citizens (2:13–17), as servants or slaves (2:18–25), as wives (3:1–6), as husbands (3:7), as officials in the church (5:2–5); by it they are able to maintain good conduct among the Gentiles (2:12) and live by the will of God (4:2). So they ought to stand fast in that grace. This they require to do all the more because they are in the last times; the end is shortly about to break upon them (4:7, 17); a sign of the closeness of the end is the persecution and suffering which they have already suffered in part (1:6; 3:13–17), which they endure even as he writes and will have to endure to an even greater degree (4:12–19). Only God's grace can carry them through to full salvation. The background of the letter is thus persecution viewed from an eschatological perspective, and their suffering is counter-balanced by the emphasis on (a) the position of the believer as newborn (1:3, 23; 2:2) and a member of the people of God (2:4–10) and (b) the hope they have in God which will sustain them (1:3, 13, 21).

We do not know how well author and readers were acquainted; the very nature of the writing as a circular letter excludes personal references so that even if the writer had worked previously as an evangelist or pastor in the area to which he writes this would be hidden from us; 1:12 does imply that he was not one of the original missionaries of the area.

So far we have only spoken of the author. A number of inter-locking questions are raised by this. How far is the Apostle Peter to be identified with the letter? How far is already existing material used in its composition? Is it really a letter at all, or a sermon, or part of a liturgy to which an epistolary beginning and ending have been added? To whom was it written? Had the recipients just recently become Christians or was their faith of longer standing? We require to examine these and related questions in detail before proceeding to the exposition of the letter.

## II. THE RECIPIENTS

### a. GEOGRAPHICAL AREA

The letter is addressed to the Christians in Pontus, Galatia, Cappadocia, Asia, and Bithynia (1:1). Where are these places? It might seem that a glance at a map (p. 6) would provide a quick answer; but geographical names are not always attached to the same precise area, e.g., consider how much the area termed Poland has varied in the last two centuries. The names in 1:1 could be either those of the Roman provinces which were so termed at the time when the letter was written or those of the older nations out of which the Romans created their provincial system. If the former the area would largely coincide with that

part of Asia Minor which lies to the north and west of the Taurus
mountains (so Hort, Sir William Ramsay, Beare, Schelkle, etc.);
if the latter it would consist of an area which did not extend so far
south and east (so Selwyn, Guthrie, etc.), in particular it would
not include the churches recorded as evangelised by Paul in
Ac. 13, 14 and those to which he wrote Galatians (if they were
written to the same churches). In favour of the conclusion that the
names are not those of Roman provinces we may argue:

(1) There is no mention in the letter of the work of Paul as
founder of any of the churches of the area. This argument is
however only true if we take Asia as meaning the north-western
part of the area, for Paul definitely worked in some parts of Asia,
e.g. Ephesus.

(2) Pontus and Bithynia at this stage formed one Roman province;
yet they are mentioned separately in the present list, and not
even adjacently: therefore the Roman provinces cannot be
intended.

In favour of the conclusion that the names are those of the Roman
provinces we may argue:

(1) It would be more natural to use the names as designations of
provinces since this was the officially prevailing usage.

(2) Taken together they form a natural area, which cannot be
said for the alternative hypothesis. The southern coastal areas of
Asia Minor are not mentioned because they had their natural
connections with the south and east.

(3) If they are the older district names then the large central area
of Phrygia is omitted, and it would be difficult to get from Galatia
to the cities of Western Asia without passing through this area.
These arguments indicate that it is preferable to accept the names
as indicating the Roman provinces; but even if we accept the
other hypothesis we cannot argue that the area of the recipients
does not include an area where Paul founded churches.

b. THE ORDER OF THE NAMES IN 1:1

Why are the areas named in the order in which they appear?
Hort (pp. 157–84), accepting an earlier suggestion of Ewald,
argued in great detail that they are in the natural order in which
they would be visited by a messenger sent with the letter and
landing at Sinope in Pontus and moving in a clockwise direction.
But why should anyone begin at Sinope (or at any other point in
Pontus)? If the letter had been sent from Babylon (5:13) in

Mesopotamia the messenger would have been bound to pass through Cappadocia or Galatia to reach Pontus. However it is very probable that Babylon is actually Rome (see notes on 5:13) and it may be that the messenger sailed into the Black Sea from Rome and disembarked at Sinope. But there were more natural places to land in Western Asia on a voyage from Rome and begin the journey; there is moreover no need to begin and end the journey at the same point (as if the messenger had obtained a return ticket to Sinope at excursion rates). Bigg (pp. 69f, 74f) argued that the Christians of Pontus were commencing a new mission and had asked for Peter's guidance; so they were first in Peter's thought and the messenger began with them; this is pure hypothesis since we know nothing of a mission in Pontus and cannot read it out of the letter. Beare (pp. 23f) has suggested that Pontus and Bithynia were the areas which were feeling persecution more than the others and so they are mentioned first and last, the two positions of importance; this depends on: (1) Beare's late dating of the epistle in the time of Trajan when Pliny certainly reports persecution in Pontus and Bithynia; (2) the assumption that since we have no reports of persecution in the others there was little or none in them; this is an unwarranted assumption, for it is pure chance that we have Pliny's report on Pontus and Bithynia (cf. pp. 40f).

But is there any reason to attach great significance to the order of the names? If it was a period of persecution a messenger would probably be unable to plan his itinerary in advance, least of all to plan it in an area so remote as Rome was from that in which he would be travelling; his movements would depend on local circumstances. In any case, was only a single copy of the letter sent? In a period of persecution this might easily have fallen into the wrong hands and been destroyed before the whole area had been visited (cf. Beare, p. 23). Probably we shall never know the answer concerning the question of the order of the names.

C. THE SOCIOLOGICAL AND RELIGIOUS BACKGROUND

The area in which the recipients lived was by no means homogeneous. The cities of the coast in the provinces of Asia, Pontus and Bithynia were completely hellenized but as one moved further inland the degree of hellenization decreased; it had hardly penetrated into most of the areas of Galatia (apart from the south of the area mentioned in Ac. 13:14) and practically not at all into Cappadocia; the native languages were still in use and native customs prevailed.

It was in Asia Minor that the cult of the Roman Emperor had begun and was officially demanded of all citizens with the exception of Jews. This was one factor in a very diverse religious situation. Respect was still paid to the traditional gods and goddesses of mythology in the official religious life of cities and states. In personal life the philosophical cults of Stoicism and Epicureanism competed with the newer Mystery Cults and in the hinterland native orgiastic religions still flourished. There were Jewish colonies in most of the large cities which drew some proselytes and a greater number who committed themselves to the moral tenets of Judaism though rejecting its ceremonial and ritual demands.

Socially there were great extremes of riches and poverty. In the rural areas almost feudal conditions prevailed in which the large estates were worked by vast gangs of slaves. In the cities there was a measure of industrialisation with individual small businesses. Large numbers of slaves were employed in these and in the households of the wealthier citizens; these slaves were often well educated or skilled in a trade. On the whole in this period Christianity was found largely in the cities, an urban phenomenon. From the letter we learn a little about the composition of the churches. Slaves are addressed in 2:18–25, but there is no direct ethical instruction of masters; we dare not assume there were no masters in the congregations since 2:13–17 is directed to free men who may possibly have had civic duties; moreover what is said about wives in 3:1–6 suggests that some at any rate were wealthy. The churches must therefore have contained a cross-representation of society as a whole, with exceptions, e.g. the army, the administrative classes. (See further, D. C. Pellett, 'Asia', *I.D.B.* I, pp. 257ff).

## d. THE EVANGELISATION OF THE AREA

At what period were these areas evangelised? How long have those addressed been Christians? According to the account of Pentecost (Ac. 2) there were men from Cappadocia, Pontus, Asia, Phrygia present to hear Peter's sermon and it has been argued that these took back the Gospel to their own areas (so Wand, Selwyn, etc.). The evidence is very doubtful, for: (i) Those who heard Peter, although they are said to have come from these areas, were at that time domiciled in Jerusalem; they were not

temporary pilgrims (Ac. 2:5); (ii) The whole list of Ac. 2:9–11
is an artificial construction and cannot be regarded as a list of
those who were actually present (cf. C. S. C. Williams, *The Acts of
the Apostles*, London, 1964, *ad. loc.*). It may be that by the time
Luke composed this section of Acts there were Christians in all the
areas which he mentions, and this is why he refers to them.

Ac. 13,14 and Paul's letter to the Galations suggest that
Galatia was the first of these areas to be evangelised. A few years
later Paul was preaching the Gospel in Ephesus in Asia and was
the first missionary there. If Colossians is by Paul then the church
had spread there during his lifetime, though through the efforts of
others than himself; it must in any case have expanded through
the area as Christians either deliberately went as missionaries to
new towns or as their work took them there. In 1 Cor. 16:19 Paul
speaks of the churches of Asia in the plural and in 2 Cor. 2:12 of
his own preaching in Troas (cf. Ac. 20:5ff). By the date of the
writing of Revelation the church is well established in Asia; the
letters to the seven churches (Rev. 2,3) indicate the width of its
expansion. The final form of Revelation probably dates from the
end of Domitian's reign (96 A.D.) but the letters might be earlier.

Our best evidence for the existence of the Church in Bithynia
and Pontus comes, curiously, not from Christian sources but from
secular. Pliny, who was Governor of the area, writing to the
Emperor Trajan in 112 A.D., describes the impact of the new
faith; some had been Christians and abandoned their faith as
long as twenty-five years before; the church had spread beyond
the cities into the villages and rural districts (*Epistles*, X, 96).
Twenty-five years brings us back prior to 90 A.D., and probably
earlier, for those who had given up their Christianity must have
been Christians for at least a short period. It is possible that
Christians were already active in the area as early as 50 A.D.;
Ac. 16:7 narrates how Paul turned away from this area, an
action which Luke attributes to the instruction of the Holy Spirit;
behind this may lie Paul's known unwillingness (Rom. 15:20) to
preach where the church already existed.

Of Christianity in Cappadocia nothing is known until long
after the period in which we are interested (on the foundation and
spread of the church in all these areas see J. Weiss, *Earliest
Christianity*, New York, 1959, II, pp. 774ff; F. V. Filson, *A New
Testament History*, London, 1965, pp. 308ff).

Does 1 Peter itself provide any evidence of the length of time its

readers had been Christian? It could be argued that at least part
of the letter (1:3–4:11) was written to new converts and intended
for them at their baptism (see pp. 21ff); this is doubtful, but even
if it were true it would not give any indication as to the length of
time the churches had existed. Those addressed have been
Christians long enough to have been gathered into regular
congregations with ministers (5:2–5); the kiss of peace is a
recognized liturgical action (see notes on 5:14); the sacrament of
baptism is known to them well enough for arguments to be based
on it (3:21). The evidence could imply a period of existence
lasting anything from two or three years to a couple of generations.

### e. JEWISH OR GENTILE CHRISTIANS?

The majority of members of these congregations were of Gentile
origin, though a superficial glance at the letter might suggest that
the author had Jewish Christians in mind. From the time of
Origen many of the Church Fathers held the latter view, but the
unanimous opinion of scholars today rejects it. 'The Dispersion'
(1:1) was a phrase used by Jews for those of their number who
lived outside Palestine and therefore might indicate Jews in
Pontus, etc.; but the letter clearly shows that the homeland of the
readers is not Palestine but the heavenly kingdom (1:4; 3:21f;
5:10 etc.). In 2:4–10 many OT terms are applied to the readers,
but the early Christian tradition regarded the church as the
people of God and used OT terms to describe it (see notes on
2:4—10). The writer certainly uses the OT widely in his letter but
Paul did this also and he wrote to Gentile churches. Peter 'had
been entrusted with the gospel to the circumcised' (Gal. 2:7) and
therefore we might expect him to write to Jewish Christians only;
but Peter may not have been the author (see pp. 49ff) and even if
he was this need not have prevented him writing to Gentile
Christians; Paul, whose special responsibility was the latter
(Gal. 2:7), was accustomed to begin his mission work in each
town by preaching in the Jewish synagogue (Ac. 13:5,14; 14:1;
16:13; etc.).

   Apart from these negative arguments there are many positive
indications in the letter that its writer had Gentile Christians in
mind. References to their way of life before they had become
Christians show that they were not Jews. The manner of life of
Jews would never have been described as 'futile ways inherited
from your fathers' (1:18; cf. 1:14; 4:3), for the OT which set out

these ways was still authoritative for Christians. In 2:10 the readers are described as once having been 'no people', i.e. outside God's people, and therefore Gentiles (cf. Rom. 9:25). In 3:6 the women in the community are considered to be the children of Sarah by their conversion; Jewish women would always have been such (see on 3:6 and cf. Gal. 3:29).

In addition to this internal evidence we can also say that if the area covered by the letter included, as is very probable, churches of Pauline foundation, then these were churches composed for the most part of Gentiles; if purely Jewish Christian churches existed in these areas it is surprising that neither Acts nor any other Christian writing inside or outside the NT shows any trace of them. None of this should be taken to imply that there were no Jewish Christians within the churches addressed, but they would only have been a minority. The later we date the epistle the less reason there is to expect to find this to be a self-conscious Jewish minority.

## III. THE UNITY OF THE LETTER

Difficulties relating to the connection of the earlier part of the epistle to the later have led many scholars to deny its unity; a variety of solutions have been offered of which we can only consider the more important.

Bornemann, 'Der erste Petrusbrief—eine Taufrede des Sylvanus?' *Z.N.W.*, 19 (1919–20) 143–65, considered that 1:3–5:11 was a baptismal sermon preached by Silvanus, based on Ps. 34 and dating from around 90 A.D. His rather fanciful reconstruction of the origin of the sermon and then of its attribution to Peter cannot be sustained and the change from a sermon to a letter by the addition of a few verses (1:1f; 5:12–14) is hardly a rejection of the original unity of the writing.

We need to take much more seriously the view that 1:3–4:11 was originally associated with an act of baptism and that 1:1f and 4:12–5:14 are additions. This was apparently first proposed by R. Perdelwitz (*Die Mysterienreligion und das Problem des 1 Petrusbriefes*, Giessen, 1911), and supported later by B. H. Streeter (*The Primitive Church*, London, 1929, pp. 115ff) and by H. Windisch in his commentary. In his additional notes to the third edition of Windisch's commentary Preisker took the suggestion further interpreting 1:3–4:11 as a baptismal liturgy. Before examining the more general reasons for a break at 4:11 we shall outline and consider Preisker's view and that of F. L. Cross which is related to it, for if 1:3–4:11 does turn out to be a liturgy then this is in itself a strong ground for suspecting that the letter is composed of two different sections.

## a. 1:3–4:11—A LITURGY?

Preisker holds that in 1 Peter we have the baptismal liturgy of the Roman church (1:3–4:11) plus a general sermon to the whole community (4:12–5:11) and he outlines the letter as follows: (i) 1:3–12: an opening prayer-psalm in which the present participle 'guarded' (*phrouroumenous*, 1:5) is to be given a relatively future sense; the hearers are just about to be brought into God's care through baptism; (ii) 1:13–21: a didactic section character- ised by OT references and relating to the behaviour to be expected from those about to be baptised; (iii) 1:22–5: a short baptismal dedication following the act of baptism, which is supposed to have taken place between 1:21 and 1:22. Directly after this we have a succession of past tenses, 'having purified' (1:22), 'born anew' (1:23), 'have tasted' (2:3; here the imperative of the LXX has been changed to the aorist indicative). All this indicates that they have just been born anew in baptism (notice also 'newborn babes', 2:2); (iv) 2:1–10: a hymn in three strophes; verses 6–8 are an insertion in the original hymn; (v) 2:11–3:12: a paraenetic (i.e. exhortation based on moral instruction) sermon introduced by 'Beloved' and 'I beseech'; (vi) 3:13–4:7a: a 'revelation' in which an 'apocalyptic prophet' discloses the new situation of the baptized; (vii) 4:7b–11: the liturgy would normally have closed with a prayer; the present passage is substituted as more suitable in a letter; (viii) 4:12–19: from 4:12 onwards to the end the whole congregation, of which the baptized are now full members, is brought within the ambit of the service; 4:12–19 is another 'revelation' which assumes the hearers have already suffered persecution (the existing congregation would have: the newly baptized would not); (ix) 5:1–9: a paraenetic section addressed to the whole church; (x) 5:10–11: closing blessing to the worship. To all of this a beginning and ending were added transforming it into a letter which was then despatched to the areas mentioned in 1:1.

It is exceedingly difficult to see how such a detailed liturgy would have been comprehensible to its readers without the necessary rubrics which Preisker's analysis provides (cf. C. F. D.

Moule, 'The Nature and Purpose of 1 Peter', *N.T.S.* 3 (1956) 1–11). Moreover what would interest Christians in Asia Minor in the baptismal liturgy of the church at Rome? If it was very different from their own liturgy they would have required explanatory notes to understand it; if it was similar they would not have required it at all. If they were suffering persecution, or about to suffer it, they might have needed to be recalled to the meaning of their baptism—but why to the liturgy of another church? It is impossible to envisage the situation in Asia Minor which would have called out the need for the liturgy, nor the circumstances in Rome which would have led to its communication. The whole document does bear the stamp of one hand possessing a constancy of style (see pp. 26f); the various elements which Preisker envisages would have left a greater impression of variation than we in fact discover; the existing variations are more easily accounted for by the use of traditional material than by his suggestion. There are a number of details which conflict with his view: if the act of baptism took place after 1:21, why in 1:3 are the hearers of the 'liturgy' described as already reborn ('born anew' is a past tense)? Why is the perfect tense used for 'born anew' in 1:23, for if the act of baptism has just taken place and if rebirth took place in it we would have expected an aorist? Is it even certain that the reference to 'born anew' (1:23) is linked to baptism in the context, since it is not said that the new birth is effected by water, as in Jn 3:3,5, but by the word of God? Preisker also takes 4:12ff as addressed to the whole congregation; it reads much more like part of a letter. 'Instead of discourse on the general principles of the Christian life . . . we find advice directed to a definite historical situation' (Streeter, *op. cit.*, p. 124).

F. L. Cross, *1 Peter, A Paschal Liturgy* (London, 1954) has modified and extended the suggestion of Preisker. He finds in 1:3–4:11 'the part of the Celebrant' in 'the Baptismal rite of Easter' (p. 38). This is an improvement on Preisker's thesis in so far as it obviates the necessity to attribute different sections of 1:3–4:11 to various persons or groups of persons, but it is still open to the objection that without the rubrics it is difficult to see of what use it would be to someone who wished to celebrate baptism or how it could be applied as part of a letter to the situation of Christians in Asia Minor. Further, unlike the original suggestion it accounts only for 1:3–4:11, and fails to show how 4:12–5:11 came to be added and the whole turned into a letter.

Cross relates the letter not to baptism in general but to the baptismal liturgy of Easter. From about the middle of the second century we find the Greek word for suffering (*paschein*) connected to the similarly sounding Hebrew word *Pascha* (the etymology is erroneous), from which comes our word Paschal for Easter, and both related to the Passover festival (cf. Melito, *Homily on the Passover*, 46); the suffering of Christ took place at the time of Passover. The Greek word for suffering is used in 1 Peter much more often than in other parts of the NT; therefore the liturgy in the letter was performed at Easter. Cross discovers further Paschal references within the letter: 1:18f implies that Jesus was the Passover lamb; 1:13, 'gird up' goes back to Exod. 12:11 and the Passover; the theme of 'joy' which runs through the letter is appropriate to Easter. Cross also finds certain resemblances between 1 Peter and the known baptismal rite of Hippolytus's *Apostolic Tradition;* the latter reflects practices in Rome in the late second century and 1 Peter was written from Rome. These references and resemblances are much too general; they have been severely criticised by C. F. D. Moule, *op. cit.*, and T. C. G. Thornton, '1 Peter, A Paschal Liturgy?', *J.T.S.*, 12 (1961) 14–26. A. R. C. Leaney, '1 Peter and the Passover: An Interpretation', *N.T.S.* 10 (1964) 238–51, has attempted to sustain the view of Cross by linking 1 Peter to the Jewish Passover liturgy of the first century A.D.; he is able to find links, but Christianity emerged out of Judaism and it would be surprising if there were none. Thornton (*op. cit.*, pp. 17f) points out that while the frequency of the Greek word for suffering is exceptionally high in 1 Peter this can be accounted for by the subject matter—the letter is about persecution and suffering and relates this to the suffering of Christ. Most interestingly the word occurs more frequently in 4:12–5:11 (the portion of the letter which does not belong to the alleged paschal baptismal rite) than in 1:3–4:11. Moule (*op. cit.*), following Bornemann (see p. 20) recalls the large part Ps. 34 plays in 1 Peter, and points out that this Psalm has no paschal associations. There may indeed be eucharistic allusions in 1 Peter (cf. M.-E. Boismard, *D.B.S.*, VII, 1435ff) and in the notes on 2:1–3 we draw attention to some that may be possible; this is not surprising; where a rite is regularly celebrated it will affect thought and language; but this does not make 1 Peter, or any part of it, a baptismal or eucharistic liturgy.

b. 1:3–4:11—A BAPTISMAL HOMILY?

If we reject the suggestion that 1 Peter includes a liturgy, this does not mean that 1 Peter may not contain a baptismal homily or sermon; if it did this would account for the baptismal references and for the apparent lack of unity between the earlier and later parts of the letter. If there are strong grounds for dividing the letter at 4:11 then we must account for that division and this is as likely a solution as any; discussion of the nature of 1:3–4:11 and the possibility of division cannot be separated. What then are the grounds for division?

(i) In the earlier part of the epistle persecution appears to be only a threatening possibility (1:6; 3:13–17) but in the later part it is a present reality (4:12–19; 5:9; see the notes on the four passages and pp. 36ff). This variation could be accounted for on the supposition of differing periods of composition for the two sections of the letter: the situation changes and the state initiates deliberate persecution. Alternatively it could be explained by arguing that 1:6; 3:13–17 are addressed to those just baptized who cannot therefore have suffered persecution, but who may well do so, whereas 4:12–19; 5:9 is addressed to those who have been Christians for some period and therefore have already been persecuted; for them persecution is a present fact and not just a future possibility. When we examine the persecutions more closely (pp. 36ff) we shall see that the differences between the two sets of passages have been much exaggerated; they may arise from the eschatological pressure which is felt from 4:7 onwards (4:7 belongs to the earlier section); 1:6; 2:12; 4:4 assume that the readers have been or are being persecuted.

(ii) The references to baptism come in the earlier part: in 3:20f it is explicitly mentioned; elsewhere there are a number of allusions: the use of the rebirth imagery (1:3,23; 2:2); the quotation of a creed (3:18ff), for creeds appear originally to have been linked to baptism; the quotation of baptismal hymns (1:3–5; 3:18–22); the reference to milk (2:2f), the use of which in baptism was certainly a recognized custom of the church from the beginning of the third century (cf. Cross, *op. cit.* pp. 32f) and therefore must go back to a much earlier period; the 'put away' of 2:1 alludes to the putting off of clothes by the baptized. Many of these references must be admitted; others are too vague (cf. Thornton, *op. cit.*, Moule, *op. cit.*); their identification depends too frequently on the use of later liturgies (Boismard uses the *Apostolic Tradition* of Hippolytus and the *Catecheses Mystagogicae* of Cyril of Jerusalem). E. Lohse, 'Paränese und Kerygma im 1 Petrusbrief', *Z.N.W.*, 45 (1954) 69–89, argues that apart from 3:20f all the certain allusions occur in the portion 1:3–2:10; if it is a baptismal homily they should be more widespread. If we accept the more remote allusion to a baptismal hymn that Boismard finds in 5:5b–9 (cf. *Quatre Hymnes baptismales*, pp. 133ff) then it could be argued that the baptismal material is not confined to the earlier part of the letter. It should also be remembered that allusions to baptism were part of the general language of the early church; Paul builds an argument on the *fact* of baptism in Rom. 6:3ff and constantly refers to it in his letters; in the church of that period baptism entailed such a tremendous change in the life of the convert that it became something he always recalled and from which preachers and writers could argue.

(iii) The recipients of 1:3–4:11 appear to have only recently left paganism and become Christians whereas 5:2–5 is addressed to leaders of the church. In the earlier part the present way of life of its recipients is contrasted with the life they have left (4:3f; cf. 2:10; 1:18f). The word 'now' is frequently used, e.g. 3:21, implying that they have just now been saved by baptism, and 1:12, implying that the Gospel has just now been proclaimed to them (cf. 2:10,25; 1:6,8). But the fact that the present way of life of the readers is contrasted with that of their past heathen existence does not necessarily imply that they have just become Christians, cf. 1 Cor. 6:11; Eph. 2:3,11f; nor do references to rebirth imply that all are converts and that the community could not have been in existence long enough in their area for some to have been born in its time (cf. 2 Clement 1:4–8 which comes from around the middle of the second century). The use of 'now' does not necessarily imply their recent baptism. 'This "now" is an important feature of the Epistle (1:6,8,12; 2:10,25; 3:21), not to be confined to the moment of conversion or of baptism, but indicating a period and a situation when the new Israel comprising both Jew and Gentile had been brought into being and the tide of the universal Gospel was felt to be in full flood' (Selwyn, 'Eschatology in 1 Peter' in *The Background of the New Testament and its Eschatology* (ed. W. D. Davies and D. Daube), Cambridge 1956, p. 394f: cf. also Moule, *op. cit.*, p. 6 and the notes on the passages).

(iv) Beare (p. 7) suspects a difference of style between the two sections, arguing that in 4:12–5:14 'the style is direct and simple.

There are no carefully constructed periods or nicely balanced rhythms and antitheses, such as mark the preceding discourse'. The variation in style may be accounted for in a number of ways: traditional material is used throughout the epistle in varying degrees (cf. pp. 29ff); from 4:7 onwards the parousia becomes more urgent. Apart from this Beare has overdrawn the difference in style; can it be said that there is really a great change between 3:13–17 and 4:12–19, the two passages which deal with persecution? Preisker (p. 160) notes that the stylistic peculiarities of 5:1–9 are similar to those of 2:11–3:12 (and both are those of primitive catechetical material).

(v) There is one individual matter of grammar which has been held to support the conception of a division, viz., the use of the aorist imperatives in the earlier section. Of one occurrence at 1:22 Beare writes (p. 84f), 'The use of the aorist should be noted as supporting the interpretation that this is an injunction to newly converted Christians. Otherwise the present would be more appropriate, as an exhortation to continue loving one another: the aorist . . . has rather the force of inculcating the adoption of a new attitude, the necessary consequence of their admission to the Christian brotherhood'. Whatever be the explanation of the frequent aorist imperatives in the letter we must note that they occur in the later section (5:2,5,6,8,9,) as well as in the earlier, and in the later section they cannot be said to inculcate a new attitude.

(vi) The doxology of 4:11 suggests a formal ending: but see notes on 4:11.

There are also positive arguments in favour of the unity of the letter:

(i) Beare acknowledges 'in recognizing the composite structure of the book, there is no need to postulate two different authors; on the contrary, there is every indication that the writer of the letter to the persecuted also composed the discourse to the newly baptized' (p. 8). The unity of style is seen in the writer's love of concrete imagery rather than theological argument, his choice of illustrative words, of compound rather than simple forms, and in the way he expresses his thoughts both negatively and positively (see E. Scharfe, *Die Petrinische Strömung der Neutestamentlichen Literatur*, Berlin, 1893, pp. 3–22), and these indications of style are found uniformly throughout the epistle. Equally uniform in the letter is the use of traditional material and allusions and brief quotations from the OT; Boismard (*D.B.S.* VII, pp. 1442ff) has shown that the author has dealt with the traditional material which he has incorporated in a similar fashion in 1:3–4:11 and in 4:12–5:14, in each case adapting it to the persecution situation of the readers (cf. E. Lohse, *op. cit.*, pp. 85–9). It must be allowed that if the writer first preached a sermon and then incorporated it into a letter with additional material this would account for the unity of style.

(ii) If the letter is held to be composite then we require to re-construct the conditions under which a baptismal homily was made part of a letter considered appropriate to those suffering persecution and sent to them without any explicit indication that this was being done. It does not appear that any such satisfactory historical reconstruction has yet been offered.

(iii) A number of minor points sustaining unity may be offered: the theme of 'glory' which appears in 4:11 is taken up again in 4:13f; the eschatological pressure visible in 4:12–19 and 5:6–9 was already present in 4:7a.

(iv) The real reason for arguing for a sermon in 1:3–4:11 is to provide an explanation of the presence of baptismal references; this section has never been considered to be any kind of sermon, but a *baptismal* sermon. If however the baptismal allusions can be equally accounted for by the use of traditional material, hymns, creeds, catechisms (see pp. 29ff) then there seems no reason to maintain the argument that the earlier part is a sermon.

In the light of these considerations there would not seem to be sufficient evidence to compel the acceptance of 1:3–4:11 as a baptismal homily and we would therefore hold to the unity of the epistle over against any such theory which necessitates its division.

C. TWO LETTERS?

Recently C. F. D. Moule (*op. cit.*) has suggested that 1 Peter is actually the combination of two forms of one letter written by the same person to a number of communities some of whom 'were actually suffering persecution, while for others it was no more than a possibility' (p. 7). In this way he accounts for the difference in attitude to persecution. (On earlier attempts to see more than one letter in 1 Peter cf. Moffatt, *An Introduction to the Literature of the New Testament*, Edinburgh, 1927, pp. 342ff, Guthrie, pp. 124f). Moule determines the two letters as (a) 1:1–4:11; 5:12–14 and (b) 1:1–2:10; 4:12–5:14. It is easy to see how the two, if they ever existed, could have been put together to form one letter. But did they ever exist? It is extremely difficult to see why 2:18–3:7 should have been omitted from (b) (2:13–17 might be considered inappropriate in view of the actually existing persecution) when 5:1–5 has been included; both are advice for moral living and have nothing directly to do with persecution. 4:7–11 appears not inappropriate to a tense situation; 3:17–22 which links suffering to the death of Jesus would have been very suitable for those actually undergoing persecution. The suggestion must be rejected.

## IV. THE USE OF EARLIER MATERIAL

There are many similarities between 1 Peter and the other NT epistles. This may have arisen either through the literary dependence of one on the other or through the use of common material, probably, but not necessarily, oral. We leave the relationship of 1 Peter to the Gospels until the discussion of authorship (pp. 49ff), because the writer's acquaintanceship with the Gospel tradition can be an argument in support of his identification with the Apostle Peter.

Before we discuss the common material with the other epistles we need to mention the use in 1 Peter of passages, phrases and words drawn from the OT. There are longish quotations deliberately introduced as Scripture (e.g. 1:24f; 2:6–8; 3:10–12); there are also many phrases and sometimes complete clauses which the writer uses, not to support his argument, but to advance it, i.e. he expresses the steps in his reasoning through them (e.g. 1:25b, 'the good news which was preached'; 2:3, 'you have tasted the kindness of the Lord'; 2:11, 'aliens and exiles'); brief allusions lie in words like 'inheritance' (1:4), 'gird up' (1:13), 'lamb' (1:19); often as in the last instance a whole theology is implied. The way in which these quotations are used shows us that the writer can make formal quotations but more often incorporates OT material without informing us; if we did not possess the OT we should never have been aware of his extensive use of it. It is therefore probable that if there was other material to hand he would also use this without telling us; since this other material, e.g., catechisms, hymns, creeds, would not have the authority of the OT in the eyes of the church he would never make formal quotations from it.

With a single exception (it is not really an exception; see notes on 4:8b) all the citations from the OT and the allusions to it are drawn from the LXX, the Greek translation of the original Hebrew; if there is a divergence between the two the writer always follows the LXX and never displays any knowledge of the Hebrew text. It ought to be said finally that he makes more extensive use of the OT in proportion to the size of his letter than any other book in the NT except Revelation; Hebrews has approximately the same amount of OT material, but it is used in a very different way since the author of that epistle or homily deliberately bases his argument on the OT. The frequent use of the OT by our author shows us the way his mind works—through the compilation of material ready to hand rather than through his own words; this again suggests that he will be predisposed to use material in circulation in the church.

### a. USE OF TRADITIONAL MATERIAL

When examining the material common to 1 Peter and other NT writings older commentators considered exclusively the possibility of literary dependence; more recent work has argued that all the NT epistles have drawn on common material, probably oral, but possibly written. Through an examination of this common material P. Carrington (*A Primitive Christian Catechism*, Cambridge, 1940), Selwyn, Boismard (*D.B.S.*, VII, 1419ff) and others have attempted to isolate its original form. In many instances this is impossible because we do not possess sufficient evidence (cf. Lohse, *op. cit.*). But this is not to deny that common instruction must have been given to converts and that a liturgical, credal and paraenetic tradition would have shaped the life of all congregations. The common instruction need not necessarily have been given prior to baptism, for the evidence of Acts suggests that baptism followed directly on belief (Ac. 8:36–8; 10:44–8; 16:30–3), but may have been part of the nurture of Christians; if Acts, as is probably true, reflects the period of its composition in this matter, this would still hold true for the time of 1 Peter; the two are of approximately the same date (on the date of 1 Peter see pp. 63f).

The vast majority of those who came into the church did so from various Gentile backgrounds in which the standards of behaviour fell far short of those required in the primitive Christian community whose ethics had been moulded in Judaism. In 1 Th. 4:1 (one of the earliest of Paul's epistles) the word which Paul uses for 'learned' suggests the handing on of tradition, and he does in fact go on to impart ethical instruction; similarly in 2 Th. 3:6 he refers to the ethical teaching he has given as 'the tradition that you received from us'.

(1) *The common paraenetic tradition.* This consisted of material of different kinds, *Haustafeln* or social codes, catalogues of virtues and vices, special forms for particular occasions, e.g. baptism, persecution, the teaching of the Two Ways; the last named does not appear in 1 Peter but was found in Jewish tradition and is an important feature in the *Didache* and *Barnabas*. In addition to these, and in part moulding them, would be the tradition of the sayings of Jesus.

There is a very good example of a *Haustafel* (a German word that came into use at the time of the Reformation for catechisms of social behaviour; 'social code' is the nearest English equivalent) in 1 Peter, viz., 2:13–3:7 and probably also 5:2–5 (see notes there), in which instruction is given in regard to behaviour towards civil authority, of slaves towards masters, of wives towards husbands, of husbands towards wives, and of the ministry to the church. The social code was a regular method of instruction in the early church and forms containing similar items are found in Eph. 5:22–6:9; Col. 3:18–4:1; 1 Tim. 2:8–15; 5:3–8; 6:1f; Tit. 2:1–10; *Barnabas* 19:5–7; Polycarp, *Philippians* 4:2–6:2. These codes were already well-known in Hellenistic Judaism (cf. Tob. 4:3–21; Sir. 7:18–35; Josephus, *Contra Apionem* 2:199–208) which had taken them over from the Hellenistic world where they were especially popular with the Stoics. The Christian church probably did not take them directly from this latter source but indirectly through Judaism. We find in them a usage of the participle where we should expect the imperative; this practice was also found regularly in contemporary Hebrew; normal Greek usage would be the imperative (cf. D. Daube, 'Participle and Imperative in 1 Peter' in Selwyn, pp. 467–88). The codes must therefore have passed through a Jewish or Jewish Christian stage. This would imply a fairly early origin within Christianity for these rules and a respect for their verbal formulation in that they were not accommodated to more normal Greek grammar. When Christians accepted these social codes, they were considerably modified, e.g., the example of Jesus for slaves could not have been in them in their Hellenistic or Jewish forms. Within the NT the codes are also adapted to the particular situation of the readers of each epistle as the differing emphasis within them shows. (On these social codes cf. A. M. Hunter, *Paul and His Predecessors*, 2nd edn. London, 1961, pp. 52–7; 128–131; K. E. Kirk, *The Vision of God*, London, 1932, pp. 111ff and K. Weidinger, *Die Haustafeln*, Leipzig, 1928.)

Besides these social codes there are other sections of the epistles which strongly resemble one another in the paraenesis they provide. Selwyn (pp. 363ff), following Carrington, has attempted to identify various underlying forms, e.g. a baptismal catechism for the instruction of new converts, a persecution form to guide the behaviour of those under trial and sustain them. Here again we find the use of the participle for the imperative indicating an early origin. The details of these forms and catechisms must probably escape us, but this is no reason for denying their existence. W. Nauck, 'Freude im Leiden', *Z.N.W.*, 46 (1955) 68–80 isolates a much briefer persecution form which he discovers in greater or less completeness in Mt. 5:11f; Lk. 6:22f; 1 Pet. 1:6; 4:13f; Jas. 1:2,12; there are traces of it in other epistles. In it suffering and joy are brought together. Its basic form is

> Blessed are you, when you are persecuted;
> Rejoice, you will be rewarded.

While the Christian usage of the form may be traced to Jesus it goes back beyond him in Judaism, perhaps as far as Maccabean times. Boismard (*D.B.S.* VII, 1419ff) probably goes to the opposite extreme from Selwyn; he constructs a common catechetical order of instruction lying behind 1 Peter, James, 1 John, Titus, Romans, Colossians; this gives the call of the Christian to the new life and shows the change required from him in a new morality. The common instruction that Boismard unearths is so general that it is difficult to deny its existence, but it is doubtful if he really proves more than that the Christians had a common faith and morality.

At least one catalogue of vices is found in 1 Peter (2:1; cf. 4:3); there are many more in the NT, e.g. Rom. 1:29ff; 2 Cor. 12:20; Gal. 5:19ff; Col. 3:8. Like the social code their origin lies in Hellenism (cf. notes on 2:1).

(2) *Liturgical material* (See G. Delling, *Worship in the New Testament*, London, 1962; C. F. D. Moule, *Worship in the New Testament*, London, 1961). There was an accepted tradition in regard to the

Lord's Supper of which Paul made use (1 Cor. 11:23–5); there were brief statements of belief, a credal tradition, such as 1 Cor. 15:3–5; hymns are quoted at Eph. 5:14 and 1 Tim. 3:16. Liturgical material of one kind and another is also thought to be present in 1 Peter. Boismard (*Quatre Hymnes baptismales*) isolates four portions of hymns at 1:3–5; 2:22–5; 3:18–22; 5:5–9; Selwyn (pp. 268–81) regards 2:6–10 as based on another hymn. Credal statements have also been detected in 3:18–22 and 1:18–21. For a fuller discussion of such alleged liturgical material see the notes on these and other passages.

b. DEPENDENCE ON OTHER EPISTLES

Admitting, as we must, that 1 Peter and the other NT writings were affected by a common tradition, does this account for all the similarities of 1 Peter with other epistles? Discussion has centred especially on the relation of 1 Peter to Romans and Ephesians. There is much common material shared with sections of 1 and 2 Thessalonians, the Pastorals and James but it is usually regarded as adequately accounted for by the supposition that the various authors drew on the common stock of tradition. A direct literary connection has been suspected in the case of Romans and Ephesians. Sanday and Headlam in their *I.C.C.* commentary on Romans (pp. lxxivff) found that 1 Peter depended on Romans; Bigg in the *I.C.C.* commentary on 1 Peter denied this (pp. 17ff). Bigg lists the suspected passages and it is at once obvious that most of them go back to common liturgical and catechetical material: e.g., (i) Rom. 4:24 and 1 Pet. 1:21; it is now generally recognized that Rom. 4:24f is a primitive confession; (ii) Rom. 8:34 and 1 Pet. 3:22, 'at the right hand of God'; this is a liturgical phrase, and once the concept it affirms is accepted there are few other ways of expressing it; (iii) Rom. 12:9,10,14–19 and 1 Pet. 1:22; 3:8f; catechetical material, partly allied to sayings from Q; (iv) Rom. 6:7 and 1 Pet. 4:1b; both probably depend on a legal tag.

There are however a number of places where such dependence on a common tradition is not so easily seen:
(i) Rom. 6:11 and 1 Pet. 2:24b. The verbal resemblance here is greater in the English than in the Greek (see notes on 2:24b). The conception of a dying and living connected to the death and resurrection of Jesus appears to be Pauline and 1 Peter would therefore have been affected by Pauline ideas at this point;

literary dependence would be excluded by the lack of close verbal similarity.

(ii) Rom. 12:1f and 1 Pet. 1:14; 2:2,5. These passages are linked by the general conception of the priesthood of Christians and by the use of two words which do not occur elsewhere in the NT, viz., *logikos* (spiritual) and *suschēmatizesthai* (conform). The general conception did not originate with Paul but entered Christianity from the OT via Qumran (see notes on 2:5). Rom. 12:1f is a complex short section, closely constructed and bearing the stamp of Paul's vocabulary, style and thought; the two rare words will then not have been part of traditional material but will have entered Christian vocabulary because Paul used them; as a part of Christian vocabulary they were adopted by the author of 1 Peter. Thus again we do not find literary dependence on Romans by 1 Peter, or the use of common material, but an indirect dependence.

(iii) Rom. 13:1–7 and 1 Pet. 2:13–17. Selwyn (pp. 426ff) suspects catechetical material and refers also to 1 Tim. 2:1–3; Tit. 3:1–3,8. There is no trace of similar Pauline teaching on the state in the other genuine Pauline letters nor is there any reference to it in Eph. 5:22–6:9 and Col. 3:18–4:1 which represent earlier forms of the social code than 1 Peter 2:13–3:7 (cf. pp. 47f). We note also the change of style between Rom. 12 and Rom. 13:1–7; brief clauses frequently formed around the participle instead of the imperative are replaced by material in Paul's normal style; this suggests that he composed the passage and did not lift it from a traditional code. He apparently introduced it into Romans and not his other letters because of the special position of the church in the capital. Its ideas derive from strains in Judaism with which as a Rabbi he would have been familiar and which, over against zealot ideas of revolution, taught the submission of the citizen to authorities as appointed by God; his thought was probably also influenced by Jesus' own words about the payment of tax (Mk 12: 13–17). This conception of submission to legal authority therefore entered the stream of Christian instruction in Rom. 13:1–7 and thereafter began to form part of catechetical instruction; on this 1 Pet. 2:13–17 depends; confirmation lies in the absence of participial imperatives in 1 Pet. 2:13–17 as in Rom. 13:1–7.

(iv) 1 Pet. 2:6–8 and Rom. 9:33 both combine OT texts with the same variations from the original. Here both are probably making use of OT material which had been already put together

B

for apologetic purposes in the primitive church (see notes on 2:6f). But it may be that if we suspect some dependence of 1 Peter on Pauline thought and terminology then other passages like this and those previously dismissed as explicable in terms of common catechetical and liturgical material ought rather to be taken as further evidence of Pauline influence, e.g. 1:3 in relation to 2 Cor. 1:3; Eph. 1:3.

To sum up: it seems that the theology and expressions of Romans had worked their way into the life of the Roman church and were derived by our author from there; this is inherently probable if Romans was in use in the Roman church, as it surely was, and if 1 Peter was written from Rome (see on 5:13 and pp. 64f). This, moreover, is in keeping with the links which exist between 1 Peter and Pauline theology especially as expressed in Romans. In both a large part is played by the passion of Jesus as the event of salvation (1 Pet. 2:24; 3:18—Rom. 3:24f; 6:10; 8:17, etc.); the resurrection occupies an equally important place (1 Pet. 1:3; 3:21—Rom. 4:25; 6:1ff, etc.). The salutation follows those of the Pauline letters (see on 1:1f and 1:3). Paul's formula 'in Christ' recurs three times (3:16; 5:10,14); the intimate personal and social relationship indicated by this phrase does not re-appear in 1 Peter, where it is merely a formula without vigour. Equally the conception of suffering and rising with Christ re-appears, if it does re-appear, in a completely weakened form at 4:13; 5:1. A whole range of Pauline teaching is missing, e.g., justification by faith, the law, the two Adams, but this may only be because the controversy about the admission of the Gentiles to the church which led to their formulation has been settled and is no longer an issue. On the other hand the failure of the author of 1 Peter to use 'Lord' to describe Jesus, apart from OT quotations, and the absence of words like 'crucify' and *thlipsis* (for persecution: 1 Peter uses *pathēma*) suggest that part of the author's vocabulary was formed under an influence other than that of Paul. The evidence suggests that Paul's theology had entered the church, some of its terms appropriated, but its vigour lost; incidentally this suits best the period of the end of the first century, being similar to what we find in the Pastorals, but it would not be entirely out of keeping with the conclusion that the Apostle Peter, coming to Rome shortly before the Neronic persecution, learnt something of Paul's theology, came to know Romans, and allowed both to influence his writing.

When we turn to 1 Peter and Ephesians we again find that there must be some kind of relationship: either 1 Peter was used by the writer of Ephesians (so Moffatt, *Introduction*, pp. 381–3) or Ephesians was used by the writer of 1 Peter (so C. L. Mitton, *The Epistle to the Ephesians*, London, 1951, pp. 176ff; 280ff) or Ephesians and 1 Peter both depend on liturgical, catechetical and confessional material from the tradition (so Selwyn, Boismard). Mitton's table of parallels shows that there are a great many points of contact between the epistles and that these contacts are widely scattered through both epistles (contrast 1 and 2 Thessalonians where the contacts with 1 Peter are concentrated into a few passages). They are not primarily paraenetic, though each contains a social code (Eph. 5:22–6:9; 1 Pet. 2:13–3:7); similar subjects are covered therein but there are few verbal similarities. The contacts lie rather in the area of creed and liturgy. Boismard (*Quatre Hymnes baptismales*, pp. 15ff) argues that 1 Pet. 1:3–5 represents a baptismal hymn which was known to the author of Ephesians also; the parallels are, however, widely scattered through Ephesians (1:3,18f; 2:4f); this implies that whereas the hymn is quoted in 1 Peter, in Ephesians it has been worked into the material as a whole. It seems easier to assume that the author of 1 Peter knew Ephesians well and used its phrases, which once they had become part of his vocabulary he is able to recombine, than that the author of Ephesians had deliberately broken up a hymn; all our knowledge of the two authors goes to suggest that the approach in Ephesians is much more original while that in 1 Peter depends much more on other thinkers and writings. Parallels to this alleged hymn in 1 Peter are found also by Boismard in Romans; here they are scattered even more widely, and so the argument applies yet more strongly that 1 Peter is the dependent epistle. More generally it needs to be said that there comes a limit to the number of times in which we find a parallel in 1 Peter to a passage in some other epistle and say that the writers of both have used common material; such arguing from parallels to common material was at one stage offered as a solution to the parallels between Matthew, Mark and Luke; there are few scholars today who would deny some form of literary dependence; the more frequently we find parallels in the case of 1 Peter the more difficult it becomes to accept the common tradition solution. We are driven to the conclusion that, as in the case of Romans, the author of 1 Peter knew Ephesians, or at least its author and his

vocabulary, whether this author be Paul or not. If the date of
Ephesians is post-Pauline this necessarily implies a contemporary
or later date for 1 Peter. In this connection C. L. Mitton ('The
Relationship between 1 Peter and Ephesians', *J.T.S.* 1 (1950)
67–73) has pointed out that the borrowings of 1 Peter from Ephesians are often in passages in which there is no parallel to Ephesians
in other Pauline epistles; they cannot then have been borrowed
from earlier genuine Pauline epistles.

The number of parallels between 1 Peter and 1 Clement is
noteworthy; similar ideas recur and a number of expressions are
used which are peculiar to both epistles (cf. Lohse, *op. cit.*, p. 84f;
Bigg, p. 8). The probability of literary dependence is low because
of other extensive differences but the resemblances would confirm
the conclusion that both emerged from the same church milieu;
1 Clement was certainly written in Rome, 1 Peter very probably
(see on 5:13); it would also suggest that they were of roughly
contemporary date.

## V. THE IDENTIFICATION OF THE PERSECUTIONS

### a. THE NATURE OF THE PERSECUTIONS

We have already seen that it has been argued that the references
to persecution in 1:3–4:11 and in 4:12–5:11 relate to different
periods of persecution (see p. 24). We have now to examine to
see if this is so and to determine what were these periods (if there
were two or more).

The persecutions are mentioned on four occasions: 1:6; 3:13–
17; 4:12–19; 5:9. The beginnings of Christian work in the
so-called missionary countries remind us that where Christians
are a minority rejecting much of the traditional cultural, religious
and social set-up, they are open to sporadic persecution at the
hands of mobs, groups who may feel their position or privileges
threatened, or even of individuals to whom they may stand in
some special relationship (slave to master, or wife to husband).
1:6 and 3:13–17 imply no more than such activity, and clearly
do not apply to official persecution at the hands of the state.
1:6 indicates that these trials are a present reality but 3:13–17
makes of them rather a possibility, 'even if you do suffer for
righteousness' sake' (3:14) and 'if that should be God's will'
(3:17). (On the use of the optative mood see notes on 3:14).

At 4:12-19 persecution is either already in progress or just about to break out; it is not just a contingent possibility. 5:9 also makes it reality rather than possibility. While it might be possible to suppose that the author received fresh news in the interval this seems too feeble; we would expect him to refer to the messenger or the information. (The argument of 'fresh news' to explain breaks in the NT letters as we have them now is used so often that we must imagine couriers dashing hither and thither with new information every time a writer sat down to send an epistle.)

In addition to the more pressing nature of the persecutions in the later part of the letter, it is argued that 4:12-19 relates to persecution by the state rather than to sporadic outbreaks of mob-violence or group enmity. Is then a different situation in regard to persecution envisaged in 4:12-5:14 from that in 1:3-4:11?

'If you are reproached for the name of Christ' (4:14; cf. 4:16, 'if one suffers as a Christian') is often understood as implying that persecution is endured by the church because its members profess Christianity. This can be looked at either from the point of view of the persecutor or the persecuted. The former would imply that the offence which led to persecution was that of being a Christian *simpliciter* and it would also imply that the persecution was official. Often later, or at least our evidence comes from later, when Christians did suffer persecution it was not because they were regarded as Christians *simpliciter* but because they were accused of atheism (they did not sacrifice to the gods who were publicly worshipped by others) or cannibalism (they ate 'flesh' and 'blood' in the Eucharist). Such charges would emerge easily when in some way Christians had attracted unfavourable attention, and public sentiment would be roused against them (cf. outbursts of anti-semitism in Christian countries). Christians were put to death for many reasons other than the simple charge of being Christian. Polycarp was martyred (155 A.D.) because he refused to swear by the genius of the Emperor. He could not do this as a Christian but it was his obstinacy in rejecting the deity of the Emperor that led to his execution. He was not then martyred 'for the name of Christ', but Polycarp, if he had been asked, would have said that he had suffered 'for the name of Christ'. The 'name' was so common a concept among Christians that everything they did could be said to be done 'in the name of Christ', e.g. preaching (Ac. 4:17; 9:27), healing (Ac. 3:6; 4:30), suffering persecution

(Ac. 5:41; 9:14,16; 21:13), being forgiven sins (Ac. 10:43); the Christians are those who invoke 'the name' (Ac. 9:21; 22:16); they are baptized 'in the name' (Ac. 2:38; 10:48). This form of expression is therefore perfectly natural on the lips of a Christian writer to describe persecution of any type, whether mob-violence or official, and does not necessarily therefore refer to state persecution against Christians as such.

The persecution was widespread; the 'brotherhood throughout the world' was suffering, 5:9; cf. 4:17, where 'the household of God' is the whole Christian Church and not just an individual congregation. The world-wide nature of the persecution is not stressed in 1:6; 3:13–17, but there is nothing there or in any other part of the earlier section of the epistle which militates against it.

Was the death penalty involved in this persecution, not just through mob lynching, but as a sentence inflicted by a civil court? Those who suffer are said to 'share Christ's sufferings' (4:13); his sufferings involved his death; have these Christians then to face death as he did? When we examine this passage we shall see that another interpretation of the phrase is preferable. The term 'suffer' is also used at 4:15f; does it necessarily imply death? It does so at 2:23 (and in the marginal reading at 3:18) but it does not at 2:19–20 where it is used for the ill-treatment of slaves by their masters which they are expected to survive; this also is the meaning at 3:14,17; at 5:10 the suffering lasts for a period and therefore cannot refer to death alone. In the passage 4:12–19 'reproach' (4:14) hardly seems a strong enough word to refer to death; in 4:15 while the death penalty would be exacted from a murderer or a thief it would hardly be from a mischief-maker (the meaning of this word is doubtful, see note on it); finally 4:19 implies that despite their suffering the readers will continue their good works (see notes on 4:19) and this does not suggest that the author expects them to die.

If the letter is a unity then 2:13–17 implies that these Christians should pray for the civil authorities; would they have been ready to do so if they were being persecuted? But 1 Clement 61 contains the same idea and it was written after the Neronic persecution of which it is very much aware; 1:1 may also refer to persecution. In any case Christians are required to pray for those who persecute them (Mt. 5:44). When we come to examine the statements on persecution in 4:12–5:14 we shall see that they

are written not so much from the perspective of the state as from
that of the eschatological expectation of the Parousia.

On the other side there are certain positive links between the
earlier references to persecution and the later. The same Greek
word is used to describe them at 1:6 and 4:12, and it is not the
normal word in the NT for persecution. Both at 3:14 and 4:14
there is an obvious reference to a more original form of the
beatitude underlying Mt. 5:10–12 (there is no reason to suppose
the writer knew Matthew's Gospel). In both 3:17 and 4:19 the
suffering of the readers is said to be in accordance with the will of
God (see further Walls-Stibbs, pp. 50f). These are not definite
links since they might be expected to turn up in any discussion of
persecution, but they do not appear in all the other references to
it in the NT. It is also possible that if 'wrongdoers' in 2:12 (see
notes) means 'criminals' then state action may be intended, and
this lies in the earlier section of the letter.

We may therefore conclude that there is nothing in the references to persecution in 4:12–19; 5:9 which necessitates regarding
them as relating to a period other than that of 1:6; 3:13–17, that
the references in 4:12–19; 5:9 do not necessarily imply that
Christians suffered in the eyes of those who persecuted them simply
because they were Christians, that nothing in 4:12–19; 5:9
compels acceptance of the view that the persecutions were
officially conducted by the state, and that the evidence is satisfied
by the situation in which Christians lived at all times and in
which violence might break out against them at any moment—in
this they might suffer death, or the loss of goods, or be regarded as
murderers or just mischief-makers. However in 3:13–17 the
persecutions are less likely, a possibility rather than an actuality,
than in 4:12–19; 5:9; this change may arise from the greater
emphasis on the nearness of the end which commences at 4:7
(within the 'earlier' part of the letter).

b. DATE OF THE PERSECUTIONS

Can we connect this account of the persecutions with any of the
periods in which persecution is known to have taken place?
Three periods of persecution are relevant to our discussion:
in the time of Trajan (112 A.D.), towards the end of the
reign of Domitian (95 A.D.), under Nero at the time of the
burning of Rome (64 A.D.). We know more about the first and
third of these than about the second. (See W. H. C. Frend,

*Martyrdom and Persecution in the Early Church*, Oxford, 1965, pp.
151–77; 210–35).

(i) Beare has put forward a strong case for the view that the
situation envisaged in 4:12–19; 5:9 corresponds to the time of
Trajan. During his reign Christians certainly suffered in one of the
areas to which 1 Peter was directed. Our knowledge comes from a
letter of Pliny the Younger to the Emperor Trajan and his reply
(Pliny, *Epistles*, X. 96, 97). We do not know how the persecution
began. If the Emperor had ordered that persecution should be
instituted against the Christians he would certainly have given
some guidance as to its conduct; Pliny is completely ignorant of
such guidance and writes for instructions; the Emperor's reply
shows that he himself had no plans. 'This correspondence makes
it clear that neither the counsellors of the highest court in Bithynia,
nor the officials of the imperial secretariat in Rome, possessed any
juristic material which would provide an answer to the legal
question proposed by Pliny, and, therefore, that there was no such
material' (Lietzmann, *A History of the Early Church*: Vol. II, *The
Founding of the Church Universal*, London, 1961, p. 157). It is equally
clear that this was not a universal persecution but was localised in
Bithynia-Pontus where Pliny was imperial legate; there is no
evidence for a widespread persecution in this period. From
Pliny's letter it appears that after some Christians had suffered a
great many more were anonymously denounced. He wishes to
know whether he should punish those who have been Christians
and have repented, which they demonstrate by cursing Christ and
offering sacrifice, or only those who are still Christians, and
whether the latter should be punished merely because they are
Christians or because of the crimes associated with the profession
of that faith. He has not been able to discover any particular
crimes and has inflicted the death penalty because their 'contu-
macy and inflexible obstinacy deserved chastisement' (Loeb
translation of Pliny). 'It follows that the governors did not
concern themselves at all about the faith and conduct of Christians,
but required any accused persons to make known the correctness
of their attitude to the state by offering sacrifice before the
images of the gods and the Emperor' (Lietzmann, *ibid.*). Christians
were therefore punished in Pliny's eyes, not because they were
simply Christians, i.e., for the name, but because they refused to
fulfil duties that the court required from them. Though Pliny's

letter and its reply do not imply a widespread persecution yet there were certainly other incidents in this period, e.g. Ignatius, the bishop of Antioch, was sent to Rome and martyred.

The references in 1 Peter cannot be made to harmonise with this persecution for: (1) it is not world-wide as 5:9; 4:17 imply; (2) it was not specifically 'for the name', if that is to be deduced from 4:14–16 as indicating a crime in Roman eyes; (3) in it the death penalty was automatically inflicted, but it was not in 1 Peter.

(ii) We have much less definite knowledge about the persecutions in the time of Domitian. A number of prominent people were put to death in Rome probably because they were Christians. Clement refers to 'the sudden and repeated misfortunes and calamities which have befallen' the church in Rome (1 Clement 1:1), but we cannot be certain of the exact date of his letter; it would be within the period 75–110 A.D. Moreover it relates to persecution in Rome and not in Asia Minor. There is no reason to believe that even in Rome it amounted to much (cf. Frend, *op. cit.* p. 217). Revelation testifies certainly to persecution in Asia Minor and is probably to be dated 90–100 A.D. in its final form. Pliny says that there were Christians who at various times renounced their Christianity, some as far back as 25 years prior to his letter; this might, but need not refer to persecution at a similar time to that in Revelation; Christians frequently abandon their faith for reasons other than persecution (cf. the parable of the sower, Mk. 4:3–20). Certainly there is no evidence of a worldwide persecution at this time; we do not even know the nature and cause of what there was. There is thus no especial reason to connect the persecutions of 1 Peter with those of Domitian.

(iii) We do have quite definite information about persecution under Nero from the Roman historian Tacitus (cf. *Annales* 15:38–44). When Rome was burned (64 A.D.), Nero persecuted the Christians in order to divert suspicion from himself; it was a ludicrous charge but the Christians in Rome suffered greatly; they were convicted 'not so much on the count of arson as of hatred of the human race' (Tacitus, 15:44). This may suggest that Christians were now regarded 'as a sect dangerous to the public safety' (Ramsay, *The Church in the Roman Empire*, London, 1893, p. 241). There does not appear however to be sufficient reason for arguing that from 64 A.D. onwards Christianity itself became a crime (cf. Frend, *op. cit.*, pp. 165ff). Tacitus says that 'there arose a sentiment of pity due to the impression that they (the Christians) were being sacrificed not for the welfare of the state but to the ferocity of a single man' (Loeb translation). Governors would therefore not have wished to follow Nero's example in this persecution unless they were compelled to do so, and there is no evidence that they were. This then was a persecution confined to Rome and cannot be that referred to in 1 Peter.

Ramsay argues (*op. cit.*, pp. 245ff; 256ff; 279ff) that somewhere between the time of Nero and Trajan the profession of Christianity itself became a crime and suggests that this happened in the reign of Vespasian, at which period he dates 1 Peter, supposing Peter to have survived the Neronic persecutions. But 'there is no evidence to show that the legal and political situation of Christians changed significantly for the worse in the reign of Vespasian, or that the Church in any part of the Empire was persecuted under his administration' (Beare, p. 12).

In view of the difficulty of associating the references to persecution in 1 Peter with any of the known periods of persecution it would appear more satisfactory to abandon the attempt at identification. Persecution of Christians in the ancient world was endemic (cf. Moule, *op. cit.*; van Unnik, 'Christianity according to Peter', *Expository Times*, 68 (1956–7) 79–83) and might thus well be described as worldwide; this would be all the more likely if it was believed that the end was coming and persecution was one of its signs (see on 4:12–19). In the NT and in early Christian literature we find many references to persecution for which the dates are indefinite and which cannot easily be fitted into the three known periods. Ignatius of Antioch was martyred in Rome (probably between 107–117 A.D.) but this does not appear to have been connected to any general persecution; Revelation was written in a period of persecution; Heb. 13:3 tells of members of the church in prison, and 10:32–4 refers to previous suffering; 1 Th. 2:14–16 shows that much earlier the Thessalonians were persecuted; at a later period *Hermas* and *Barnabas* demonstrate that persecution was an ever present possibility.

We may note finally that since the references to persecution are not sufficiently definite to permit us to connect them with any known period of persecution and since they do not relate particularly to state action against Christians they are of little assistance in the determination of the date of 1 Peter.

## VI. EXTERNAL TESTIMONY

At what period was the epistle first quoted? To establish this sets an upper limit to the date of composition.

In 1905 the Oxford Society for Historical Theology published an exhaustive examination of the use of the NT by the Apostolic Fathers (*The New Testament in the Apostolic Fathers*, Oxford, 1905). They concluded that only in Polycarp's letter to the Philippians was there revealed any certain knowledge of 1 Peter, although it was just possible that there might be some knowledge in some of the other writers. This examination was carried through before our present understanding of the large part which the common worship and paraenesis of the early church played in forming its life and shaping its writings. We have already seen how what was supposed by earlier scholars to be a literary dependence of the NT letters upon one another is now more adequately explained as the use of this common tradition (pp. 28ff); the same must be held to be the true explanation of the Apostolic Fathers' (apart from Polycarp) occasional coincidences of phrasing with 1 Peter; e.g. *Barnabas* 5:6 'manifest in the flesh' may be compared with 1 Pet. 1:20, he 'was made manifest', but we need also to take into account 1 Tim. 3:16, 'he was manifested in the flesh', which is a line from an ancient Christian hymn. We therefore restrict ourselves to Polycarp. It is indefensible to argue that the resemblances between 1 Peter and the other NT epistles imply common material rather than literary dependence and then to argue from even slighter resemblances between 1 Peter and the Apostolic Fathers to the literary dependence of the latter on the former.

Within Polycarp there are a sufficient number of references to 1 Peter to suggest that he was thoroughly acquainted with the letter, as he was with a number of other NT writings. We may compare Polycarp, *Philippians*, 1:3, 'without having seen him you believe with unutterable and exalted joy', with 1 Pet. 1:8, 'Without having seen him you love him; though you do not now see him you believe in him and rejoice with unutterable and exalted joy'; or *Philippians* 10:2, 'maintaining your conduct blameless among the Gentiles that you may receive praise for your good deeds'; with 1 Pet. 2:12, 'Maintain good conduct among the Gentiles, so that in case they speak against you as

wrongdoers, they may see your good deeds and glorify God.'
Polycarp was bishop of Smyrna which lay within the area of the
circulation of 1 Peter and we need not be surprised by this
evidence. He does not identify the letter by name, but since he
rarely does this in his quotations from other NT writings we
cannot determine whether he considered Peter to be the writer
or not.

It is difficult to date Polycarp's letter. At 9:1f he writes as if
Ignatius, the bishop of Antioch, was already martyred; this took
place in the reign of Trajan. In 13:2 he asks for information about
Ignatius and this suggests that he is still alive, though he may be
just dead and Polycarp be requesting news of his martyrdom.
P. N. Harrison (*Polycarp's Two Epistles to the Philippians*, Cambridge,
1936) suggested that our present letter combines two letters of
which chapters 13,14 formed the earlier; if so we note that all the
certainly identifiable references to 1 Peter are in the later (chapters
1–12). It may be that 13:2, which exists today only in a Latin
translation, was wrongly rendered into that language and that
Ignatius was really dead at this time. More recently W. R.
Schoedel, *The Apostolic Fathers*, ed. R. M. Grant, Vol. V, New
York, 1967, (contrast R. M. Grant in Vol. I pp. 64ff) has argued
that 9:1f does not imply the death of Ignatius, though he considers
it and 13:2 to have been written about the time of his death.
If Polycarp's letter was written at that period then 1 Peter must
almost certainly be dated earlier than the time of Trajan but
could be as late as the end of the first century, i.e., the time of
Domitian: this would permit sufficient time for 1 Peter to become
known to Polycarp and his readers. If Polycarp's letter dates from
later, or if that portion of it which contains the Petrine references
does, then 1 Peter could belong to the reign of Trajan.

2 Peter testifies to the existence of an earlier epistle by Peter:
'this is now the second letter that I have written to you' (3:1).
The reference is almost certainly to our first letter and indicates
that the author of 2 Peter, who passes himself off as Peter, thought
that Peter wrote 1 Peter. 2 Peter was not written by the same
person as 1 Peter so this represents independent evidence for the
existence of 1 Peter by the time 2 Peter was written. The probable
date of the latter is the second quarter of the second century and
nearer to the beginning of that period than the end (cf. W. G.
Kümmel, *Introduction to the New Testament*, London, 1966, p. 305;
E. M. Sidebottom, *James, Jude, 2 Peter, New Century Bible*). This

dating of 2 Peter easily allows for the appearance of 1 Peter at any period in the first century and probably up to a period as late as that of the reign of Trajan.

Eusebius, *Ecclesiastical History*, III, 39:17, says that Papias knew and used 1 Peter; unfortunately Papias is difficult to date; he may belong to any time between 100–150 A.D., but probably nearer to the beginning of that period. Van Unnik, 'The "Gospel of Truth" and the New Testament' in *The Jung Codex*, ed. F. L. Cross, London, 1955, claims echoes of 1 Peter in this writing; since he dates it at 140–5 A.D., and it may well be a generation later, this gives us no additional information.

Irenaeus (*c.* 180 A.D.) is the first to refer to Peter by name in relation to the letter; increasingly thereafter quotations from it are so attributed.


## VII. THE PLACE OF 1 PETER IN THE DEVELOPING LIFE AND THOUGHT OF THE EARLY CHURCH

a. As we have already seen it is impossible to date accurately the period at which Christianity reached the various areas to which 1 Peter is directed (pp. 17ff). The general feel of the letter is that Christianity is not a new phenomenon in those areas but that the church is established, expanding and drawing the attention of outsiders. 'We get the impression . . . of a flood-tide which has been running strongly in the Church and accounts for much in the temper and atmosphere of' 1 Peter (Selwyn p. 39). This would indicate that Christianity had been present for at least a few years, more probably a decade, and would not at all be out of harmony with the view that it had been established much longer.

b. There is no trace of the dispute between Jewish and Gentile Christians which was in danger of splitting the church at least as late as the early fifties and which was still sufficiently alive by the time Paul wrote Romans (in the mid or late fifties) to lead him to discuss the issue, though the virulence had by that time gone out of it.

c. There is equally no trace of the church's fight with Gnosticism which occupied it during the second century. Conflict with gnostic ideas had certainly appeared much earlier and is seen in some of Paul's letters, more so in the non-Pauline portions of the

Pauline corpus and also in the Johannine literature, 2 Peter and
Jude. Less trace of the conflict is observable in Hebrews and little
if any in 1 Clement; the latter was written from Rome, the
probable place of writing of 1 Peter, and the former certainly has
some connection with Italy (13:24).

d. There is an acknowledged ministry but no developed doctrine
of it. There are no references to bishops but clear indications that
elders were in positions of authority in the church (5:1ff). The
nomenclature of offices in the church was not standard until well
into the second century and these two offices may well have been
equivalent for the writer and his communities (the verbal form of
'bishop' appears in some manuscripts at 5:2 in relation to the
ministry of elders). There is, however, a clear doctrine of the
church as the people of God; it is worked out more fully than in
any other NT writing but it does not contain any fundamentally
new thought. It was commonly accepted in the early church that
the Christians were the continuation of the OT people of God;
here the theme is expounded systematically. It could have
appeared at any time after Paul's major letters.

e. There is an expectation of Christ's speedy return; the writer
may even believe that the period of suffering which would
inaugurate that return has begun or is just about to begin (see
notes on 4:13,17). Paul's earlier letters show that he expected to
survive until the parousia; his later letters indicate that he had
begun to reckon with the possibility that he might not; he still
appears to have expected that the end would come soon (e.g.
Rom. 13:11–14). Such eschatological hope remained alive in the
church for a considerable period as Revelation, 2 Peter, Jude,
Mark 13 and its parallels testify. An outbreak of persecution
would easily revive eschatological expectation. There would be
constant interplay between the two ideas of persecution and the
parousia; a little persecution would suggest the nearness of the
end which in turn would lead to a belief in a more widespread
persecution.

f. Selwyn raises the point that the use of terms like 'aliens',
'exiles' (1:1; 2:11) implies 'people who do not properly belong to
the society in which they reside' (Selwyn, p. 57) and that Christians
would have become aware of this just after James' martyrdom in
62 A.D. This view might as easily have emerged after the martyr-
doms of Stephen or James the brother of John, both of which took
place at a much earlier period. From a very early period Christians

must have realised their foreignness in the world. In any case
we find the idea in Phil. 3:20 and its presence in 1 Peter
might be taken to indicate dependence on Paul, i.e., the writer
had reflected on a conception formulated by Paul and
produced his own form of it. There is certainly no need to see
here a gnostic motif (cf. H. Jonas, *The Gnostic Religion*, Boston,
1963, pp. 49ff).

g. The epistle is full of OT quotations and allusions (cf. pp. 28f).
Paul certainly uses the OT when arguing about the relative
position of Jews and Gentiles in the people of God or when
verifying his arguments about the law or justification by faith; in
each case he will have had Jewish objectors principally in mind.
Apart from these subjects his letters contain relatively few
quotations and allusions. Both Paul and the writer of our letter
were normally addressing a Gentile constituency. The increased
usage of the OT in 1 Peter would therefore indicate that it had
become more fully absorbed into its readers' thoughts. We find a
similar usage in Mark but largely only in relation to the passion;
we know however that from the earliest days Christians explained
the passion in OT terms in order to demonstrate that it was part
of God's plan of redemption: so Mark is not quite a fair parallel to
1 Peter.

h. There is an ambivalent attitude to the state: 2:13–17 implies
respect for it; 5:13 with its allusion to Rome as Babylon regards
the state as under the judgement of God. This would suggest a
situation in which some persecution had already been experienced
from the state but not one in which the state had come to be
conceived as necessarily inimical. This is similar to what we find
in 1 Clement.

i. The social code (see pp. 30f) appears in a number of different
forms in the NT and early Christian literature. The simplest and
most direct is that of Colossians (3:18–4:1), though even here
there is some expansion beyond simplicity in the section on
slaves. In Ephesians (5:22–6:9) this section is similar to that in
Colossians, but that on wives has been greatly enlarged and related
to teaching on the nature of the church. In both these codes there
are sections dealing with masters and children but none on duty
towards the state. In Titus (2:1–3:2) there are sections on slaves,
wives, duties towards the state and also sections on younger and
older men and women; there is also a reference to Titus' own
behaviour; he is to set an example of what a minister ought to be.

In 1 Timothy there are sections on duty towards the state (2:1–7), on women though not explicitly on wives (2:9–15), on slaves (6:1–2), on widows who appear to be as much an ecclesiastical as a social class (5:4–16), on church officials (3:1–13; 5:17–19) and Timothy himself as a representative minister (5:20–5; 4:1–5:3), and on the wealthy (6:3–19). Here we find social and ecclesiastical codes intermingled in a way reminiscent of, but more advanced than in Titus. 1 Clement is much more brief but includes sections on children, wives, duties toward the aged, respect for church leaders, humility and subjection in general, and citizenship (1:3–2:8; 21:6–9). *Didache* 4:9–11 and *Barnabas* 19:5–7 mention a good many of the various categories but without particular expansion of any one. Polycarp's letter to the Philippians contains sections for wives, widows (again partly as a social and partly an ecclesiastical class), church officials, the younger men, virgins (4:2–6:2). We can trace here a development from a fairly simple form (Colossians) of the social code through varying complexities of development of individual sections to a form in which an ecclesiastical code is intermingled with the social. If we now attempt to place 1 Peter in this sequence we see that each section of the social code which it has appears in a fairly expanded form (except in the case of husbands), that it includes a section on the state unlike Colossians and Ephesians but like the later codes, and that an ecclesiastical code is beginning to appear (5:1–5a) which is not as yet intermingled with the social code. It thus appears to be more advanced than Colossians and Ephesians and somewhat similar to Titus and 1 Clement but not as developed as 1 Timothy, where indeed the code as code is breaking down through over-great expansion of each item.

j. Of particular doctrines that of the Spirit suggests a period after the first flush of enthusiasm has died away. In 1:11 if the Spirit inspires (a recognized Jewish usage); in 3:18; 4:6 we have the contrast of flesh and Spirit; 3:18 is probably credal; 4:14 gives the promise of the Spirit in time of persecution; 1:2 teaches his general presence with the believer. This does not sound like the way in which the first generation of Christians appraised the Spirit, and certainly not like someone (e.g. Peter) who had experienced Pentecost.

k. We note that most of the parallels from credal, catechetical and liturgical material come from the books which are generally regarded as later in the NT, e.g. Ephesians, the Pastorals, James,

1 John. The relationship to Romans and Paul in general (pp. 32ff) suggests the absorption of some of that apostle's ideas. The one exception in relation to common material is the Thessalonian correspondence.

## VIII. AUTHORSHIP

Three main theories have been advocated: that the Apostle Peter wrote the letter; that it was written by Silvanus, either in Peter's lifetime under his instructions or after his death to continue his teaching; that it is pseudonymous.

### a. PETER AS AUTHOR

(On Peter, see O. Cullmann, *Peter: Disciple, Apostle, Martyr*, 2nd edn. London, 1962).

Authorship by Peter has been held to be untenable for the following reasons:

(i) The vocabulary and style. Peter was an 'uneducated' man (Ac. 4:13). His original language would have been Aramaic but he would have picked up in his early days a smattering of colloquial Greek. Such a smattering could never have grown in an uneducated man into the command of the language we find in this epistle. Selwyn says of its style that it 'is not only natural and unforced, indicating that it belongs to one who not only wrote, but also thought, in Greek; but it exhibits a felicity of phrase, a suppleness of expression, and a wealth of vocabulary which betoken a mind nourished in the best Greek spirit and tradition' (p. 25). We may compare Beare, 'He is a stylist of no ordinary capacity, and he writes some of the best Greek in the whole New Testament, far smoother and more literary than that of the highly-trained Paul' (p. 28).

(ii) The quotations of the OT are drawn from the Septuagint, the Greek translation of the Hebrew OT. This would not have been the version to which Peter, as a Galilean Jew, would have been accustomed; he would have been brought up on either a Hebrew version or an Aramaic translation of it, i.e. a Targum. What it is important to observe here are the allusions to the OT. Direct quotations would obviously have been put in the version to which the readers were accustomed, i.e., the LXX, even though the writer himself was accustomed to another version. The indirect allusions imply that the writer thought in terms of the LXX rather than the Hebrew text; as F. H. Chase says, 'Apart from quotations, however, the writer continually weaves into his own language words and phrases which are (possibly unconscious) reminiscences of the LXX' (*H.D.B.*, III, p. 781b; Chase appends a list of these allusions).

(iii) If Peter was writing to areas which had been evangelised by Paul (see p. 18) then in view of his previous clash with Paul (Gal. 2:11–14), his known warm-hearted though impulsive nature and his humility expressed at 5:1 in calling himself 'fellow elder', we might have expected that he would have made some reference to his brother apostle's previous work. We should expect this even more because Paul was in Rome at or about the time when Peter would have been writing the letter, and Peter must therefore have renewed his fellowship with him. In a somewhat parallel situation Clement in his letter to Corinth alludes to Paul because Paul had evangelized Corinth (47:1ff); cf. Ignatius, *Ephesians*, 12:2; *Romans* 4:3; Polycarp, *Philippians* 3:2; 9:1.

(iv) We have seen the indebtedness of the epistle to Pauline conceptions (pp. 32ff). Peter would only have encountered Paul's letter to Rome fairly late on in his life after his own presentation and understanding of the Gospel had become fixed and would not then have easily accepted new ideas and new forms of expression. Zahn (*Introduction to the New Testament*, II, Edinburgh, 1909, p. 176) however argues: 'But from all that we know of Peter there is not the slightest reason to assume that he was original, in the sense that James or Paul or John was original.' This is simply not so if we leave aside the evidence of the letter itself. Peter was the first of the disciples to express in public (even if he understood it wrongly) a statement on the nature of Jesus: 'You are the Christ' (Mk 8:29); he was also the first of the apostles to preach the gospel to Gentiles (Acts 10); there is no unwillingness in either case to express himself in new ways. But the whole letter, with its dependence not only on Paul but also on the common catechetical and liturgical material of the early church, suggests a writer without a characteristic view of his own (cf. pp. 29ff). Since Peter's commission was to the circumcised whereas Paul's was to the uncircumcised (Gal. 2:7f) we might reasonably have expected that this would have produced a different outlook on, and expression of, the Gospel.

(v) If it appears as we shall show (pp. 63f) that the letter suits a date later than that of the death of Peter (assumed to be in or about the time of the Neronic persecution, viz., 64 A.D.) then the letter cannot be by Peter. There is no evidence for Ramsay's assumption (*op. cit.* pp. 282f) that Peter survived the Neronic persecution.

(vi) There are a number of minor additional arguments: (a) If the letter was written by Peter why was it accepted so slowly in the early church? (cf. pp. 43ff). (b) There is nothing in the history of Peter to connect him with Asia Minor; but then our knowledge of his life is very scrappy. (c) If the letter was written in Rome by Peter we might expect that some of the Asian Christians there would send their greetings home (cf. Col. 4:10–14); but then this might not be suitable in a circular letter.

These arguments might appear to lead at once to a rejection of Petrine authorship; yet there are other considerations which suggest he was concerned in its composition and these must be examined.

(i) The ascription of the letter to Peter in 1:1 combined with the absence of explicit doubt in the early church about his authorship is an argument that cannot be passed over lightly.

(ii) There are certain passages which suggest that the author of the epistle was present at events in the earthly life of Jesus: (a) 5:1, 'a partaker in the glory that is to be revealed'. This is taken to be a reference to the transfiguration (cf. Selwyn, p. 30f; Walls-Stibbs p. 33f) and since Peter was present at this event the letter must be by him. It could be argued alternatively that the reference is a deliberate attempt to build up Peter as the author, but it is much more likely that in agreement with most commentators we should reject altogether the reference to the transfiguration (see notes on 5:1). (b) 2:20–5 is a description of the passion of Jesus; Selwyn says, 'This great passage recalls many incidents which St. Peter himself had witnessed' (p. 30). Certainly Peter did witness these events but the language in which they are described is drawn almost entirely from Isa. 53; it does not have the ring of an eye-witness account. If it is argued that Peter deliberately chose these words because they carry with them an interpretation of the passion (Walls-Stibbs p. 33), it must be answered that any preacher of the early church might have chosen them for this very reason and could not indeed have chosen words which would have about them the ring of an eye-witness. (c) Selwyn lists other passages (1:3; 1:7,9; 1:8; 1:10–12; 3:15; 5:2; cf. pp. 28–31) of which he says that they 'are not only consonant with Petrine authorship, but take on fresh meaning and reality on that assumption' (p. 31); he does not however attempt to use them to prove Petrine authorship but only to confirm it; they are too general for firm conclusions to be drawn, e.g. 1:3 is explicable given Peter's experience of the resurrection but it could equally have been written by any first century Christian who believed in the wonder of the risen Lord.

(iii) If the author of 1 Peter heard Jesus teach on as many occasions as Peter did we should expect to find strong reminiscences of Jesus' words in the letter. It is possible to list a considerable number (cf. Walls-Stibbs, p. 35 n.1; Chase, *H.D.B.*, III, pp. 787f). We note: (a) Almost all the reminiscences have their parallels in Matthew and not in Mark, the allegedly Petrine gospel. (b) There are no direct quotations; the authority of the Lord as teacher is never invoked; the same holds true incidentally of Paul's letters; it is the attitude of a writer to 'tradition' rather than to a 'person' whom he knew. (c) When we examine the parallels in detail we find that the majority are only vaguely similar in thought; verbal parallels are extremely rare. Moreover the general sentiment expressed in the Petrine form of the parallel is normally one common to early Christianity. Thus Walls parallels 1 Pet. 1:17 with Mt. 22:16; but Rom. 2:11; Eph. 6:9; Col. 3:25; Jas. 2:1 are also parallels; have we then to argue that Paul and James were witnesses of the teaching of Jesus? The closest parallels are: (1) 1 Pet. 3:14 and Mt. 5:10; but Nauck (*op. cit.*) has shown that there was probably a basic persecution form and 1 Pet. 3:14 depends on it. (2) 1 Pet. 1:18 and Mk 10:45 in relation to the death of Jesus as a 'ransom'; but if 1 Peter was written in Rome and Mark was the gospel of the Roman church it is likely that the interpretation in that gospel of the death of Jesus would find its way into 1 Peter. (d) Often when we find parallels these lie between passages in 1 Peter and passages in the Gospels which reflect developed tradition. The probable parallel to 1 Pet. 1:4 is Lk. 12:33 rather than Mt. 6:19a, 20a though the latter represents more faithfully what Jesus said; cf. 1 Pet. 4:10f and Lk. 12:42; 1 Pet. 4:14 and Lk. 6:22; 1 Pet. 1:18 and Mk 10:45. The author of 1 Peter does not therefore know the original form of the tradition but only its development and he was therefore not present when it was originally spoken (cf. E. Best, '1 Peter and the Gospel Tradition', *N.T.S.*, 16 (1970) 95–113).

(iv) In a recent article R. H. Gundry ('*Verba Christi* in 1 Peter:

Their Implications concerning the Authorship of 1 Peter and the Authenticity of the Gospel Tradition', *N.T.S.*, 13 (1967) 336–50) has attempted to show that not only are there many verbal reminiscences of Jesus in 1 Peter but that these mostly come from contexts in which Peter was involved. When we omit those passages in 1 Peter which have their parallels in sayings of Jesus in John (e.g. 1:22 and Jn 13:34f; 15:12), those passages which have parallels in the other NT epistles as well as in the gospels and for which a general knowledge of the tradition of the teaching is sufficient to account (see (iii) above) and those passages which are part of the general Biblical imagery (1:13; 2:25; 4:19) we are left with 2:4 (but only possibly; the stone imagery was probably part of the early tradition and therefore does not need to be explained in terms of Peter's name; see notes on 2:4), 2:19f (recalling Lk. 6:32–5 or Mt. 5:46f, but the resemblance is not very great), 3:14 (see (iii) above), 5:3–5 (recalling Lk. 22:25–30; Mk. 10:42–5 but 1 Pet. 5:2–5 is probably part of an ecclesiastical code; see notes *ad loc.*). Of these only 2:4 can be said to have a specific Petrine reference; even if the allusion is accepted it is not enough on which to build a theory.

(v) It is suggested that there are certain affinities between the thought of 1 Peter and the speeches attributed to Peter in Acts. A great many have been listed (cf. Selwyn pp. 33–6; Wand, p. 27f). Walls (Walls-Stibbs pp. 35f) selects the most important: 'the same sense of prophetic fulfilment' (Acts 2:16ff; 3:18; 1 Pet. 1:10ff, 20; this conception is universal in the NT, e.g. the Matthean formula 'this was to fulfil what the Lord had spoken by the prophet'); 'the same insistence on the cross as the foreordained action of God' (Ac. 2:23; 1 Pet. 1:20; this is again common NT teaching, e.g. Lk. 22:22; 24:26; Mk 8:31; Eph. 1:3–12; Jn 11:49–53); 'the same close connection of the resurrection and exaltation' (Ac. 2:32ff; 1 Pet. 1:21; 3:22; but if we omit Ac. 1:3 we find this everywhere else in the NT, e.g. Phil. 2:8–11; Eph. 1:20; Col. 3:1; 1 Th. 1:10); 'the same call to repentance and faith-baptism' (Ac. 2:38,40; 1 Pet. 3:20ff; but the close connection between new conduct and baptism is basic to the Christian teaching on baptism, e.g. Rom. 6:1–14; Col. 2:11–3:11; Tit. 3:5); 'the same sense of the certainty of Christ's judgement of the living and dead' (Ac. 10:42; 1 Pet. 4:5; but the conception of judgement is common throughout the NT; apart from 2 Tim. 4:1 these are the only places which speak of the living and the dead, but this is such a natural phrase that too much weight cannot be laid on it). Walls also refers to the same 'joyous recognition of the Gentile mission and the blessings attending it' in 1 Peter and in Peter as portrayed in Acts; but in what writing in the NT is there not this joyous recognition? (On the widespread nature of a common preaching in the NT, see C. H. Dodd, *The Apostolic Preaching*, London, 1936). There is however a general difficulty in drawing such a parallel between 1 Peter and the Petrine speeches in Acts: the latter are not verbatim accounts of Peter's words. Even if we were not to go as far as many scholars and hold that they reflect the gospel as preached in Luke's own time (so Haenchen, Dibelius, Conzelmann, O'Neill) we cannot deny that they represent the rewording of traditional material by Luke or the Christian community prior to him; it is interesting to observe that almost all the points listed in Peter's speeches in Acts by Walls re-appear also in Paul's speeches in Acts. It is therefore much more likely that these parallels arise from the common catechetical and evangelical instruction of the early church than from an exclusively Petrine factor.

(vi) It is suggested that there are affinities of thought between 1 Peter and Mark. This has been covered partly in our discussion of possible reminiscences of the teaching and activity of Jesus in 1 Peter (see (iii) above). Peter explains the death of Jesus in terms of the servant of Isa. 53; it cannot be said that this bulks largely in Mark (cf. M. D. Hooker, *Jesus and the Servant*, London, 1959, pp. 62–102; E. Best, *The Temptation and the Passion: The Markan Soteriology*, Soc. for N.T.S., Monograph Series No. 2, Cambridge, 1965, pp. 140ff). There is in both 1 Peter and Mark the attempt to interpret the death of Jesus as 'ransom' (see (iii) above and notes on 1:18) and a close relationship of persecution to the parousia (see on 4:13). These affinities are however explicable because both Mark and 1 Peter embody the theology of the Roman church (cf. p. 60).

We conclude that (ii)–(vi) show that there is some, though not much, evidence that is consonant with a connection between Peter and 1 Peter. We have however found nothing which enforces such a connection, though there is certainly nothing to be detected which is contrary to it. If then we take into account the objections raised to Petrine authorship which we considered earlier we are compelled to reject his claim to be the author.

## b. SILVANUS AND THE AUTHORSHIP

Many scholars who accept the arguments against direct Petrine authorship but are impressed by the evidence suggesting a connection between Peter and the letter attempt to solve this dilemma by supposing that Silvanus (see on 5:12) wrote it under the guidance of Peter. It is known that in the ancient world writers not only employed scribes who took down verbatim what they said but also secretaries who, given some guidance as to what a letter should contain, would write it and after approval send it in their master's name; the degree of guidance given would vary from writer to writer. Obviously Silvanus must be regarded as a secretary in the latter sense; if he is taken as scribe in the former sense then he is not responsible in any way for the language or content of the letter and Peter is still its full author and all the objections to his authorship would continue to stand.

In recent years Selwyn (pp. 7ff) has made out a strong case for the participation of Silvanus in the composition of the letter; in this he has followed such earlier scholars as Zahn, Bigg, Moffatt.

Selwyn begins by identifying the Silvanus of 1 Pet. 5:12 with the Silvanus mentioned by Paul (1 Th. 1:1; 2 Th. 1:1; 2 Cor. 1:19); this Silvanus is almost certainly to be identified with Silas, Paul's companion in Acts 15:40 etc. (Silas and Silvanus are probably the Greek and Latin forms of the same Jewish name). This Silas is again almost certainly to be identified with the Silas who with Judas Barsabbas (they were both prophets, Ac. 15:32) took the letter of the Jerusalem Council to the Gentile churches (Ac. 15:22,27). He disappears from the narrative of Luke after Ac. 18:5, where he is stated to be with Paul in Corinth; the reference in 2 Cor. 1:19, though later, refers back to this period. Selwyn surmises that at some time after this he became the companion of Peter. In confirmation of the identification of the Silvanus of 1 Pet. 5:12 with Paul's erstwhile companion Selwyn finds (i) an affinity between 1 Peter and 1 and 2 Thessalonians, and (ii) an affinity between 1 Peter and the apostolic letter of Ac. 15:23–9. It must be noted that if this indirect evidence is not found to be sufficient there is no reason for the identification of these two other than the name itself, and it was not uncommon.

The affinities which Selwyn finds between 1 Peter and 1 and 2 Thessalonians are set out in a long essay (pp. 363ff); with them he proves two things: (a) the existence of a primitive Christian catechism which has been used in both 1 Peter and 1 and 2 Thessalonians; (b) a common writer for both. It is very doubtful if these affinities are as great as Selwyn alleges (cf. B. Rigaux, *Saint Paul: Les Épîtres aux Thessaloniciens*, Paris and Gembloux, 1956, pp. 105–111). Even if they existed they can hardly be used to prove both of Selwyn's points: the more the primitive catechism is emphasised the less evidence there is to show the hand of a particular author, and vice versa. The resemblances Selwyn produces with other NT epistles suggest that the hypothesis of a catechism is correct (see pp. 29ff above). Further there is no evidence that Silvanus had any direct share in the composition of 1 and 2 Thessalonians; he might have acted as scribe, but even that cannot be proved. Of 1 Thessalonians W. Neil (*Thessalonians*, London, 1950, p. xviii) says: 'The actual Greek vocabulary and phrasing are definitely Pauline' (cf. Frame in the I.C.C. volume, pp. 28–34).

While there may be similarities between Ac. 15:23–9 and 1 Peter the former is so short in extent and the ideas it contains of so great importance to the early church that it would be impossible to prove contact; the ideas would have entered into the stream of primitive Christianity. In any case the details of the letter are probably Lukan.

According to Papias (Eusebius, *op. cit.*, III, xxxix, 15) Mark was the interpreter (*hermēneutēs*) of Peter in the writing of the second gospel. The precise meaning of 'interpreter' is not clear; probably we should understand that Mark wrote after Peter's death recalling what he had often heard Peter teach about Jesus. This then does not provide a proper parallel to Silvanus who would have been a secretary writing under the direction of Peter; it does not prove that Peter always depended on secretaries.

If there is then no external evidence to prove that Peter employed a secretary is there any internal evidence from the letter itself which might suggest this? The reference in 5:12 gives us no clue to the particular part played by Silvanus. Assuming for the moment that he did compose the letter, does the character of the writing fit that of the Silvanus whom we know from Acts and Paul? When we first encounter him it is as a delegate taking the decrees of the Council of Jerusalem (Ac. 15) to the Gentile churches; afterwards Paul chooses him as his companion and he can be assumed to have been a successful missionary in Hellenistic towns. These two facts would imply a good knowledge of Greek, though no greater dependence on the Hellenistic spirit than Paul himself, since the Jewish-Christian church in Jerusalem trusts him. But the dependence of 1 Peter on Hellenism is much greater than that of Paul. It could be argued that in the period between the Jerusalem council and the writing of the letter he came under considerable Hellenistic influence. It would not then have been impossible for Silas to have written this letter.

Any theory, however, which attributes a share in the composition of the letter to a secretary must indicate what that share is. It is certainly impossible to distinguish between one part of the letter and another and say that this portion is due to Peter and that to Silvanus; as Selwyn himself allows: 'The magic of Greek style is equally distributed throughout the Epistle, and distinguishes those parts which may be assigned to St. Peter's own testimony and definite direction no less than those in which he left to his amanuensis a wider discretion' (p. 27). If then the style, and the language cannot be isolated from the style, is to be credited to Silvanus it is fair to ask how far the thought is that of Peter. We may perhaps envisage Peter instructing Silvanus to write to the churches of Asia Minor preparing them for persecution and to base his remarks on known catechetical and liturgical material; Silvanus would then read over to Peter what he had written, Peter would approve and add 5:12-14 including reference to Silvanus as a faithful brother; Silvanus would hardly have written this himself. If we take as an example the social code of 2:13-3:7 we see that the expansion which it has received in this letter is in the language and style of Silvanus; of course Silvanus can be presumed to have known that when Peter used this code in instruction he expanded the section on slaves by a reference to the example of Christ as the true slave and the section on wives with an attack on costly apparel, but he has quite definitely expressed this in his own language and style and not Peter's, and therefore all the subtler nuances of thought belong to him and not to Peter. When we add to this the extensive use of traditional material that we find in the letter there does not appear to be a great deal which we can pin down as Peter's. When we further add the way in which LXX phrases and allusions are worked into the epistle, we can only conclude that while the letter may bear the authority of Peter, Silvanus must be its real and effective author. But we are then compelled to ask why Peter does not acknowledge Silvanus's real share in the authorship; the allusion to him in 5:12 is far too ambiguous for such a conclusion to be drawn from it. This would not be of so great importance if Silvanus were an unknown Christian, but since, by hypothesis, he is one of the known companions of Paul and a missionary in his own right and will have been-known by reputation, if not by person, to those to whom the letter is written we should expect more credit to have been given to him.

It further needs to be pointed out that small affinities of thought between 1 Peter and Mark, the speeches of Peter in Acts and reminiscences of Jesus' teaching cannot be attributed to Peter; if the final form of expression is Silvanus's then we cannot make these verbal similarities into arguments for Petrine authorship. If the hypothesis of co-authorship by Silvanus is advanced to preserve some connection between Peter and the epistle because of arguable affinities with Peter in other writings then it is precisely this argument that we are not able to use because we cannot be sure that any expression in 1 Peter is attributable to Peter.

There are a number of positive objections to Silvanus as part-author. We have already pointed out that some Pauline ideas have been accepted, but without their Pauline vigour (p. 34f); while this could be understood in the case of Peter it is much more difficult to understand in the case of a known companion of Paul. If Silvanus had a share in authorship we should have expected a greater proportion of Pauline expressions and conceptions. If, as is likely, the date of writing of the letter suits a later period than that of Peter, this is equally an objection to co-authorship by Silvanus. We therefore conclude that there is little positive evidence which compels us to see Silvanus as part-author; indeed it could well be argued that there are greater objections to this than to authorship by Peter alone.

We have not as yet examined the suggestion that Silvanus is the actual author, not co-author, and that he issued the letter after Peter's death in Peter's name as a faithful disciple to continue the ideas of his master (cf. von Soden, Bornemann, and perhaps Schelkle). If after Peter's death Mark wrote up his memories of Peter's teaching about Jesus, may not Silvanus have done the same with some of the instruction he recollected Peter using so often? This seems at first sight an attractive suggestion in that it retains some connection between Peter and the epistle, but it has not gained the support of scholars because of one insuperable objection, viz., the reference to Silvanus in 5:12 'a faithful brother as I regard him'; as Moffatt remarks 'the self-praise of 5:12 becomes offensive on such a view', *Introduction* (p. 334). There are two further difficulties: if it is supposed to be the teaching of Peter why does it contain so much traditional material? Why did not Silvanus who had been a companion of Paul in writing to an area where he knew Paul to have been active, and Peter probably not, address encouragement to the readers in Paul's name?

## C. PSEUDONYMITY

If there are difficulties in attributing the epistle to Peter, to Peter and Silvanus as co-authors, or to Silvanus writing after the time of Peter's death, then it is necessary to examine the theory that an unknown put out this letter in the name of Peter at some time after Peter's death. It must be frankly allowed that it is the difficulties in the above theories that suggest pseudonymity; there is nothing explicit within the body of the epistle, no anachronisms, no historical facts contrary to what we know of Peter, which necessitate this conclusion; the only internal evidence which is positively in its favour is the probable date (see pp. 63f). But in this period pseudonymous literature was common and the practice was not regarded with the same abhorrence as today.

Within the OT the later parts of Isaiah are attributed to the prophet of that name though not written by him; Deuteronomy consists almost entirely of words supposed to be spoken by Moses though dating from a much later period. In the time of the NT the apocalyptic literature is pseudonymous (e.g. the books of Enoch, the Apocalypses of Baruch); amongst non-apocalyptic material we find the Wisdom of Solomon (though his name is not explicitly used, yet it is implicitly suggested that he wrote the book), the Letter of Jeremiah and the Letter of Aristeas. A number of factors led to the production and acceptance among the Jews of this pseudonymous literature, e.g. the strong concept of contemporaneity of the past with the present, the idea of corporate personality, the conception of the name as the extension of a man's personality (see D. S. Russell, *The Method and Message of Jewish Apocalyptic*, London, 1964, pp. 127ff; L. S. Brockington, 'The Problem of Pseudonymity', *J.T.S.*, 4 (1953) 15–22). But would this have continued in Christianity? 2 Peter is almost certainly pseudonymous. Many scholars attribute the Johannine literature to disciples of John who continued to develop his witness and thought after his death (e.g. C. K. Barrett, *The Gospel according to St.John*, London, 1955, pp. 83ff; R. E. Brown, *The Gospel according to John*, Vol. I, in The Anchor Bible, New York, 1966, pp. lxxxviiff). The existence of the Pastorals as post-Pauline suggests the same process. Such schools, extending the thought of apostles, fit in with the explanation of the origin and acceptance of pseudonymity among the Jews.

We may then suppose that some time after Peter's death a disciple or disciples will have issued our letter. It will not then be unrelated to Peter's own thought and testimony, but since we have little sure knowledge of the content of these we cannot point to particular traits in the letter and say that this reference or allusion is ultimately Petrine. We certainly cannot agree with Boismard (*D.B.S.* VII, 1452f) that an underlying liturgical form is to be traced to Peter. It is possible that Peter was known as one who strongly upheld the use of traditional material and his disciples continued to utilise it. The existence of a Petrine school is confirmed by the Gospel of Mark, written after Peter's death but traditionally held (since the time of Papias) to contain his witness to Jesus; many scholars would doubt if the association of Peter with the Gospel was as close as Papias suggests, but there is no smoke without some fire.

There are also some theological similarities between 1 Peter and Mark, e.g. an overall similarity of interpretation of the death of Jesus in that Christ bears punishment and men's sins are forgiven (as over against an interpretation which sees Christ's death as one of victory over evil powers), a particular similarity in the use of the ransom concept to interpret that death, a like interest in the Woes of the Messiah as involving persecution for the church and not just terrible times for the world as a whole.

Clement of Alexandria reports that the Gnostic Basilides obtained information from Glaucias the interpreter of Peter (*Stromata*, VII, 17) but since it was a common claim of the Gnostics to have received information from the apostles not too much should be made of this. From the middle and later part of the second century a considerable body of literature professedly written by Peter began to appear, but this happened in the case of many of the apostles and there is no need to see in it an argument for the existence of a Petrine school.

Carrington (*op. cit.*, pp. 68ff) suggests that as a group of tannaite disciples termed 'elders' descended from Rabbi Hillel, who lived just prior to the time of Jesus and who was called 'the elder', so 'According to Papias and Irenaeus a full tannaite system of elders and disciples existed in Asia Minor, deriving their succession from the disciple John (called, like Hillel, *the* Elder), and from other disciples of the Lord'. He further argues, 'there is evidence, therefore, that one element of great importance in the Christian *ekklēsia* was the propagation of *tōrāh* by teachers who had received it in true succession, and that the process was oral'. This accords well with what we have been arguing in the case of 1 Peter. We note that in 5:1 the author describes himself as an elder and addresses some of his readers in responsible positions in the community as elders, but since he addresses them he thereby implies some form of distinction between his eldership and theirs.

If the book is pseudonymous then the references to Silvanus, Mark and Rome will be part of the way in which this is built up. Silvanus and Mark, whether identical or not with those we know elsewhere in the NT by these names, will have been believed to be associates of Peter and Rome will have been used as the place of writing because Peter was known to have been there (see pp. 64f). However Rome probably was the actual place of writing since the Petrine school would have continued in the place where Peter died.

We must now enquire whether there are positive considerations militating against pseudonymity.

(i) Walls (Walls-Stibbs pp. 20–3) says that 1 Peter was known and used by Polycarp and Papias who were 'very conscious, like all their generation, of the great gulf fixed between the original apostles and themselves'; would they have used it if they had been conscious that it was not by an apostle? We can answer quite simply that they may not have been conscious that it was not by an apostle; if the letter was issued in the time of Domitian its origin could quite easily have been obscure by the time these two authorities came to know it. In any case they may have accepted the conception of its emergence from a Petrine school as equivalent to Petrine authorship; there is no need to equip them with modern minds.

(ii) Walls also argues (*ibid.*) that there was no reason why it should not have been issued without a name; Hebrews is not attributed to any author and was accepted. But Hebrews was only confidently accepted by all when they came to believe that it

had been written by Paul. If 1 Peter had been issued without a
name it might never have been accepted.

(iii) Walls also remarks that the references to Peter in 1 Peter are
restrained and therefore unlike what we normally find in pseudepi-
graphical books; 'the contrast with such writings as we can
reasonably regard as undoubtedly pseudonymous could hardly be
greater' (p. 22). The best answer to this would seem to lie with
Guthrie who has examined in detail the problem of pseudonymity
(cf. *New Testament Introduction: The Pauline Epistles*, London, 1961,
pp. 282–94); in his third volume, *The General Epistles and Revelation*,
he writes, 'The fact is that the general tendency among pseudepi-
graphists was to avoid rather than include supporting allusions to
their main heroes' (p. 169). The amount of biographical build-up
in 1 Peter is very similar to what we find in the Pastorals and the
Johannine literature and we have suggested that the origin of all
three lies in schools of disciples.

(iv) 'Pseudonymity is a device mostly adopted when a writer
has a specific purpose for which he borrows the authority of a
greater name' (A. H. McNeile, *An Introduction to the Study of the
New Testament*, 2nd edn. rev. C. S. C. Williams, London, 1953,
p. 218), e.g. to denounce a heresy, teach a particular doctrine,
lay down rules for church life and organization; it is argued that
there is no such motive in 1 Peter. But if 1 Peter is primarily
written to prepare its readers for the eschatological persecution
which will bring in the End then such a purpose does exist.
In any case it is doubtful if the statement in quotations is entirely
true; does 2 Clement fall under it? In any case the production of
1 Peter from a Petrine school is not quite the same as borrowing
the authority of a greater name.

(v) The rejection of pseudonymous literature by the church in the
later part of the second century and in succeeding centuries might
suggest that the church was always alert to sieve out such literature. But by the middle of the second century the church was
engaged in a ferocious struggle for its existence against gnostic
perversion of its gospel and it was already accepting some writings
as authoritative; this would lead it to examine carefully new
literature of which it had not been previously aware. These
conditions did not exist at the end of the first century. (On
pseudonymity cf. also, K. Aland, 'The Problem of Anonymity
and Pseudonymity in Christian Literature of the First Two
Centuries', and D. Guthrie, 'The Development of the Idea of

Canonical Pseudepigrapha in New Testament Criticism', both in *The Authorship and Integrity of the New Testament* (S.P.C.K. Theological Collections 4), London, 1965.)

We conclude that the epistle was pseudonymous but emerged from a Petrine school. We should point out that the understanding of the epistle is not greatly affected by such a decision about authorship; indeed, if it were, the determination of authorship would probably have been much easier.

## IX. DATE

There are many factors to be taken into account in any attempt to estimate the date of writing of 1 Peter.

(i) The use by 1 Peter of other NT writings fixes a lower limit to its own date. We have seen (pp. 32ff) that 1 Peter pre-supposes a knowledge of Pauline doctrine as found in Romans and Ephesians (if by Paul), if not a knowledge of the actual writings themselves. If Ephesians is by Paul this could be satisfied by a date in the middle sixties but is more easily explicable in terms of a somewhat later date; this would allow for Pauline concepts to have entered the general stream of church thought long enough for their particular bite to have been lost (this is more important in the case of Romans than Ephesians) and for Ephesians to have been published, if it was not by Paul.

(ii) The use of 1 Peter by later writers and their testimony to it fixes an upper limit. We have seen that it was known to Polycarp, Papias and the writer of 2 Peter (pp. 43ff). If Polycarp's letter was written about the time of the death of Ignatius this puts an upper limit of 112, but this supposition about Polycarp is unlikely. 120–30 A.D. is more probable as an upper limit. We need to allow some time for the circulation of the letter, but both Polycarp and Papias were in a position to encounter it in its own area (even if pseudonymous we assume it was still sent to Asia Minor) fairly soon after its composition even if the date lies near their own time. We should note the absence of general testimony to the letter in the church until the time of Irenaeus.

(iii) The nature and extent of the persecutions referred to in the epistle have been used to date it to a particular known persecution. We have argued that the references do not relate to official state persecution (pp. 39ff) and so we cannot use them to help us ascertain the date. We need to note that if there is no reason to associate them with those described by Pliny this removes one of the main arguments for a date in the reign of Trajan.

(iv) If we can identify the author then we have a strong clue to the possible date. Our discussion of authorship has led us to the conclusion that the letter post-dates the death of Peter and emerges from a Petrine school (pp. 49ff). It is difficult to know how long Peter's disciples would have remained together as a school but probably not much more than a generation.

(v) The setting of the epistle within the stream of development of the thought of the church in the early period gives another clue. This appears to be satisfied preferably by a date towards the end of the first century. If we refer back to our discussion of this (pp. 45ff) we see that such a conclusion is supported by (a), (b), (g), (h), (i), (j), (k); (c) suggests a somewhat earlier date; (d), (e), (f) provide no clue. There is a general similarity of approach and feeling to what we find in 1 Clement without it being possible to argue that there is indebtedness of either writing to the other (cf. Lohse, *op. cit.*, pp. 83–5).

(vi) The later the letter is dated the easier it becomes to account for the spread of Christianity into all the areas to which it is addressed (cf. pp. 17ff).

(vii) Amongst minor matters the use of Babylon for Rome may only have arisen after the conquest of Jerusalem (70 A.D.); see notes on 5:13.

The evidence is best satisfied by a date between 80–100 A.D., or, put differently, it was written during the reign of Domitian. Since there is no need to tie it to Domitianic persecutions, if there were such, it could well have come from the beginning of this period. If this period is unacceptable then the evidence would indicate an earlier date rather than a later.

## X. PLACE OF WRITING

It is generally assumed that the letter was written from Rome (5:13, Babylon is Rome); other places of origin have been suggested (e.g. Streeter, *op. cit.*, pp. 130ff who prefers Smyrna; Beare, 1st edn. 1947, p. 31, who prefers the area to which the letter is directed) but have not been found acceptable by other scholars (Beare, 2nd edn., 1958, reverts to the traditional solution).

That the earliest external witnesses to the letter are found in Asia Minor (Polycarp, Papias, cf. pp. 43f) cannot be used as an argument against Rome; a letter is likely to be known and quoted in the area to which it is written before it is used in the place from which it is written.

In favour of Rome as the place of composition are:

(i) Babylon is a pseudonym for Rome; see notes on 5:13.

(ii) There is a traditional association of Peter with Rome. It is difficult to gainsay the verdict of Cullmann (*op. cit.*, p. 114) that the evidence 'is sufficient to let us include the martyrdom of Peter in Rome in our final historical picture of the early Church, as a fact which is relatively though not absolutely assured'. (On the archeological evidence about Peter's burial in Rome, cf. Cullmann, pp. 131ff; J. M. C. Toynbee and J. W. Perkins, *The Shrine of St. Peter and the Vatican Excavations*, London, 1956; E. Kirschbaum, *The Tombs of St. Peter and St. Paul*, London, 1959; the evidence in this case is much more ambiguous.)

(iii) The dependence of 1 Peter on Paul's letter to the Roman church (cf. pp. 32ff); the most natural place for this to have come about would be the area of circulation of Romans, i.e. Rome.

(iv) Affinities with Mark (see pp. 54, 60).

(v) Similarities of thought and language with 1 Clement (cf. Lohse, *op. cit.*, pp. 83–5).

(vi) Absence of gnostic ideas; these affected Christian literature in Rome later than in many other areas, e.g. Asia Minor.

(vii) Any affinity that may exist with the later Roman baptismal liturgy (cf. F. L. Cross, *op. cit., passim;* Boismard, *D.B.S.* VII 1430ff). Such affinity does not prove that 1 Peter was itself a baptismal liturgy (see pp. 21ff) but results from the continuance of liturgical and linguistic formulae in the Roman church.

(viii) Any Petrine school which continued the work of its leader can be assumed to have done so in the place where he was martyred, i.e. Rome, as Mark's Gospel indicates. Although Peter can only have been in Rome for a short period before his death he will have brought disciples there when he came.


## XI. TEXT


Since the publication of the RSV one important new Greek manuscript of 1 Peter has been discovered, viz., $P^{72}$, in the

Bodmer collection of papyri; it dates from the third, or possibly fourth century. Normally it supports the text used in the translation of the RSV; at a few points in the notes attention has been drawn to its readings where these are important (cf. S. Kubo, *P72 and the Codex Vaticanus*, Salt Lake City, Utah, 1965).

# THE FIRST LETTER OF
# Peter

1

The customary opening words in letters in the Hellenistic world were 'A to B, Greetings' (cf. Ac. 23:26); these were sometimes followed by a thanksgiving to the gods and a prayer or wish for the prosperity of the readers. Each element was capable of expansion. Our letter contains the thanksgiving (1:3–12) but not the prayer. The normal Hellenistic epistolary introduction was profoundly modified in the early church, probably under the influence of Paul, by the alteration of the normal Greek word for 'greetings' to the much more theological word 'grace' from the same Greek root, and by the addition of the usual Jewish greeting, 'peace' (cf. Jg. 19:20; Mt. 10:12f; Jn 20:19,26; the Greek and Hebrew greetings are already found together in 2 Mac. 1:1ff).

1. **Peter:** on the question of authorship see pp. 49ff. Peter is the Greek rendering of the Aramaic name 'Cephas' which Jesus gave to Simon (Mt. 16:18; Mk 3:16); both mean the 'rock'; for Gentile communities the Greek form is the more appropriate.

**Apostle:** *lit.* 'one who is sent', 'missionary'. The word was used in the early church with a wide meaning referring to any missionary (e.g. Rom. 16:7), and, more restrictedly, to the twelve disciples chosen by Jesus; Paul used it of himself as an equal of the Twelve. In Judaism the apostle (Hebrew *shaliach*) of a man was his agent or ambassador who for a limited time and in a certain sphere of action could act in his principal's name and with his authority (cf. T. W. Manson, *The Church's Ministry*, London, 1948, pp. 31–52; K. H. Rengstorf, *T.D.N.T.*, I. pp. 407ff; M. H. Shepherd, *I.D.B.* I, pp. 170–2). If Jesus' disciple Peter wrote this letter he claims with this term the right and authority of Christ to address his readers; if the letter is pseudonymous this right and authority are claimed for it. Like Paul the writer exercises a supervisory ministry.

**dispersion:** (cf. Jas 1:1) this eventually became a technical term for the Jewish people outside Palestine their homeland; its origin lies in the OT (Dt. 30:4; Neh. 1:9; Ps. 147:2). It thus denotes those who live away from their homeland and hope to return to it. (On **dispersion** see K. L. Schmidt, *T.D.N.T.* II, pp. 98–104; J. A. Sanders *I.D.B.*, I, pp. 854–6). It does not imply that the Christians were only scattered groups or individuals.

**exiles:** (cf. Gen. 23:4; Ps. 39:12) conveys a similar meaning to 'dispersion', but with the additional emphasis that the separation from the homeland is only temporary. Both words are used metaphorically. There are frequent references in the NT to the transitory nature of the life of Christians in this world with the implied accompanying thought that they will eventually come to their true home, the heavenly Jerusalem (1 Pet. 1:17; 2:11; Eph. 2:19; Phil. 3:20; Heb. 11:13; 13:14; *Didache* 9:4; a classic exposition of the conception is found in *Epistle to Diognetus*, 5). We shall find that our writer continually uses OT terms to describe Christian existence; for him, as for the remainder of the NT, the church is the continuation of the OT people of God. The existence of the church thus lies far back in the purpose of God, and this is the thought to which he passes in verse 2, viz., 'chosen and destined'.

**Pontus . . . Bithynia:** see pp. 14ff.

2. **chosen:** another concept derived from the OT (cf. 2:9 and see H. H. Rowley, *The Biblical Doctrine of Election*, London, 1950; G. E. Mendenhall, *I.D.B.* II, pp. 76–82). Israel believed itself to be chosen, selected or elected by God (Hos. 11:1; Ezek. 20:5; Isa. 41:8f; 51:2; Ps. 105:43). This belief was emphasised in the inter-testamental period, e.g. the faithful in 1 Enoch are known as 'the elect' (cf. 1QS 8:6; 11:16). The early Christians, viewing themselves as the people of God, realised also that they had been 'chosen' by God to be so (cf. Rom. chapters 9–11; see also notes on 2:4). Here the thought is closely linked to verse 1: it is because they are 'chosen' by God that they are now exiles of the dispersion in the world.

**destined:** the whole of verse 2 from this word onwards may qualify all verse 1 so that the readers are not only set out as 'destined' to be believers but also to be exiles of the dispersion and Peter to be an apostle (So Hort, Selwyn, Beare, etc.). **destined:** *lit.*, 'fore-known'. When God foreknows (people and not events) he achieves his purpose, here defined as 'obedience to Jesus Christ. . . .' It is not just that he knows beforehand what is going to happen, but that he brings to pass what he foreknows. His fore-knowledge and choice of believers are a common NT belief, e.g. Rom. 8:29f; 11:2; Eph. 1:4,11f; 2 Thess. 2:13. Christians are set **down** as

'chosen and destined' for 'obedience to Jesus . . .'; nothing is said
about the certainty that they will be brought from their present
exile to the New Jerusalem; 4:15–19; 5:9f appear to leave this as
yet undecided (even if these later passages come from another
epistle, it is from one by the same author, cf. pp. 26f). The author
does not show himself to be as aware of the problem of human
responsibility in relation to God's election as was Paul (see Rom.
9–11).

**sanctified by the Spirit:** note the capital S in Spirit; God's
Spirit as his agent in sanctification is meant. What God had
destined them to be, he now makes them to be, viz., holy. The
believer does not sanctify himself but is sanctified by God's
Spirit (cf. 2 Th. 2:13). The close association of the Spirit with
baptism in the early church (cf. 1 Cor. 12:13; 6:11; and Jesus'
own baptism, Mk 1:9–11) suggests that the moment of sanctification would have been baptism: from that time forward Christians may be termed 'saints', i.e. 'holy' (cf. Rom. 1:7; 1 Cor. 1:2;
etc.), though they still have to produce in their lives the fruits
of actual holiness; 1:15 shows that our writer is quite aware of
this requirement.

**obedience, sprinkling:** these are two concepts which are
difficult to fit together since the first suggests the moral response of
the Christian to the second. The literal translation is 'for obedience
and sprinkling with the blood of Jesus Christ'; the RSV rendering
has understood a 'to Jesus Christ' with 'obedience'. It is grammatically possible that a reference is being made to the obedience
of Jesus (this would take 'Jesus Christ' in the same way in the two
halves of the phrase) but it is hard to see how the obedience of
Jesus Christ is related to the believer in any way similar to that in
which 'sprinkling with blood' is. We thus take 'obedience' as
rendered in the RSV but do not understand it of the believer's
daily moral obedience; it denotes his once-for-all obedience
which led to his acceptance of reconciliation through the blood of
Jesus Christ. Paul often uses 'obedience' in this way (Rom.
1:5; 6:16; 15:18; 2 Th. 1:8), an obedient response in faith
which brings first justification and then actual righteousness.
This faith-obedience would have been publicly manifested in
baptism.

**sprinkling with his blood:** probably a reference to the story of
the enactment of the covenant (Exod. 24:3–8) when Moses
sprinkled the people with the blood from the same animal which

he had poured on the altar (signifying reconciliation between
God and people) and in which a decision for obedience was
given by the people prior to the sprinkling (the same order of
events as in this verse, thereby confirming our view of 'obedience').
The covenant story is used with this reconciliatory significance in
Heb. 9:15–22. **Blood** necessarily carries a reference to the death
of Jesus, but the emphasis lies not on the violent nature of his
death but on its redemptive nature (cf. Heb. 9:22, 'without the
shedding of blood there is no forgiveness of sin'). Exod. 29:19–21,
the consecration of Aaron and his sons to the priesthood, also
refers to the sprinkling of blood; this might be in mind here since
the epistle later stresses the priestly nature of the people of God
(2:4–10), but it is probably not, because 'obedience' and 'sprinkling' are not linked in this story as they are in Exod. 24.

In this verse we have **God the Father,** the **Spirit** and **Jesus
Christ** mentioned alongside one another; we have here the
beginnings of Trinitarian doctrine (cf. Mt. 28:19; 1 Cor. 12:4–6;
2 Cor. 13:14; Eph. 4:4–6; 2 Th. 2:13–14). The present formulation was not created in order to bring Father, Son and Spirit
into parallel egalitarianism but has emerged from the description
of the readers' Christian existence; this is true of the other
expressions of Trinitarian doctrine in the NT (Mt. 28:19, which
gives the baptismal formula of Matthew's community, may be an
exception). Thus both the order, Father, Spirit, Christ, and the
description of the Second Person as Christ and not Son, arise from
the context and are not indicative of pre-eminence or dignity.
God is not termed 'Father' primarily as the Father of all men, or
all believers, but as the Father of Jesus (cf. 1:3). In Judaism God
was sometimes addressed as Father, but the very common
Christian usage does not derive directly therefrom but through
Jesus' own use of the word in relation to God.

**grace:** in the Pauline theology means God's goodness toward
those who do not merit it; while something of the wonder of this
is lost in our writer's usage it still stands for the gracious activity of
God towards men.

**peace:** when this is used in Jewish greetings 'something is given,
which means well-being for the other' (Pedersen, *Israel* I–II,
London, 1954 p. 303). 'When we consider the rich possibilities of
shālōm (peace) in the OT we are struck by the negative fact that
there is no specific text in which it denotes the specifically spiritual
attitude of inward peace' (v. Rad, *T.D.N.T.*, II, 406). Thus

peace is objective, almost equivalent to salvation, rather than a subjective feeling of harmony.

**May grace and peace be multiplied to you:** this formula (cf. 2 Pet. 1:2; Jude 2) differs from that which Paul normally uses in that (i) Paul says that grace and peace are from God (except 1 Th. 1:1), and (ii) our writer introduces 'be multiplied' which he probably takes from the Greek versions of Daniel (4:1 and 6:26 in the version of Theodotion and 4:37c in the LXX). This addition accords with his conception of 'grace' as an 'object' of which more or less can be given by God, rather than with Paul's conception of it as God's favour. These gifts of grace and peace are mediated by the letter itself.


## PRAYER: THANKSGIVING FOR THE HOPE THAT IS IN CHRIST 1:3-12

In one long skilfully constructed paragraph (in the original the separate sentences of the RSV are linked by relative pronouns) the writer follows the initial address with a prayer of thanksgiving. God's greatest mercy is the resurrection of Jesus Christ and on this all salvation rests (1:3-5); the recollection of salvation brings joy and this upholds the church through the various trials that threaten so that at last salvation is attained (1:6-9); a long preparation was made for this salvation in the history of Israel (1:10-12). These thoughts have all been welded together so carefully that some scholars (e.g. Windisch, Schneider) have regarded it as a hymn. Exact analysis into hymnic form cannot however be carried through successfully. Alternatively it has been suggested that it may be based in part, or in whole, on a hymn. J. Coutts ('Ephesians i:3-14 and 1 Peter i:3-12,' *N.T.S.* 3 (1957) 115-27) sees behind both 1:3-12 and Eph. 1:3-14 a form of liturgical prayer whose original form is more easily detected in Ephesians than in our text. Boismard (*Quatre Hymnes baptismales,* pp. 15-56) has pointed to a number of parallel expressions and thoughts in Tit. 3:4-7; the latter concludes with the words, 'the saying is sure' (Tit. 3:8), indicating that the author is using a known source (cf. 1 Tim. 1:15; 3:1; 4:9; 2 Tim. 2:11). Boismard therefore deduces a short baptismal hymn lying behind both 1 Pet. 1:3-5 and Tit. 3:4-7 which he considers the former reproduces more faithfully. But an examination of the use of the

phrase 'The saying is sure' in the Pastorals shows that it itself
indicates the faithful reproduction of a source and not just
indebtedness to, or the redaction of, a source; we should therefore
expect Tit. 3:4–7 to be the original. Boismard, moreover, does
not explain satisfactorily why certain similar ideas are expressed
with different words (e.g. 'regeneration' and 'born anew').
While therefore a hymn may underlie part or all of 1 Pet. 1:3–12
its form has been much altered.

## DOXOLOGY I :3–5

3. **Blessed be ...** this form of prayer is Jewish rather than Greek
(cf. Ps. 68:19; 72:18 and Jewish liturgical prayers, in particular
the Eighteen Benedictions); it was adopted by the Christian
church (cf. 2 Cor. 1:3; Eph. 1:3; Lk. 1:68). Though 1 Pet. 1:3a
is verbally identical with 2 Cor. 1:3 and Eph. 1:3 this does not
imply literary dependence; the phrase will probably have been
created by Paul in 2 Cor. 1:3 or earlier through the adaptation of
the existing Jewish form and passed into the liturgical and epistolary usage of the church, and so been adopted by our author.
**The God and Father of our Lord Jesus Christ:** God is praised,
not as creator and ruler of the world, but as the redeemer who is
the Father of Jesus Christ and through whom men enjoy new life.
'Of our Lord Jesus Christ' is probably to be understood as
dependent on both 'God' and 'Father' (see also 2 Cor. 1:3; 11:31;
Eph. 1:3; Rom. 15:6; cf. Eph. 1:17; Rev. 1:6; 3:2,12); as we saw
in 1:2 there is as yet no developed Trinitarian doctrine. But any
inferiority that is thereby implied is balanced by the description
of Jesus as **Lord;** this title was used in the OT for God and in
contemporary Hellenism for its gods and for the Roman Emperor
when he was given divine honour. It was one of the most common
titles used by the early Christians for Jesus (cf. V. Taylor, *The
Names of Jesus*, London, 1953, pp. 38–51; W. Kramer, *Christ,
Lord, Son of God*, S.B.T. no. 50, 1966, pp. 65–107; 151–182, 215–
222). It frequently forms the centre of confessional formulae
(1 Cor. 12:3; Rom. 10:9). Verses 3b–5 develop the ground on
which Christians bless God: by his gracious act they have been
redeemed and are being guarded to inherit eternal salvation.
**mercy:** this word may have been chosen rather than 'love' or
'grace' because it is often used in relation to God's election (cf.
2:10; Rom. 9–11) which has been one of the themes of 1:1–2, and

in relation to the admission of Gentiles to the church (Rom. 15:9; 11:30-2; Eph. 2:1-4; cf. Hort); the communities which are addressed are largely Gentile.

**born anew:** the desire for a new beginning is widespread in religion; in the contemporary Mystery Religions the initiates underwent ceremonies of rebirth; in Judaism the proselyte was regarded as a new born child (cf. A. D. Nock, *Conversion*, Oxford, 1933; M. Grant, *The World of Rome*, London, 1960, pp. 154ff; J. M. Robinson, *I.D.B.* IV, pp. 24-9). Apart from 1 Peter the conception is found in Jn 3:3,5; 1 Jn 3:9; Tit. 3:5; Jas. 1:18; it does not appear in Paul, but he uses the related idea of the Christian as a new being (2 Cor. 5:17; Gal. 6:15; cf. Eph. 2:10; Col. 3:9-11). It cannot be doubted that our author is using imagery familiar to his readers, but with an eschatological reference and an ethical seriousness foreign to the Mystery Religions (cf. Preisker); it is unlikely that he introduced it into Christian terminology. It expresses vividly the completed change in life for the pagan who turned to Christ—a change so great that former friends could not understand his new life (4:4). On the one hand the phrase is not to be reduced to a vivid metaphor, and it may have been no more than this in Judaism: the Christian is not like one who is born anew; he *is* born anew. On the other hand no naturalistic or metaphysical change takes place in his nature. Essential to rebirth is the response in faith-obedience (1:2) to the Word of God (1:23) preached about the resurrection (1:3). The new life flowing from the new birth only exists because of the new risen life of Christ; we are close here to the ideas of Rom. 6:3-11, viz., new life through dying and rising with Christ. The Christian is reborn neither by simply passing through the ceremony of baptism, though rebirth cannot be dissociated from it, nor by righteous living, for he is as incapable of starting himself on the new life as he was of conceiving himself for his first life. It is only by God's mercy, his unlooked for and undeserved gracious act of love in the giving of his Son, that a man can be born anew (cf. Tit. 3:5). The new life is real, but there is also a constant demand made on the Christian (as is shown by the remainder of the letter) to live an actual new life of obedience to God.

**living hope:** this with 'inheritance' (verse 4) are the purpose and end of the new birth. While 'living' appropriately accompanies the idea of rebirth we should have expected it in the form

'born anew unto life'. 'Hope' emphasises that the new life is not a
present possession alone but contains a future element. He who is
born has hope; in ordinary life hope can prove vain and delusive
(Job 7:6; Sir. 34:1; Eph. 2:12); in the new life hope is 'living',
i.e., it is vigorous and cannot fail; it can no more pass away than
can the living God; it is 'a hope by which one may live' (Reicke).
The nature and content of this hope is further explained in
verses 4,5 (cf. C. F. D. Moule, *The Meaning of Hope*, London 1953).

4. New birth implies entrance into a new family and therefore
the possibility of a new **inheritance**; similarly in Paul those who
become sons of God become heirs to a new inheritance (Gal. 4:7;
Rom. 8:17). The use of the image of inheritance to describe
salvation goes back to the OT where God gave the Jews the
Promised Land as their inheritance. Already in the OT inheritance
comes to be regarded as something other than material possessions
(e.g. Ps. 16:5; 73:26); this is even more true of the NT (cf. Col.
3:24; I Cor. 6:9; 15:50; Mk 10:17; Tit. 3:7; Heb. 1:14). In
contrast to an inheritance as material as Palestine our writer
describes what he has in mind as **imperishable, undefiled and
unfading,** using three negative adjectives (it is often easier to
define theological terms with negative rather than positive
statements); their meaning is well brought out by Beare's paraphrase: 'the inheritance is untouched by death, unstained by evil,
unimpaired by time'. Believers do not create it; God has made it
and preserves it until the time he is ready to introduce them to it.
**kept:** a perfect participle in the Greek underlines the fact that the
inheritance already exists and is being preserved for those who
are now being 'guarded' (verse 5). Hidden **in heaven** (Col. 1:5;
Mt. 5:12) it will one day be revealed. We may contrast this
picture with that of Rev. 21:1,5 where the new heaven and earth
are created at the last day.

5. **guarded:** the inheritance is not only kept for Christians but
they are preserved for it. The daily life of the Christian is a
warfare against evil and at times he may wonder if he will endure;
let him be assured, God guards him.

**God's power:** the phrase emphasises God's ability to preserve
the Christian. This protection by God was felt to be all the more
necessary as the end of all things drew near since Christians
believed that the end would be introduced by a period of severe
stress, the so-called Messianic woes (see on 4:13): the writer and
readers are already in this period (cf. 4:12-19) for salvation is

**ready to be revealed** (the nearness of the end appears also in
1:6,20; 4:5,7,13,17; 5:10).

**salvation:** not the individual salvation of the believer but the
eschatological consummation of all God's plans for the universe;
in it Christians receive their full salvation. The roots of the
Christian conception of salvation lie deep in the OT where God
is seen as the saviour of his people. The concept was also used
widely in pagan religions in relation to their gods and deified
mortals, e.g. the emperor. The inadequate ideas of salvation in
paganism and the never fully realised conception of the OT form
the background to the NT usage of the term.

**through faith** the Christians are guarded for this salvation.
They do not receive it because of their faith (which would
have been a different case in the Greek); they trust God
and so he is able to guard them. To interpret faith as a 'steadfast
determination to cling to God in all trials' (Wand) makes their
faith the cause of their preservation by God, i.e. they are saved
because they cling steadfastly to God; this really makes the
reference to God's power unnecessary and provides no assurance
to the believer since what he doubts is his own power to cling to
God in trial.

## JOY IN SALVATION (1:6–9)

6. **In this** does not refer to 'in the last time' (verse 5) but to all
of verses 3–5; they should rejoice because God has brought about
their rebirth, keeps an inheritance for them and guards them for it.

**you rejoice:** this can be taken either as an indicative (so RSV) or
as an imperative (so RSV mg., 'Rejoice in this'); the former is
preferable, for the latter breaks the flow of thanksgiving which
began at verse 3 by the introduction of hortatory material and it
does not suit the epistolary form at so early a point in the letter.
The Greek word used for 'rejoice' occurs only in Biblical Greek
(and Greek influenced by it) and is used of religious, not secular,
joy. 'It includes the happiness expressed in worship, which praises
God for His beneficent acts, and also the joy of the Last Day,
viewed under the aspect of a religious festival (cf. Ps. 96:11ff;
Rev. 19:7)' (Wand).

**trials:** the persecutions and sufferings which pertain to the
Christian life as such and not to life generally; they are an ever-
present possibility (cf. p. 42 and 3:13–17; 4:12–19; 5:10), but
their duration can only be brief (**for a little while**) compared to

the eternal nature of the inheritance (verse 4) which they precede.
**may** conceals a word (cf. W. Grundmann, *T.D.N.T.*, II, pp. 21-5)
which expresses the divine necessity of their trials; it is in God's
hands and not man's whether they take place or not, just as it was
in God's hands that the Messiah had to suffer (Mk 8:31; Lk.
22:37). The Christian in suffering neither complains nor is
stoically indifferent but rejoices (cf. Mt. 5:11f; Lk. 21:28; 2 Cor.
4:8-10) because of the inheritance (verse 4) for which he is
purified by this very suffering (verse 7). Since such suffering fell
so often on Christians the paraenetic material used in the early
church is full of references to their attitude to it (Rom. 5:3-4;
8:18; Jas 1:2; 2 Cor. 4:17; 7:4; Mt. 5:12; Ac. 5:41). The whole
eschatological tenor of the passage suggests that the Messianic
**woes** (cf. verse 5 and 4:13) may still be in mind, for they will
last for 'a little while', but the attitude depicted remains true of
persecution in general.

**7. the genuineness of your faith:** 'faith' is a word with a
wide range of meaning; here it has the sense 'faithfulness to God'.
Its genuineness is brought out by the test of suffering (cf. Jas 1:2f);
this is one, but not the only, answer to the question of suffering in
the Christian life.

**gold . . . fire:** as gold, which in the raw state may be compounded
with impurities, is tested and cleansed by fire (an OT metaphor,
cf. Prov. 17:3; 27:21; Ps. 66:10; Jer. 9:7; Mal. 3:3; Sir. 2:5) so
the quality of faith is revealed by suffering. A genuine faith is far
**more precious than gold** which belongs to this world and will
perish with it, and therefore all the more in need of the refinement
that comes through the fire of persecution (cf. 4:12; 1 Cor. 3:13).
Such faith will receive its reward when God reveals Jesus Christ
'in the last time' (verse 5).

**praise and glory and honour** from God will be its reward
(Rom. 2:10,29; 8:30; 1 Cor. 4:5; Ps. 8:5; 1 Mac. 2:51) and it
itself will also be 'praise and glory and honour' to God (Phil. 1:11)
who will have guarded those with faith and sustained them in
their suffering (verse 5). They will in fact enter into and enjoy the
divine 'praise and glory and honour' (Rom. 8:17; 5:2; 2 Cor.
3:18; Col. 3:4). Thus they have reason to rejoice.

**the revelation of Jesus Christ:** he is always present with them
as the risen Lord but 'in the last time' his presence will become
visible. It is therefore preferable to speak of his 'revelation' than
of his second coming (von Soden).

**8. you love him:** the Christian is one who loves Christ, cf. Jn 8:42; 14:21; 21:15f; 1 Cor. 16:22; Eph. 6:24; 2 Tim. 4:8. The first of the two great commandments is as important as the second (Mk 12:28-31).

**believe in him:** faith whose object had been unidentified earlier (verses 5,7) is now related to Christ; there is no virtue in an undirected though strong 'faith'; it too rapidly descends into faith in self. Christ the object of faith is not seen (cf. Jn 20:29; 2 Cor. 5:7; Heb. 11:27). Once Christianity spread beyond the original disciples who followed Jesus in Palestine it became increasingly important to emphasise that the absence of a visible relationship does not mean there cannot be a real relationship expressed by faith and love. It is said that Christians love Christ **without having seen** (past tense) him, but that they believe in him though they do not now **see** (present tense) him; the difference, if it is other than stylistic (and it is sometimes difficult to see the reason for the writer's choice of tense), may arise because it is possible to continue to love someone who was once seen (the reading 'known' of the RSVmg is inferior; the choice of reading in the RSV over against its margin is confirmed by $P^{72}$) and has passed from sight, but normally only to believe in someone with whom there is a present acquaintance; or (cf. Hort) it may be because 'seen' refers to the past nature of the Christ-event as a single act—you did not (an unusually emphatic negative) see him die and rise. In any case there is no need to see in the contrast a claim on the part of the writer to have been a personal disciple of Jesus. The RSVmg takes the verse as an exhortation but as in verse 6, and for the same reasons, the RSV itself is to be preferred.

**now:** this serves to bring out the brevity of the present stage of 'not seeing'; this time will shortly pass and that of verse 9 arrive with the revelation of Jesus Christ (verse 7).

**with unutterable and exalted joy:** the extent of their joy, which is neither a masochistic joy nor a joy despite suffering, is underlined in these concluding words; even now through his love and his faith, though he suffers, the believer begins to experience the joy of the heavenly kingdom (Jn 16:22-4; Rev. 19:1-8).

**9.** In the original this is not an independent sentence but gives the reason for the Christian's great joy (verse 8).

**faith:** note how often this word appears (verses 5,7, and verse 8 has the verbal form 'believe'). Here it means either the Christian's

faithfulness to God or his responsiveness to God's action in Christ
or, more probably, the two are not to be distinguished.

**salvation:** throughout the NT this is linked to faith (Ac. 16:31;
Eph. 2:8; 2 Th. 2:13; 2 Tim. 3:15; Heb. 10:39). Here as in verse 5
ultimate eschatological salvation is in mind and **obtain** should
be given a partially future sense: they now obtain it by their faith
but will only fully enter into it at the last.

**soul:** (Greek *psuche*). This is not a special part of man's physical
or mental structure, or a divine spark within him, or his higher
nature, but man as a whole; it is a Jewish rather than a Greek or
modern usage of the word. In 1 Peter it is used in a somewhat
different way from Paul who tends to apply it to the natural and
not the redeemed man. It is almost the equivalent of the personal
pronoun (it can be so replaced at 1:9,22; 2:25; 4:19); it is the
man himself (at 3:20 the plural is translated 'persons'), the whole
man, who is saved (cf. Mk 8:35–7 where 'life' is the translation of
the same word).

## The OT Anticipation of Salvation 1:10–12

10. **The prophets** before Christ (on Selwyn's view that they
were Christian prophets see on verse 12) foresaw the salvation
that would come to the writer and his readers and for which he
has just been giving thanks (1:3–9). OT scholars have drawn
attention to the way in which the prophets spoke to their own
times but this must not be over-stressed as if there were no future
reference or relevance in their utterances. On the other hand the
NT writers at times go too far, as if the only importance that the
prophets possessed lay in their predictions; Matthew continually
refers to the fulfilment of OT sayings in the events of the life of
Jesus (1:22f; 2:5f,15 etc.; cf. Rom. 1:2; Ac. 3:18 etc.); Paul
argues that the prophets spoke not only for their own time but for
that of the Christian church (Rom. 4:23f; 15:4; 1 Cor. 9:10; 10:11).
For the NT writers the content of OT prophecy, and indeed of all
of the OT, is Christ.

**yours:** this is not to be contrasted with 'mine', i.e. the author's,
but with the prophets who spoke and wrote.

**grace:** as in 1:2 this is used in a more objective way than in Paul;
here it is the result of God's favour and almost equivalent to
salvation rather than God's favour itself: it is not so much God's
attitude to sinful men as the outcome of his attitude to those who

respond in Christ. Though Paul often uses 'grace' of God's
mercy in bringing the Gentiles into the church there is no reason
to confine it here in that way, as if the writer were limiting the
words of the prophets to the forecast of the entrance of Gentiles
into the church.

11. **what person or time:** these words can also be translated,
'what time (i.e. what precise moment of time) or what manner of
time (i.e. with what attendant circumstances or at what opportune
moment)'; this rendering is accepted by the majority of commentators and appears in most other translations. There is no
essential difference in meaning in so far as it is the 'time' of the
'person' which is at issue. In the OT (Dan. 12:6-13) and much
more in the literature of inter-testamental Judaism (1QpHab
7:1-8, indeed the whole book, re-interprets Habakkuk; 2 Esd.
4:51f; cf. Ac. 1:6) we find the desire to know the 'time' of God's
salvation.

**the Spirit of Christ:** the belief that the prophets were inspired
by the Spirit of God was commonly accepted in Judaism and passed
from there into Christianity (2 Pet. 1:21; Ignatius, *Magnesians*
9:2); to the early Christians the Spirit of God, the Spirit of the
Lord and the Spirit of Christ were identical and this may account
for the present phrase (cf. Rom. 8:9; Phil. 1:19; Ac. 16:7; Gal.
4:6). It is however possible that our writer views Christ as active
in the period prior to the incarnation with his Spirit inspiring the
prophets about himself; such pre-incarnate activity of Christ is
found in 1 Cor. 10:4; Jn 12:41; *Barnabas* 5:6 (cf. A. T. Hanson,
*Christ in the Old Testament*, London, 1965, pp. 133-6).

**when predicting the sufferings of Christ:** we do not know
what prophets the author has in mind; he quotes elsewhere from
Isaiah; probably he would have regarded the whole OT as
witnessing to Christ.

**the sufferings . . . the subsequent glory:** *lit.*, 'the sufferings
into Christ and the subsequent glories'. 'Into' is probably used
with the pregnant sense 'destined for', written from the situation
of the prophets and referring forward to the historical sufferings
(a Christian looking back would speak of the sufferings *of* Christ;
so Hort); as sufferings were destined for Christ so is grace for the
Christian (verse 10 where 'into you' is the strict rendering of 'that
was to be yours'); sufferings are also destined for the Christian
(3:17; 4:12-19). The plural 'glories' probably refers to the succession of events—resurrection, ascension, heavenly session,

return in power. The author regards the OT prophets as concen-
trating their attention on the passion and glory of Christ; these
were the kernel of the early Christian preaching rather than his
birth, miracles or teaching (Lk. 24:26f; 1 Cor. 15:3f; Ac. 17:3).

12. **It was revealed . . . but you:** the same conception is found
in Paul (Rom. 15:4; 1 Cor. 9:10; 10:11). There are certainly
places in the OT where the writers, or their editors, realise that
their words contain a meaning beyond the contemporary situation
(Gen. 49:1,10; Num. 24:17; Dt. 18:15; Hab. 2:1–3) but there is
no idea that they relate explicitly to the Christian church; the
prophets spoke very much to their own times even if their words
also carried a further import.

**serving:** the same word (*diakonein*) is used widely in the NT of the
Christian ministry in all its forms; the prophets are ministers to
the church. We can see how closely the author, in common with
the other writers of the NT, joined the OT and its story to themselves subordinating it to the life of the church in a way that
Christian scholars would not adopt today. For them the OT has a
relative independence of the NT and a message directed to its
own time; but it is incomplete, pointing beyond itself and only
finding completion in the event of Jesus Christ. When in contra-
distinction to the NT attitude the church has cut itself off from
the OT (as with Marcion and the Gnostics) its faith has been so
severely impoverished as in the end to be no longer recognizable
as truly Christian. Cf. *The Old Testament and Christian Faith*, ed.
B. W. Anderson, London, 1964.

**the Holy Spirit:** the same Spirit who inspired the prophets was
active in the missionaries who had **preached the good news** to
the readers, and there is an identity of message in both, viz., 'the
sufferings of Christ and his subsequent glory' (verse 11). There
must have been a considerable number of missionaries who had
worked in the area to which this letter is written; the author does
not claim to have been one of them.

**now,** i.e. in the time of the church, in distinction from that of the
prophets.

**sent from heaven:** not a precise reference to Pentecost; it means
'given by God' and is more general.

**things into which angels long to look:** it is not clear whether
the angels succeed in seeing the salvation offered to the church,
or whether their desire to look arises from a wrong curiosity or a
true desire for spiritual insight. Although angels are commonly

regarded as possessing supernatural knowledge of salvation there
is much in the NT which implies their inferiority to believers
(I Cor. 6:1ff; Heb. 1:14; 2:16); their knowledge may be limited
(I Cor. 2:8; Eph. 3:10; cf. I Enoch 16:3; Ignatius, *Ephesians* 19:1);
at 3:22 they are subordinated to Christ in a way that Christians
are not. The desire of the angels to understand God's salvation
serves to emphasise in the eyes of the letter's readers the greatness
of what God has done for them. The references to the OT and to
angels thus fitly round off I:3-12 in building up the wonder of
God's salvation.

Selwyn (*ad loc.* and pp. 259ff) following Wohlenberg argues
that the prophets of I:10-12 are not the OT prophets but those of
the NT. (For their existence cf. Ac. 13:1-3; Eph. 2:20; 3:5f;
Lk. 2:36 etc.). Selwyn points to certain difficulties in the traditional
interpretation:
(a) 'search', 'inquire' are peculiar words to use of OT prophets;
they proclaimed the message God gave them; (b) 'Spirit of Christ'
is a more natural phrase to apply to NT prophets than OT
prophets; (c) the difficulties in the phrase 'the sufferings of
Christ and the subsequent glory'; he renders it 'the sufferings of
the Christward road' and the subsequent 'triumphs', referring it
to the sufferings of Christians and their eventual coming to
glory (this allows him to take the plural 'glories' more easily;
cf. 2 Cor. 1:5). Thus the prophets predict the time of the Messianic
woes (see on 4:13) after enduring which Christians will be
glorified. Our discussion of the passage has shown that (b) is no
necessary objection to the traditional view. Nor does the use of the
words 'search, inquire' apply more easily to NT prophets than
those of the OT; the former were either 'proclaimers' of the Word
of God or the vehicles of prediction (Ac. 11:28; 21:10f; cf. Rev.
1:3; 22:18 which describe Revelation as a prophecy); they were
not rational searchers after truth nor was their activity any less
ecstatic than that of the OT prophets; within the OT there is
evidence of prophets seeking truth (Dan. 7:16; 9:3ff; Isa. 6:11);
furthermore 'revealed' in verse 12 removes any conception of the
prophets reaching their predictions through quiet study. Thus
there is no substance in Selwyn's (a). He may be allowed to have
the better of the argument in (c), though many commentators
include the 'glories' of Christians with the 'glory' of Christ and so
explain the plural; if this is accepted it would probably be better
to see also a double reference in 'the sufferings of Christ' to his

historical sufferings and to the Messianic woes (see on 4:13)
which his followers will endure. There is, however, at least one
serious objection to Selwyn's view. We are required to imagine a
central core of scholars who search and inquire about the time of
the End and whose results are communicated to the church by
missionaries; there is no evidence for such activity in the early
church; in particular we do not find any of the results given or
even alluded to in 1 Peter. 'Now' (verse 12) suggests a considerable
time-interval between the work of the prophets and that of the
missionaries and is more suitable if they are taken to be OT
prophets. Finally, it is impossible to sustain Selwyn's hypothesis if
the translation 'what person' is allowed to stand in v.11.


## EXHORTATION TO CHRISTIAN BEHAVIOUR
### 1:13-2:10

On the basis of what God has done for Christians as set out in
the thanksgiving (1:3-12) they are encouraged to true conduct;
the hope of full salvation is to be the driving force in daily duty.

### (a) BE HOLY BECAUSE GOD IS HOLY 1:13-16

13. **Therefore:** a transition verse which takes us from the
expression of the greatness of God's salvation in 1:3-12 to the
conduct which those who are beginning to experience that
salvation ought to display.
**gird up your minds:** a common metaphor (cf. Prov. 31:17;
Jer. 1:17; Lk. 12:35; Eph. 6:14 etc.) drawn from the Easterner's
long flowing robes which would impede physical activity unless
tucked up under a belt (Exod. 12:11; 2 Kg. 4:29; 9:1); in view
of its obvious nature and its frequent use there is no need to see
dependence of the metaphor on Lk. 12:35 or in any special way
on the Exodus event (Exod. 12:11). The Christian is to be pre-
pared for tough work, but in the mental and spiritual sphere
rather than in the physical.
**mind** is not used in a narrow intellectualised sense but of that
which guides and directs conduct; the importance of thinking is
stressed for the Christian.
**be sober:** a favourite exhortation of our writer (cf. 4:7; 5:8).
Although the basic meaning is the avoidance of drunkenness it is

used in our letter more widely of temperance in general, i.e. of disciplined behaviour which avoids extremes of conduct. Actual drunkenness would have been a return to non-Christian ways and is rebuked at 4:3 (cf. Rom. 13:13; 1 Thess. 5:7f). If sobriety is closely linked to the preceding reference to 'minds' then it suggests the need for steadiness in the face of strange ideas; in the eschatological atmosphere in which 1 Peter was written there might well be wild and disorderly movements of thought and action by which Christians who were not standing firmly in a clearly thought out position might easily be swept away; in 1 Th. 5:5-8 there is a similar warning.

**fully:** this adverb might be also taken with 'be sober'; our letter is too brief for us to learn enough about the author's style to be able to settle with any definiteness to which word it should be attached.

**set your hope:** they had been given hope by Christ's resurrection (1:3—see there for the meaning of hope); now hope is related to his parousia. The Greek verb is the first of a number of aorist imperatives in the letter; they are unusual and have caused much discussion; see p. 26.

**the grace that is coming to you at the revelation of Jesus Christ:** as in 1:2,10 grace is objectified and has become almost equivalent to 'salvation'. The whole reference is eschatological (cf. 1:5).

**revelation** does not refer to the truth about God made known in the incarnation nor to the progressive enlightenment of the Christian's mind with knowledge, but to the second appearance of Christ which is even now on its way (**coming**) to them and is, as the Greek word suggests, a favour conferred by God rather than an objective to be worked for. We have here another indication of the nearness of the end for our author (cf. 4:7).

14. **As obedient children:** *lit.* 'as children of obedience', a semitic idiom (cf. Lk. 16:8; Eph. 5:8; 1 Th. 5:5) in which little emphasis lies on the word 'children' in distinction from adults, though obedience is appropriate to 'children' and may have suggested the idiom; it could be rendered 'as obedient people'. **obedient** refers back to 1:2; God has chosen them for obedience. This virtue is the key-stone of Jewish ethics, an emphasis which reappears in Christianity in that love is always a commandment (Mk 12:28-31; Jn 13:34; 15:12,17; Rom. 13:9f). Throughout our letter great stress is laid on obedience (1:22; 2:13,18; 3:1; 5:5).

**do not be conformed . . . ignorance:** addressed to those who were once Gentiles (cf. Ac. 17:30; Eph. 4:18); Jews knew God's ways and could not have been accused of ignorance (cf. pp. 19f).

**passions,** *lit.* 'desires', need not have a bad sense and can be neutral (i.e. 'do not be swayed by desire but be ruled by God'), but in the NT it often possesses the bad connotation. It is used to characterise Gentile behaviour in Rom. 1:24; Eph. 2:3; 4:22; 1 Th. 4:5; 1 Pet. 4:2.

**conformed:** a rare word found also at Rom. 12:2; on the question of dependence see p. 33. In the Greek it is a participle and not an imperative, the first example in the letter of the frequent use of participles for imperatives (see p. 30 and D. Daube, 'Participle and Imperative in 1 Peter' in Selwyn, pp. 467–80).

15. **but:** we move to a more positive expression of the nature of Christian behaviour than that of verse 14.

**as he who called you is holy:** this could be rendered 'as the Holy One who called you;' for the Holy One as a title for God, cf. Isa. 40:25; Hos. 11:9; 1 Jn 2:20; 1 Clement 23:5 (In Mk 1:24 it is used of Jesus). Whichever translation is chosen the meaning is that the character of the Christian is to be conformed to that of God (cf. 1 Jn 3:3; Mt. 5:48). The movement of thought from verse 14 to verse 15 is similar to that within Rom. 12:2.

**called:** see also 2:9; 5:10. The word expresses the strong belief of the early Christians that God had chosen and destined (1:1f) them to be his people (cf. Rom. 8:28–30).

**holy:** the etymological derivation of this word is probably 'separation'. Ideas of *tabu* and *mana* were originally associated with it but by the time of the later OT writings and certainly by that of the NT these connections were almost wholly forgotten. God's holiness is primary and from it is derived the holiness of what belongs to him, e.g. the temple, the angels, the levitical priesthood, his people. The idea of 'separation', in so far as it continues to flavour the word, is separation to God rather than separation from the world; naturally separation to God means separation from sin because God and sin have no common meeting point. Thus understood it teaches a positive rather than a negative conception of conduct. Within the NT it is applied to the church: Paul calls its members 'the saints' (*lit.* 'the holy ones'); in our letter the church is termed 'a holy nation' (2:9); it is the new people of God chosen to express God's nature in its conduct (cf. the call to imitate Christ in 2:21; 4:1). On holiness see N. Snaith, *The Distinctive Ideas of the Old Testament*, London, 1944, pp. 21–50; E. Jacob, *Theology of the Old Testament*, London, 1958, pp. 86–93; J. Muilenburg, *I.D.B.*, II, pp. 616–25.

**in all your conduct:** holiness is not just an inner pietistic ideal but a quality to be expressed in the whole of life.

16. **since it is written:** a regular formula to introduce an OT quotation. The present quotation comes from Lev. 11:44; 19:2; 20:7.

## (b) BEHAVE BECAUSE GOD IS FATHER, JUDGE AND REDEEMER
## 1:17–21

17. **And if:** in the sense, 'and if, as you do, you invoke. . . .'
**you invoke as Father:** while the OT does sometimes refer to God as Father (Ps. 82:6; Jer. 3:19) and Judaism increasingly used the term, the Christian community derived it from Jesus who used it of God in a new and intimate manner; its use was characteristic of primitive Christianity and in Gentile Christianity it was even preserved in its Aramaic form, Abba (Rom. 8:15; Gal. 4:6). There is no direct reference to the Lord's Prayer in the phrase but it is suggestive of the invocation of God as Father in worship. To call God 'Father' is not an excuse for careless conduct; those who so invoke him should 'conduct' themselves 'with fear'.

**who judges each one impartially:** Fatherhood is not wholly disparate from judgement for a good father chastens his children (Heb. 12:5f). It was as much part of the primitive Christian tradition that God was Judge as that he was Father. As Judge his impartiality (the conception goes back to the OT, e.g. Dt. 10:17; Amos 3:2) appears in different ways: he makes no distinction between Jew and Gentile (Ac. 10:34; Rom. 2:10f) or between master and servant (Eph. 6:9; Col. 3:25); in our text it is implied that he makes no distinction between Christian and non-Christian (cf. Mt. 5:45); he will judge both, and though the Christian invokes him as Father this does not remove him from the sphere of judgement (cf. 4:17); he can escape judgement no more than the Jew who called Abraham his father (Lk. 3:8). On the judgement of Christians cf. 1 Cor. 3:12–15; 2 Cor. 5:10; Rom. 14:10–12; Mt. 25:31–46.

**deeds:** the Greek word is singular (this is unusual in the NT), implying that it is not merely the outward actions that will be judged but the whole life; cf. I Cor. 3:13–15, where the same word is rendered 'work'.

**with fear:** not abject terror, for the Christian has been set free from this (Rom. 8:15; I Jn 4:17f), nor merely the reverential attitude of worship. Fear as a motive in behaviour goes back to the OT (Ps. 33:18; 85:9; 111:10; 147:11; Prov. 1:7; Sir. 40:26) and appears often in the NT (Mt. 10:28; Lk. 12:5; 2 Cor. 5:10f; 7:15; Phil. 2:12). Our author gives more attention to this element of fear than do other NT writers (cf. 2:17f; 3:2,14f). There is a true awe before God which proceeds as much from a realisation of his goodness (Rom. 2:4) as of his greatness and it is of God's goodness that our writer goes on to speak in verse 18; he has also just referred to God as Father; this true fear is then a filial fear.

**exile:** see on 1:1 and 2:11. If the readers do not remember with fear that they are exiles they may be tempted to take out citizenship rights in this world and lose those of their true inheritance.

18. In the Greek this is a continuation of the sentence of verse 17 and adduces a further reason for Christian behaviour, viz., God's goodness in redeeming men by Christ.

**You know that:** the author is about to remind them of the commonly accepted tradition of the early church about the death of Jesus. Despite this, or rather, because of it, we are unable to determine his meaning in verses 18f with any certainty; had he been enunciating a new doctrine he would have stated it more clearly; because he is aware his readers know it he only alludes to it, and this allusiveness creates our difficulty.

**you were ransomed:** it is uncertain if this is the proper meaning of the Greek word. It belongs to a group whose root (*lutro*) occurs frequently in the LXX; it is used there for: (i) the redemption of property, sometimes by a kinsman (Lev. 25:26,33,48f) and sometimes not (Exod. 13:12f; Num. 18:15–17), for which a price is paid (the price is denoted by a noun from the same root); (ii) the deliverance of the Israelites from bondage and exile achieved by God's power, normally without mention of a price (Exod. 6:6; Isa. 44:22f; 51:10f; 52:3; Dt. 7:8); (iii) it is also used in non-Biblical Greek for the manumission of slaves where a price was paid to a god, and of the setting free of prisoners of war for whom a ransom was paid. The verb may thus be rendered 'ransomed' with the necessary implication of the payment of a price, or 'delivered' without suggesting this but implying that the death of Jesus is the means of the new Exodus of the new people of God.

In favour of the latter we may argue: (a) 'Silver, gold', the 'blood of Christ', which appear to be possible prices are not, as is normal in Greek, in the genitive case but in the dative; the datives might, however, be taken as instrumental. (b) The emphasis in the letter on the church as the new people of God entering into a new inheritance, i.e. their deliverance is the new Exodus accomplished by the death and resurrection of Christ. (c) The lamb (verse 19) refers to the Passover lamb and in the OT its death was not considered to have any atoning significance (but see on *lamb* in verse 19). (d) It is not said to whom the ransom is paid. In favour of the translation 'ransom' we may argue: (a) 'Silver', 'gold' obviously suggest the payment of a price. (b) The ransom conception is one strand in the tradition of the early church; it appears at Mk 10:45 (=Mt. 20:28) where no other rendering is possible, and may also appear at Tit. 2:14 and Heb. 9:12 (the RSV uses 'redeem' in both places); it should be pointed out that there are also places where the root clearly does not carry the ransom interpretation, e.g. Lk. 1:68; 2:38; 24:21; since Luke omits Mk 10:45 it is probable that he does not adhere to the interpretation of the atonement in 'ransom' terms. All in all it is probably better to accept the RSV translation in 1 Pet. 1:19 and regard this letter as standing in the same tradition as Mark. But we ought also to realise that the word would carry as a strong overtone the meaning 'deliver' because the whole tenor of 1 Peter shows the church as the new people of God delivered into a new inheritance. If the primary meaning of the word in 1:19 were adjudged to be 'deliver', then we could not argue for 'ransom' as a secondary meaning, for there is nothing in the context to introduce it and Luke's use of the term shows that it need not carry the 'ransom' overtone. The secular usage of the word would also immediately bring in associations of deliverance from captivity and slavery (1 Cor. 7:22f; Gal. 5:1); the slavery or captivity would be 'the futile ways inherited from your fathers'; to this we may compare the Pauline conception of deliverance from slavery to sin (Rom. 6:16–23) and demonic powers (Gal. 4:8). We have already seen that one of the difficulties in relation to the meaning 'ransom' concerned the identity of the person, if any, to whom the ransom was paid; patristic theology spoke of it as paid to the devil; there seems no trace of this in the NT. Bigg points out that if in fighting to free slaves soldiers lose their lives we can say that they gave their lives as the ransom or purchase price of the slaves' freedom, but cannot say to whom it is paid; this seems a fair parallel. On the meaning of 'ransom' etc. see L. Morris, *The Apostolic Preaching of the Cross*, London, 1955, pp. 9–59; V. Taylor, *Jesus and His Sacrifice*, London, 1943, pp. 99–105; D. E. H. Whiteley, *The Theology of St. Paul*, Oxford, 1964, pp. 141–51; F. Büchsel, *T.D.N.T.* IV, pp. 340–356.

**the futile ways:** when men live without God, as in the opinion of Jews and Christians the Gentiles did, all their ways are futile (cf. Eph. 4:17; 1 Cor. 3:20; Rom. 8:20). **futile** is used both in the OT and NT to describe idols (Lev. 17:7, LXX; Jer. 8:19; Ac. 14:15 where the RSV renders it 'vain'; cf. Rom. 1:21). These Christians to whom the letter is written had once been idol-worshippers and their pre-Christian ways could be described as idolatrous ways.

**inherited from your fathers:** they had quite naturally accepted the culture of their times.

19. **blood:** see on 1:2. On 'blood' as the means of redemption see Eph. 1:7; Heb. 9:12,22; Rev. 1:5; 1 Clement 12:7; on 'blood' regarded as a price, see Rev. 5:9. It emphasises here the place of the death of the victim in redemption rather than suggests its own life-giving power (the life is in the blood, Gen. 9:4 etc.). See L. Morris, *op. cit.* pp. 117–24; R. de Vaux, *Ancient Israel*, London, 1961, pp. 419ff.

**lamb:** since in 2:22–5 the writer draws deeply on Isa. 53 he may well have Isa. 53:7 in mind here (cf. Isa. 52:3 with its reference to redemption without money, suggestive of 1 Pet. 1:18), and once Isa. 53 came to be accepted as a prophecy of Christ's death it would be difficult to avoid such an association; but the primary reference is to the passover lamb. Jesus was regarded in this way by the early church; John times the crucifixion to coincide with its death and quotes Exod. 12:46 at 19:36; Paul makes the identification in 1 Cor. 5:7. It may be objected that the passover lamb had no atoning significance in the OT rite; however it was beginning to obtain this significance in contemporary Judaism; in Jn. 1:29,36 Jesus is described as the lamb that takes away the sin of the world, and thus atoning significance was given in the tradition of the church (contrast C. H. Dodd, *The Interpretation of the Fourth Gospel*, Cambridge, 1953, pp. 230ff).

**without blemish or spot:** the passover lamb and all animal sacrifices in the OT rites were expected to be perfect (Exod. 12:5; 29:1; Lev. 22:17–25; Ezek. 43:22f; cf. Heb. 9:14). The words serve to bring out the value of the sacrifice of Christ's blameless life (cf. 2:22).

20. **destined:** an eternal plan of God, now revealed in the Christ-event, was another element in the tradition of the early church (cf. Rom. 16:25f; 1 Cor. 2:7; Eph. 3:9; Col. 1:26; Tit. 1:2f); the idea had been taken over from the OT and Judaism (Isa. 37:26; 2 Esd. 6:1ff; 1 Enoch 48:6; 62:7). **destined,** as we saw in 1:2, is literally 'foreknown'. Of itself God's foreknowledge does not imply the pre-existence before the foundation of the world of those whom he 'fore-knows' since Christians, who are 'foreknown' in 1:2 (cf. Rom. 8:29; 11:2; Eph. 1:4f), did not exist prior to their birth. The pre-existence of Christ is implied here through the additional words **was made manifest,** i.e. at the incarnation; it was not merely a plan of God but Christ himself who was hidden until the moment for revelation. The pre-existence of Christ was accepted as early as Paul's letters and became part of the general Christian tradition (Phil. 2:6f; Gal. 4:4; Col. 1:18; Jn 1:1f; 17:24; cf. 1 Enoch 48:3,6f; see also on 1 Pet. 1:11). The two clauses of this verse form a distich and may be derived from liturgical usage (Beare).

**at the end of the times:** the Jews expected the consummation to arrive with the Messiah; since for the Christians he had already come the end must have commenced with his incarnation or manifestation (Heb. 1:2; 9:26; Ac. 2:16ff; 1 Cor. 10:11; Jude 18). This is not to say that the end is complete or that there are not other events to follow within the period of the end (cf. 1:5; 4:13).

**for your sake:** the actions of God do not take place in a vacuum but are always intended to affect the lives of men.

21. **Through him:** the relationship of believers to God is through Christ and exists because of what God has done in the death and resurrection of Christ, of which verses 18–21 tell us.

**confidence:** i.e. faith, the active response to God's actions: there is for the NT no faith in God except through Christ (cf. Jn 1:7; Ac. 3:16).

**God, who raised him from the dead and gave him glory:** the NT stresses the resurrection as the mighty act of God (Ac. 2:32; 3:15; Rom. 4:24f; 1 Cor. 6:14; 15:15 etc.). In the primitive tradition the resurrection and exaltation of Christ are associated as a single action of God indicating his triumph (Ac. 2:32f; Phil. 2:8–11; Eph. 1:20; 1 Pet. 3:18, 21f; for the ascension see on

3:22). Like verse 20 this clause of verse 21 appears to be part of a
liturgical confession; Schelkle thinks that verses 19-21 as a whole
may be based on a confession.

**faith and hope:** this rendering is to be preferred to RSVmg
'your faith is hope'. Faith and hope are closely linked conceptions
in this letter; though almost interchangeable they are not identical
nor is one transformed into the other. They are two aspects of
experience and the Christian lives by both until the final revelation
of full salvation (1:5), and enjoys both because God has raised
and exalted Jesus.

**in God:** this comes twice in the verse and is emphatic on its
second occurrence at the end of the verse; redemption begins and
ends in God.

### (c) Love one Another 1:22-5

In this and the next section we turn to the attitude of Christians
to one another; brotherly love is stressed positively here and
negatively in 2:1-3. The love of Christians for each other should
spring from the purification and rebirth they have experienced.

Preisker believes that the act of baptism took place between
1:21 and 1:22; we have taken the view that 1 Peter is not a
baptismal liturgy (see pp. 21ff) and so cannot accept this: but this
does not mean that there may not be echoes of baptism in the
passage.

22. **having purified your souls:** the Greek tense of 'purified'
(perfect participle) implies a past event whose effects continue,
and the reference is probably to the purification of baptism
(cf. Eph. 5:26; Heb. 10:22) and not to a long course of ascetic
mortification. The word is used in the OT for the ritual purification of objects (e.g. Num. 31:23) and of people (Exod. 19:10;
Num. 8:21; Jos. 3:5; cf. Ac. 21:24,26; 24:18; Christians are, of
course, a holy priesthood); in the NT it comes to be used of moral
purification (cf. Jas. 4:8; 1 Jn 3:3). Such purification is the
essential preparation for love since, if envy, passion, jealousy rule
in the soul, man cannot love.

**souls:** as in 1:9 the word denotes the whole man; it obviously
could not be a divine or immortal part of man, for this would
not require purification.

**your obedience:** as in 1:2 faith and obedience are closely
related; they are seen in the action of the new believer who offers

himself for baptism and is purified. It is not the act of baptism in itself which purifies; nor does faith itself purify, for in the early church obedience always led to baptism; an unbaptised believer would have been a contradiction in terms.

**the truth:** the man who hears the 'truth' and obeys it offers himself for baptism and is purified. The 'truth' is neither abstract or intellectual truth, nor the true philosophical system which explains the universe, but the divine revelation of the Gospel (cf. 2 Th. 2:10,12,13; Jn 14:6; Eph. 1:13; Col. 1:5; Gal. 5:7). The Qumran community believed in the purifying nature of truth (1QS 3:6ff; 4:20f—note in both cases the connection with water) and in Jn 17:17,19 Jesus prays for the sanctification of his disciples in the truth.

**a sincere love of the brethren:** it is for this they are purified. Purification is not for the sake of an inner experience ministering to the spiritual needs of the one purified but has as its purpose loving activity to build up the Christian community; it is social and not individualistic. In view of the picture painted of those who have not been purified (1:18; 4:3f) we may assume that purification is not merely helpful but necessary if men are to love; without purification and rebirth (1:23) it would be impossible to love according to the Christian pattern.

**sincere:** an adjective used also elsewhere to describe 'love' (cf. Rom. 12:9; 2 Cor. 6:6; in both cases it is translated 'genuine'); a sincere love is one without any trace of selfishness or self-seeking and not deceptive either intentionally or unintentionally as to its real motive.

**brethren:** within the OT we find already that fellow-Israelites are termed 'brothers' (Dt. 15:3,12) and the members of the Qumran community were closely knit together, regarding themselves as standing in a somewhat similar relation to one another. Jesus taught his disciples to look on each other as brothers (Mk 3:31–35; 10:30; Mt. 23:8) and the name came into use to describe the members of the early church (e.g. Ac. 1:15;14:2); Paul continually addresses his readers as 'brethren'.

**love one another:** (cf. 2:17; 4:8); these words are the heart of this section. They do not imply a love towards all men but love within the Christian community; such an emphasis is found right through the NT (Rom. 12:10; 1 Th. 4:9; Jn 13:34f; 15:12,17; 1 Jn 3:23; Heb. 13:1). It accords with the conception of the Church as a house or family (2:5; 4:17). Why should love within

the community be stressed in this way when the original word of
Jesus on love to neighbours does not appear to have been restricted
either to the fellow-Jew or fellow-member of the community of
disciples? Many factors tended to divide the Christian community,
e.g. the disagreement between Jewish and Gentile Christians,
heretical views either emerging from within or assailing from
outside, the pressure of possible persecution (cf. Mk 13:12), the
natural quarrelsomeness of men (cf. 1 Cor. 11:17-34; 12; Phil.
4:2f); mutual love would certainly help Christians to stand
together during these difficulties. It is interesting that in Rom.
13:8 Paul passes from 'love one another' to love for all men
(cf. 2 Pet. 1:7).

**earnestly from the heart:** 'earnestly' is rendered 'unfailing' at
4:8 and perhaps ought to be here also; the total phrase implies a
steady resolve to love with the whole being involved; love can
be no passing emotion.

23. In the Greek this is a continuation of the sentence begun in
verse 22 and supplies an additional ground for the summons to
love; the latter is humanly impossible and requires a new divine
life if it is to become a reality.

**born anew:** see on 1:3; it is again a perfect participle like
'purified' in verse 22.

**seed:** two types of seed are contrasted; human seed which
produces mortal human life and divine seed which produces
eternal life (cf. Jn 1:13; 3:3ff). This follows the general Biblical
teaching that the life of man is not naturally immortal but
becomes so by the direct action of God for those who believe in
Christ.

The **word of God** is not to be identified with the seed (contrast
Lk. 8:11); it is the means through which the seed produces the
new birth and for this reason it cannot be entirely dissociated from
'seed', as the use of Isa. 40:6-9 shows. It is illegitimate to push the
illustration (a variation of it appears in Jas. 1:18) and enquire
what the seed is or suggest that something of the divine nature
passes into man (cf. 2 Pet. 1:4); it is also erroneous to see the
influence here of the Stoic conception of the *logos spermatikos* or
seminal word. The English conceals the fact that two different
terms are used for 'word' here and in verses 24f; both are common;
in verses 24f the term which occurs in the quotation has to be
used; here the writer is free to chose and he selects the one (*logos*)
which had a technical meaning in the vocabulary of the early

Christians (and which had a philosophical usage especially among the Stoics). It could mean the Son of God, as in Jn 1:1–18 where there are rich religious and philosophical overtones (cf. Rev. 19:13), but it could also mean, more simply, the preached message about Jesus (Ac. 4:29; 13:44,46; 1 Cor. 14:36; 2 Cor. 2:17; Col. 1:5,25; etc.). In view of verse 25b the latter must be the meaning here. The new birth was brought into being by means of the preaching about Jesus. In 1:3 the new birth was said to take place through the resurrection of Christ; there is no real difference between that and what we have here for the preaching about Jesus was preaching about the risen Christ; in the word the hearer encounters the living Lord, living because of the resurrection. We have already seen the relation of this section to baptism; for the early Christians the response to preaching and the act of baptism were practically simultaneous and never divided in thought; but baptism is not the main thought, rather the obedient response in faith to the preacher's word about Christ.

**living and abiding:** the Greek would permit these two adjectives to be taken with God (as in the Greek of Dan. 6:27) but they go better with 'word' as in the RSV, for 'abiding' is taken up again in connection with 'word' in verse 25 and 'living' contrasts with the withering of the grass and the falling of the flowers in verse 24. If God is living and abiding (Dan. 6:27) then he will have endowed his word with these qualities. The word about Christ communicated in preaching is 'living' (cf. Heb. 4:12; Ac.7:38) and the more closely the word is identified with Christ the truer this is because he lives through his resurrection; he is described as life-giving bread and water (Jn 6:51; 4:10f; 7:38). The word itself is also described as life-giving (Phil. 2:16; cf. 1 Th. 2:13; we can also compare the creative power of the word in the OT, e.g., Gen. 1, where creation takes place when God speaks, and Ps. 33:6,9); as life-giving the word is the means of producing the new life of the one who is born anew.

**24–5.** A quotation from the LXX of Isa. 40:6–9 is used to explain and support the words and thought of verse 23; it sets out the fragile nature of human existence (cf. Ps. 90:5f; 103:15f; Job 14:1f; Isa. 51:12) and contrasts it with the imperishable nature of the gospel through which the new birth takes place.

**good news:** this takes up 'good tidings' of Isa. 40:9 where the same word is used (cf. also 1 Pet. 1:12); our English word 'gospel' has the same meaning. For the prophet the word was his prophecy

proclaiming the restoration of Israel; for our author it is the
Gospel proclaiming new life for those who believe in Christ and
intended (**to you**) for his readers.

**the Lord:** in making the quotation our author has substituted
'Lord' for 'our God', thus linking the word to Christ himself who
is the Lord (cf. 2:3).

### (d) AVOID SIN AGAINST ONE ANOTHER 2:1–3

Continuing his emphasis on the life of Christians in their community the author writes negatively of the sins that hinder
members from loving one another and must therefore be laid
aside, but also positively of the way in which they can grow in the
Christian life.

1. In the Greek this verse is subordinate to verse 2. The sequence
of thought from 1:22 runs: they are born anew; they should love
one another; they should put away their sins and grow as children
grow. The result will be the strengthening of the whole community.
**put away:** the tense of the verb implies an action prior to that of
'long for' (verse 2). The image is probably that of putting off old
clothes in order to put on new and better (cf. Rom. 13:12; Eph.
4:22–4; Col. 3:8–10) or possibly that of the washing away of dirt
(cf. 3:21, where 'removal' comes from the same root, and Jas 1:21).
The word was used frequently by the primitive church for the
elimination of sin (Eph. 4:25; Heb. 12:1; Jas 1:21; 1 Clement 13:
1). This may indicate the wide use of a catechism which stressed
the need for the Christian to purify himself from sin (cf. Selwyn,
pp. 393–400, Carrington, *op. cit.*, pp. 32–7), and may have been
connected with an act of baptismal renunciation. As in 1 Pet. 2:1
the word is often linked to lists of vices (cf. Rom. 13:12f; Eph.
4:25–32, where the list is expanded; Col. 3:8; Jas 1:21; 1 Clement
13:1). Such lists were in common use for ethical instruction
throughout the contemporary Hellenistic world and in Judaism
(e.g. 1QS 4:9–11; 10:21–3); the Christian church took over this
method of instruction (cf. pp. 30f). Because a general, and probably
familiar, list is given we are unable to draw any conclusion as to
the life of particular congregations in Asia Minor, but since it is a
list of sins which militate against Christian fellowship we may
conclude that the early church was as open to the scandal of such
sins as the church has been in every period. The writers of the
NT had no illusions about the church's perfection.

**malice:** the word could be rendered 'wickedness' and be a general introduction to the remaining four sins. If taken as 'malice' then it is another sin which hinders fellowship (cf. 1:23). The author does not merely say, 'Put away sin!', but specifies the sins to be put away; it is only possible to fight against specific sins. **all,** i.e., every possible kind of.

2. Logically the putting away of sin precedes growth in goodness and so verse 1 precedes verse 2; in actual fact both are continuous processes. The idea may also be present that the ability to receive spiritual nourishment (the 'milk') and the sharing of fellowship with other Christians are interdependent.

**Like newborn babes:** 1:3,23, have taught that this is precisely what they are. Does this imply that their new birth has only just taken place, i.e., that newly baptised converts are being addressed? 'Babes' and 'milk' suggest a beginning which would lead on to being an adult and eating solid food; it is in this way that the image is used in 1 Cor. 3:1f; Heb. 5:12ff and in each case, unlike 1 Pet. 2:2, it is used disparagingly, children being contrasted with mature adults. There is however another strand in NT thought which suggests that the true Christian character is always that of the child; when Jesus teaches that those who do not receive the Kingdom of God as children cannot enter into it (Mk 10:15) he is not implying a process of growth from childhood to adulthood; the disciple of Jesus is and remains a child (cf. Mk 9:42). In 1 Pet. 2:2 there is no contrast between the present state of the newborn and a later state and milk is sufficient food to nourish the believer to full salvation; as we shall see in verse 3 'milk' means Christ himself; there can be no food beyond Christ. The whole image need not 'necessarily mean more than "long for spiritual nourishment as eagerly as newly born babies do for physical nourishment"' (Moule, *N.T.S.* 3 (1956) 6; see also pp. 21ff). The phrase does not then imply the recent baptism of those addressed.

**milk:** as with some of the other words and ideas of the epistle there is a pagan background here which would have been very apparent to first century readers. Food is a widespread symbol of spiritual nourishment in religion; it is found in the OT (e.g. Isa. 55:1; Dt. 8:3; milk is regarded as eschatological food in Isa. 60:16; Jl 3:18). But it is more probable that the Mystery cults and gnostic ideas have provided the background to 1 Pet. 2:2; in the former milk was used in initiatory rites; in the second century gnostic hymnbook, the *Odes of Solomon*, it is the symbolical food of

D

the gnostics, representing *gnosis*, i.e., knowledge (cf. H. Schlier, *T.D.N.T.*, I, pp. 646f). By the end of the second century milk was given to newly baptised converts.

**pure:** the word is regularly used for uncontaminated or un-adulterated foodstuffs; since it is also in structure the negative form of the word 'guile' (verse 1) it carries the secondary meaning 'guileless'; English 'pure' covers both meanings. It is possible that it is implied that the 'milk' of the Mystery cults is not pure but poisonous.

**spiritual:** there are three possible renderings of this Greek word (*logikos;* it is found also in Rom. 12:1): (i) 'of the word' (AV); this is a natural meaning in the context (1:23-5) but elsewhere in Greek it does not appear to have this sense; certainly it does not have it in Rom. 12:1. If, and this is very doubtful, Jas 1:21 depends on 1 Pet. 2:2 it might be argued that James understood it in this sense. (ii) 'reasonable' (RVmg), 'rational'; this is the normal meaning among the Greek Stoic philosophers; it is however difficult to fit this meaning into the present context (though it can be made to suit Rom. 12:1). (iii) 'spiritual'; this sense is found in gnostic writings, especially *Corpus Hermeticum* (1:31; 13:18, 21) where it is applied to non-material sacrifices, e.g., prayer, which the gods prefer to material offerings. If it is argued that the Gnostics were influenced in their understanding of the word by Christian writings then this shows that at an early period the word was interpreted in the sense 'spiritual'; indeed many of the early Fathers take it in this way. (For the meaning see the discussion of the word by G. Kittel *T.D.N.T.*, IV, pp. 142f.) Our author's use is probably derived from Rom. 12:1, where again 'spiritual' is the preferable translation. It implies that milk is not to be taken in the literal sense but, properly understood, is suitable food to provide growth for man in his spiritual existence.

**grow up:** while the Christian is newborn he is also always in process of growth; it is not his status which requires emphasis but his progress.

**salvation:** the final and full salvation which comes with the revelation of Jesus Christ (1:5,7).

3. This verse is a quotation from Ps. 34:8. Believers have already **tasted** and so should continue to participate. But what have they tasted? Not the word (so AV), but Christ himself (cf. 1 Cor. 10:4; Jn 6:53). The attempt to apply this verse to the Eucharist (so E. Lohmeyer, 'Vom urchristlichen Abendmahl'

*Theologische Rundschau* 9 (1937) 296; F. L. Cross, p. 33) because
Ps. 34 later came to be considered a Eucharistic hymn by the
early church fails for lack of evidence in this period (cf. Moule,
*N.T.S.* 3 (1956) 5). Naturally if believers participate in
Christ they do this by means of the sacraments, but they do so
also by the word and through fellowship with other Christians
and in deeds of love (cf. Mt. 25:31-46); it is the word which has
been stressed in 1:23-5.

**the kindness of the Lord:** this translation conceals the full
meaning of the quotation. There is, first, a play on the word
'Christ', for the word for 'kindness' in the Greek is 'chrēstos' in
which the alteration of the vowel gives Christ (cf. Justin, *Apology*,
I, 4). Second, the meaning of the word is much wider than
'kindness'; it is regularly used for wholesome and pleasant food
(cf. Lk. 5:39); the more neutral rendering 'goodness' is to be
preferred here. Thus we may translate, 'You have tasted that the
Lord is good (=Christ)', i.e. good for food, for growth.
**Lord:** in Ps. 34:8 the 'Lord' is God. Our author in common with
the other NT writers regularly understands the 'Lord' of the OT
to refer to Christ (cf. the change in 1:25); this is made clear by the
beginning of verse 4 where 'him' refers back to 'Lord' in verse 3.
Ps. 34 is deliberately quoted twice in the epistle (cf. 3:10-12) and
was possibly more often in the writer's mind (cf. p. 20).


## (e) THE PEOPLE OF GOD 2:4-10

In 1:22-2:3 attention has been focussed on behaviour within the
community; now the writer turns to the nature of the community
which he outlines in terms and conceptions drawn from the OT,
from intertestamental Judaism and from the primitive Christian
tradition. Sometimes he uses OT citations to confirm the points he
has made; at other times he advances his argument with OT
words and phrases taken out of their precise context. The basic
image of the passage is the people of God as the temple of God and
he moves to this from his discussion of Christ as the nourishing
milk (2:1-3) through the intermediate step of Christ as the 'stone'.
On this whole section see J. H. Elliott, *The Elect and the Holy*,
(*Supplements to N.T.* Vol. XII) Leiden, 1966. Best, '1 Peter
2:4-10, A Reconsideration'. *N.T.* XI (1969) 270-93.

4. **Come to him:** in the original there is a participle here and
it would be better to translate it, 'coming to him'. Although many

participles are to be rendered as imperatives (see on 1:14) this one ought not since it does not lay down a rule of behaviour. It is actually subordinate to 'be yourselves built' (verse 5); the latter should however also be rendered as an indicative (see on verse 5) and the participle similarly. The Greek word (*proserchomenoi*), while it normally has the simple meaning 'come', is also used in the LXX of man's approach to God and frequently describes the approach made by the priest rather than by the people in the sacrificial cultus; these sacrificial and priestly overtones are appropriate to the present context (cf. J. Schneider, *T.D.N.T.*, II, pp. 683f).

**that living stone,** i.e., Christ. The metaphor now changes completely from Christ as spiritual nourishment to him as 'stone' (compare the change in 1 Cor. 3:9 from 'field' to 'building'). This latter image, associated with the OT texts quoted in verses 6–8, was part of the Christian tradition from the earliest days (cf. B. Lindars, *New Testament Apologetic*, London, 1961, pp. 169ff) in defence of a Messiah who was crucified but whom God raised from the dead (cf. Ac. 4:11; Mk 12:10f; Rom. 9:33). Thus, as so often, the author makes full use of the primitive Christian tradition, and there is no need to think of Peter meditating on the meaning of his name (the rock; cf. Mt. 16:18). In the present verse the author ignores the full description of Christ as the cornerstone (cf. verse 6) preferring to concentrate on the conception 'stone' alone; this permits him in verse 5 to make the easy jump to Christians as stones. The word used for 'stone' both here and in verse 5 signifies a stone dressed for building rather than a piece of raw rock or a boulder.

**living:** see on 1:23. Elsewhere in the primitive tradition this adjective is not attached to 'stone'; its use here alerts us to the fact that 'stone' is being used metaphorically and in addition it reminds us of the resurrection and the life-giving nature of the stone.

**rejected by men:** first of all by the Jews when they crucified Christ, and now by all who hear the Gospel and reject it.

**chosen and precious:** in words drawn from OT passages used in the primitive Christian apologetic the true value of the crucified Messiah is set out. 'Chosen' is later picked up and applied to the church (verse 9); it had already been so used in 1:2 (see notes there for its meaning). It was also applied to Christ in other parts of the Christian tradition; Lk. 23:35; Jn 1:34 (but only in some

manuscripts); Lk. 9:35 (where another word from the same root
is used).

5. **living stones:** the same description was applied to Christ in
verse 4. 'Living' again indicates that 'stones' is used metaphorically
and also that the life of Christians ('born anew' 1:23) is derived
from the life of Christ; however Christians unlike Christ are not
'life-giving'.

**be yourselves built:** the Greek can be translated either as an
indicative or an imperative; from 1:13 onwards we have had
many imperatives and this suggests the continuance of this mood,
but in 1:13-2:3 the imperatives were moral commands; there
was no instruction to be born again; the theme of 2:4-10 is not
moral instruction but a description of the church; it is therefore
preferable to translate here as an indicative, 'you yourselves are
built' (cf. Selwyn, Beare, Elliot, *op. cit.*, p. 163 note 1). It may be
assumed that God is the builder. The verb 'build' and the
cognate noun are widely employed in the NT in the direct sense
as here (Mt. 16:18; Mk 14:58; 15:29; 1 Cor. 3:9-17; Eph. 2:22)
and in the transferred moral sense of 'edification' (Ac. 9:31;
Rom. 14:19; 15:2,20, etc.). Whereas the image of building
formed a regular part of early Christian tradition, we do not
elsewhere find believers described as 'stones'; it is however
implicit in 1 Cor. 3:10-15, and becomes more obvious in Eph.
2:19-22 (where the cornerstone is particularised as Christ and the
foundations as the apostles and prophets); it would be in addition
suggested by the conception of Peter as the rock and of the Christian who endures persecution as a pillar in the temple (Rev. 3:12;
cf. Gal. 2:9); it appears quite naturally in the present context.

**into a spiritual house:** grammatically 'house' is not the object of
'built' but is a nominative either in apposition to 'living stones' or,
as 'You are a spiritual house', the beginning of a new sentence
whose structure has to be understood; the interpretation is not
affected. 'House' can mean either building or household; in view
of the preceding reference to 'stones' it must surely mean the
former. The church is thus a spiritual house built by God and its
members are the stones of the building. But what kind of a
building? In the context of 'priesthood' and 'sacrifices' it must
denote a religious building, i.e. a temple. 'The house of God' is
frequently used in this way in the OT (e.g. Jg. 18:31; 2 Sam. 12:
20) and occasionally also in secular Greek. The eschatological
expectation of a new temple begins in the OT and becomes more

frequent in inter-testamental Judaism; the Qumran community
came to regard itself as this new temple. 'This is the House which
(He will build for them in the) last days . . . He has commanded
that a Sanctuary of men be built for Himself, that there they may
send up, like the smoke of incense, the works of the Law' (4QFlor.
1:1–7 in G. Vermes, *The Dead Sea Scrolls in English*, London, 1962,
p. 243f; cf. 1 QS 5:5ff; 8:4ff; 9:3ff; 1QpHab 12:1ff; in 4QpIsa^d
frag. 1 the elect are termed stones. See B. Gärtner, *The Temple and
the Community in Qumran and the New Testament* (Society for New
Testament Studies, Monograph 1), Cambridge, 1965, pp. 22–44).
A similar conception, the church as the temple, is found widely in
the early Christian tradition (Mk 14:58; 15:29; Jn 2:19; 1 Cor.
3:16; 2 Cor. 6:16; Eph. 2:19–22; 1 Tim. 3:15; Heb. 12:18–24;
Rev. 3:12; 11:1; cf. Gärtner, *op. cit.*, pp. 49–71; 88–122). The
description of the church as the temple of God is the nearest this
letter comes to the Pauline metaphor of the Body of Christ; it is
not nearly so effective but does imply that Christ and Christians
belong to the same community and are bound together in the
same unit.

**spiritual:** this is not the same word as that rendered 'spiritual' in
verse 2. Its use signifies first, that 'house' is not intended in the
literal sense, and secondly, that the Spirit of God is to be associated
with its existence. It is the adjective from the word for 'spirit' and
does not mean 'immaterial' or 'religious'; a common word in the
Pauline corpus, it is always associated with the Spirit of God.
1 Cor. 3:16; Eph. 2:22 would suggest that the Spirit dwells in the
house.

**to be a holy priesthood:** the metaphor shifts—believers who
were the stones of the temple now serve within the temple; it is a
natural development: a temple exists for the service of God and its
component parts must be engaged in that service. The word used
for priesthood comes from Exod. 19:6 (quoted at verse 9) and
originally applied to the whole of Israel; it appears also in the
LXX of Exod. 23:22 but since it has no equivalent in the Hebrew
text is probably an interpolation there. A priesthood of all
Israel is mentioned in only one other verse in the OT (Isa. 61:6)
but re-appears in the inter-testamental period where we find it in
a number of texts dependent on Exod. 19:6, viz., 2 Mac. 2:17;
*Jubilees* 16:18; 33:20; *Testament of Levi*, Greek Fragment 67;
Philo, *De Sobrietate* 66; *De Abrahamo* 56 (See Elliott, *op. cit.*, pp.
50–128, for a full discussion). In circles where the levitical

priesthood was honoured this conception could make little headway. Many fragments of the book *Jubilees* have been found at Qumran and so it is reasonable to conclude that the idea was known there; this is confirmed when we realise that the qualifications to enter the Qumran community were very similar to those required of priests for the levitical priesthood, apart, of course, from membership in the tribe of Levi (cf. Lev. 21:17ff and 1QSa 2:3; CD 15:15–17; 4QFlor 1:3f; see Gärtner, *op. cit.*, pp. 4ff for the similarities). The position at Qumran remained ambiguous since priests occupied a leading position in the community and the term 'priest' was never directly applied to its ordinary members; with the disappearance of an official priesthood in the early church this ambiguity vanished. Thus we find that Exod. 19:6 is directly applied to Christians in Rev. 1:6; 5:10; 20:6. Moreover in the NT terms drawn from the levitical cultus are appropriated for Christian activity: in Heb. 10:22 'sprinkled' and 'washed' come from the description of the consecration of priests (Exod. 29:21; Lev. 8:6,30); in Heb. 12:23 'firstborn' recalls the Levites as the firstborn of Israel; in Heb. 13:10 Christians have an altar; in Rom. 15:16 Paul describes his work as a 'priestly service'; see also the passages quoted below in reference to 'spiritual sacrifices': cf. Best, 'Spiritual Sacrifice: General Priesthood in the New Testament', *Interpretation*, 14 (1960) 280–90.

**holy:** Israel is a holy people; everything connected with the cultus is especially holy, in particular the priesthood. At 1:15f the need for holiness on the part of believers has already been emphasised and 2:9 will revert to their status as holy.

**to offer spiritual sacrifices:** one function of the priesthood of the OT, and of the priesthoods of the contemporary heathen world, was the offering of sacrifice. With **spiritual** (cf. 'spiritual house') the writer shows that he does not mean the customary material sacrifices of the cultus but those sacrifices which belong to a priesthood serving in a temple ('house') in which God's Spirit dwells and to which it is moved by that same Spirit. Non-material sacrifices were known in the OT (Isa. 1:11–17; Hos. 6:6; Mic. 6:6–8; Ps. 50:13,14,23; 51:17; 141:2). Since the members of the Qumran community were either unable or unwilling to take part in the sacrificial cultus of the temple at Jerusalem these non-material sacrifices became more important for them: 'the life of the community in perfect obedience to the

Law is represented as the true sacrifice offered in the new temple'
(Gärtner, *op. cit.*, p. 44; cf. 1QS 8:9; 9:3ff; 4QFlor. 1:6f, quoted
above); unlike the non-material sacrifices of the OT but like the
levitical sacrifices these sacrifices at Qumran served to make
atonement for the sins of the community; otherwise there would
have been no way of reconciliation to God. Again we find these
non-material sacrifices becoming a common element in the
early Christian tradition; since the sacrifice of Christ now occupies
a unique place in atoning for sin these are no longer considered
to effect this. In the NT they are sometimes instanced without
specific content (Rom. 12:1; 15:16; Phil. 2:17; 2 Tim. 4:6; Rev.
6:9) and sometimes with particular reference, e.g. good deeds
(Heb. 13:16; Phil. 4:18; Rom. 15:27; 2 Cor. 9:12), worship
(Heb. 13:15; Rev. 7:15; 8:3-5; cf. 5:8) (see Best, *Interpretation*, 14
(1960) 284,286ff). In 1 Pet. 2:5 the reference is perfectly general
and probably Rom. 12:1 (whose ideas, as we have seen on 2:2,
were probably known to our author) forms the best parallel.
The context in 1 Peter stresses the function of the priesthood (to
offer sacrifice) rather than its status (the Christians are like
priests in possessing direct access to God). There is no idea that
the priesthood acts on behalf of the world as the levitical priesthood acted on behalf of Israel; nowhere in the references of the
NT to the sacrifices which Christians offer is there any suggestion
that these are provided by others or presented on their behalf.
The NT priesthood presents its own sacrifices. Even if there is
any reference to the Eucharist in 2:2f (and as we saw there this is
most unlikely) there is no reason to view that reference as continued here or to regard the sacrifice of the Christian priesthood as
that of the Eucharist.

**acceptable to God:** cf. Rom. 15:16; Phil. 4:18; 1 Tim. 2:3;
Heb. 12:28; 13:15f.

**through Jesus Christ:** this phrase may be attached either to
'offer', in which case Christ may be conceived as mediating these
sacrifices to God in common with the NT teaching that man can
only approach God through Christ, or to 'acceptable' in which
case the sacrifices are considered pleasing to God not because of
the one who presents them but because of Christ.

6-10. In these verses we have a selection of OT passages; they
repeat many of the words and ideas of verses 4f; what is the
relationship of the two sections? Were verses 4f written to introduce the quotations from the OT (so Selwyn and Elliott) or are

the quotations used to confirm what is said in verses 4–5? This is an unfair way of stating the alternatives. We have seen that all the conceptions of verses 4–5 were part of the common tradition of early Christianity; this tradition was neither formed by the OT nor did it take shape apart from the OT. The first Christians would have held, not only that their faith was continuous with that of the saints of the OT (indeed one of the objects of 2:4–10 is to remind readers that they belong to the same people of God), but also that there was a radical discontinuity in Jesus Christ; not merely is a new meaning given to the OT when viewed through Jesus Christ but in him God has created something new, the redemption of mankind. Verses 4–5 are not then a preparation shedding new light on the OT texts to be quoted in verses 6–10, for the sum total of what the author says goes far beyond what the OT quotations assert, e.g., the references to the Spirit and to Jesus Christ in relation to our sacrifices; it is equally true that verses 6–10 do not just confirm all that is said in verses 4–5, though they do confirm some of the statements therein: many of the statements are simply not confirmed because it is impossible to provide full support for them from the OT. As we go through verses 6–10 we see that the writer moves from a kind of confirmation by direct quotation (verse 6) to the advancing of his argument by the use of OT words and phrases which take on a meaning they did not always have in the OT.

The quotations in verses 6 (=Isa. 28:16), 7 (=Ps. 118:22) and 8 (=Isa. 8:14f) were used regularly in the early tradition and were probably already associated in it (see detailed notes on the verses). It is unnecessary to suppose (so Selwyn, pp. 268–81) that verses 6–10, or any portion of them, formed a Christian hymn which our author has quoted. *graphē* is correctly rendered 'scripture' in verse 6 and should not be taken in the general sense 'writing' as indicative of a quotation from some document other than the OT. The alleged hymn does not display normal hymnic characteristics, e.g. relative pronouns, participial clauses, and verses 9–10 are addressed to the readers and not to God (cf. Elliott, *op. cit.*, pp. 133ff).

6. Isa. 28:16 is quoted here from the LXX with the same variations as in Rom. 9:33; probably neither 1 Peter nor Romans depends on the other but both on the early apologetic tradition of the church (cf. Selwyn, pp. 268ff, C. H. Dodd, *According to the Scriptures*, London, 1952, pp. 41–3). The reference to the foun-

dation in Isa. 28 was probably omitted from this pre-Pauline and
pre-Petrine tradition because it would have suggested that the
cornerstone was part of the foundation; a foundation is buried
and it would be impossible to stumble over it (cf. Lindars, *op. cit.*,
pp. 178, 180): no special significance should therefore be attached
to its omission in 1 Peter.

**cornerstone:** this may either have been a great stone at the
corner (see R. J. McKelvey, 'Christ the Cornerstone', *N.T.S.*,
8 (1961/2) 352–9) or a top or locking stone (see J. Jeremias,
*T.D.N.T.*, I, pp. 791–3): the reference to stumbling makes the
former alternative more probable. In either case it was regarded
as a special stone in the temple in some strands of Jewish tradition
(*Testament of Solomon*, 22:7ff; 2 Kings 25:17, in the translation of
Symmachus; 1QS 8:4ff).

**Zion:** see G. A. Barrois, *I.D.B.* IV, pp. 959f; G. Fohrer and
E. Lohse, '*Sion*', *T.W.N.T.*, VII, pp. 291ff). In the OT and the
inter-testamental literature Zion is used as a synonym for Jerusalem, sometimes as a political entity, the royal city of David, but
more often as the city of God (e.g. Isa. 60:14; Ps. 48:1f), the place
of God's indwelling (Isa. 8:18; Ps. 74:2; 132:13f) and his sanctuary
(Ps. 20:2); the temple hill is Mount Zion. Zion is sometimes
personified (Lam. 1:17) and regarded as equivalent to its inhabi-
tants (Ps. 74:2; 97:8; Jer. 14:19; Isa. 51:16). This is most appropriate to the context of the building of the new Temple since there
is an eschatological expectation of a new Zion as there is of a
new Jerusalem (Rev. 14:1).

7. The author explains the quotation in verse 6 by his reference
to Christ as **precious** for believers and, quoting Ps. 118:22, as the
cornerstone (=**head of the corner**) on which unbelievers
stumble. His quotation is also a confirmation of the words
'rejected by men' in verse 4.

8. The rejection of Jesus by men is now further explained with
words drawn from Isa. 8:14f; they **stumble** on Jesus the **stone.**
**as they were destined to do:** it is better to link this with 'they
stumble' which is the main thought of the sentence than with
'they disobey'. Following Jewish reverential dislike of the use of
God's name the third person plural passive is often used in the
NT where we would attribute the action directly to God; so it is
taught here that God predestines men to stumble. Predestination
is again part of the primitive Christian teaching (1 Th. 5:9; Rom.
8:28–30; 9–11; Eph. 1:12; Jude 4) though it is normally

expounded in regard to those who are saved and not to those who perish. In verse 7f Christ is set out either as precious to men or as a cause of offence to them; there is no middle position.

9–10. In these verses the writer advances his argument with a skilful selection of OT phrases (taken from the LXX) and all originally applied to Israel, the OT people of God, but now applied to the church, the new people of God: they set out its honour and dignity: they who were once no people are now the people of God.

9. **chosen race, God's own people** (adapted), **wonderful deeds** come from Isa. 43:20f and **royal priesthood, holy nation** from Exod. 19:6.

**But you:** in contrast to those who disbelieve (verses 7–8).

**chosen:** see on 1:2; 2:4.

**royal:** the two Greek words for 'royal priesthood' follow the LXX exactly; the original Hebrew is 'a kingdom of priests' where there are two nouns rather than a noun with an adjective. The Greek word for 'royal', viz., *basileion*, can be translated either as an adjective or a noun. If it is taken as an adjective as in the RSV it indicates priests who are in the service of a king, i.e. God; cf. 'royal bodyguard'; it does not imply that the priests are kings. If it is taken as a noun then we have a fairly wide range of meanings from which to choose, all of which are associated with the concept 'king'. It is impossible from an examination of the Greek text of the LXX to determine whether the translators of the LXX regarded it as a noun or an adjective; both are grammatically possible. In texts derived from the LXX (2 Mac. 2:17; Philo, *De Sobrietate*, 66; *De Abrahamo* 56) it is taken as a noun. In the Aramaic Targums the phrase appears as 'kings and priests', which again suggests that 'royal' should be treated as a noun; Rev. 1:6; 5:10, and probably Jub. 16:18, follow this interpretation. If we interpret it here as a noun what meaning should we give to it? The use of 'house' in verse 5 suggests that we accept the meaning 'palace', which is the way Philo takes it; but 'palace' does not fit in alongside the other nouns in the list of verse 9, which all denote groups of people. We might also render it 'kingdom'; normally this would mean the territory rather than the people in it, but the extension to the latter appears natural; this may be the meaning given in 2 Mac. 2:17; it would imply the identity of the people of God with the Kingdom of God, an equation not found in this direct form elsewhere; we should expect that our writer would have prefixed to it some qualifying adjective, as is his usual custom (cf. stone, sacrifice in verses 4f), to indicate that it was not to be taken in the literal sense; moreover it is very doubtful if 'kingdom' by itself is comparable with the other titles of verse 9 as attributing honour to the people of God. A third meaning is possible, viz., 'group of kings'; although there is no actual occurrence of the word in this sense, its form indicates that it is a possible meaning; it accords with the Targumic interpretation of Exod. 19:6 and with the Christian tradition of Rev. 1:6; 5:10; in these two latter texts we have a slightly different Greek word which is correctly rendered 'kingdom', but in 5:10 it is immediately glossed with the phrase 'they shall reign on earth', indicating that they are kings (cf. Rev. 20:6 where 'priests' are said to reign): the 'reign' of the saints appears in various parts of the NT (Eph. 2:6; 2 Tim. 2:12; 1 Cor. 4:8; 6:1ff; Rom. 5:17; Jas. 2:5). We conclude that the word 'royal' is to be taken as a noun, preferably with the meaning 'group of kings', and with it is associated a word which means 'group of priests'.

**priesthood:** emphasis no longer rests as in verse 5 on the duty of the priesthood but on the privilege of the church which is called 'the priesthood'; they are a body of priests; each is a priest (cf. the plural 'priests' in Rev. 1:6; 5:10; 20:6) but never a priest in and by himself; it is only as a member of the corporate priesthood that he is such and he can only exercise his priesthood within the corporate existence of the church: the conception is not individualistic.

**holy nation:** as Israel was a people separated to God (cf. Dt. 7:6; 14:2,21) so also is the church; both are holy, made so by God, and should seek holiness; see on 1:15f for the meaning of holiness.

**God's own people:** lit. 'a people for possession' (cf. Mal. 3:17; Ac. 20:28; Tit. 2:14); they are God's people because he has purchased them by the blood of his Son (1:19; cf. Tit. 2:14).

**people:** the normal word in the LXX (*laos*) applied to Israel and distinguishing it from other nations. The Christians who come from many races and nations are now one people in continuity with the people of God in the OT (cf. verse 10 and Eph. 2:11ff; Col. 1:21ff); the history of Israel is now their history.

**that you may declare the wonderful deeds:** this phrase is not to be attached to 'priesthood' alone as 'to offer spiritual sacrifices' was in verse 5, but to all five designations of the church in verse 9 (chosen race, group of kings, priesthood, holy nation, God's own people). Christians declare God's wonderful deeds of redemption (his loving action once in Christ, now continued among them by his Spirit and seen in their new status) by their proclamation of his word (1:25; 3:15) and by the holiness of their lives (1:16; 2:11–3:7). The suggestion of Boismard (*D.B.S.*, VII, 1437-9) that we have a reference here to the thanksgivings of the Eucharist is far-fetched.

**who called you out of darkness into his marvellous light:** the contrast of light and darkness as representing that of good and evil is found in the later parts of the OT and very widely in inter-testamental Judaism. In the NT tradition the change from unbelief to belief is often pictured as leaving darkness and entering light (Mt. 4:16; 6:22f; Lk. 1:79; Ac. 26:18; 2 Cor. 4:6; 6:14; 1 Th. 5:4f; Eph. 5:8; Col. 1:12f; 1 Jn 1:6f); it came eventually to have a place in the baptismal liturgies, an association which may already be beginning to appear in the NT.

10. **no people, people; have not received mercy, have received mercy:** these phrases are drawn from Hos. 2:23 under the influence of Hos. 1:6, 9; 2:1. Hos. 2:23 is quoted more fully and accurately at Rom. 9:25; there it is used to show that the Gentiles who have come into the church have taken the place of unbelieving Jews. In 1 Pet. 2:10 much less stress lies on the rejection of the Jews and much more on the acceptance of the church; this, consisting mainly of Gentiles who seemed once wholly outside God's purpose, is **now** within that purpose and has in fact become God's people (our author has added 'once', 'now' to the quotations from Hosea): yet the very fact that in verses 9f the titles of dignity which once referred to Israel are now applied to the church implies the rejection of the Jews, who themselves rejected their Messiah.

## THE SOCIAL CODE 2:11–3:12

The need for holiness has already been emphasised (1:15f); now, using a social code (see pp. 30f), the writer shows how this will work out in particular situations in which the Christian will be in contact with unbelievers. 2:11–12 is a general introduction which points out the effect of true behaviour on the pagan world; 2:13–17, the Christian and the official world; 2:18–25, the

Christian servant or slave and his pagan master; 3:1-7, the
Christian and the other members of his family; 3:8-12, a concluding exhortation deriving its power from an OT citation.

## CHRISTIAN BEHAVIOUR AND THE HEATHEN 2:11-12

A short section introducing the social code, in which the negative
side of holiness, abstinence from evil, is stressed on the grounds of
its powerful effect on the surrounding heathen.

11. **Beloved:** a common term of address in NT times (cf. 4:12;
Rom. 1:7; 1 Cor. 10:14; 2 Pet. 3:1, etc.). Though derived from
the special Christian term for love (*agapē*) through usage it had
probably lost some of the characteristic flavour of that term.
Here it is used formally to indicate the beginning of a new section
of the letter (cf. 4:12).

**beseech:** this word is used regularly to introduce sections of
detailed instruction on behaviour; cf. Rom. 12:1; Eph. 4:1;
1 Th. 4:1.

**aliens:** from the same root as 'exile' in 1:17.

**exiles:** see on 1:1. These two words, 'aliens, exiles', which occur
together also at Gen. 23:4; Ps. 39:12 differ little in meaning.
They emphasise here the 'foreign-ness' of Christians (the new
people of God, 2:9f) to their pagan environment, to whose
culture they should not assimilate themselves, rather than their
separation from their true homeland (see notes on 1:1); the two
ideas are complementary.

**abstain:** the negative aspect of 'holiness' (see on 1:15f), the
sense of 'separation' from evil. While the conception is part of the
Jewish inheritance of early Christianity, the actual word used to
express it entered Christianity (cf. 1 Th. 4:3; 5:22; Ac. 15:20,29)
from Greek moral philosophy.

**flesh, soul:** these two concepts are set in opposition. In the OT
the former is not used to designate the material element in man
but man as a whole viewed as a weak human being when contrasted with the strength of God. Paul adapted the term, under the
influence of the Qumran community's usage, to denote man as
morally weak; as flesh man lives apart from God, unredeemed
and subject to the power of sin. The way in which the term is used
in 1 Peter lies between the usage of the OT and Paul's usage, cf.
3:18,21 (where 'body' translates the Greek word for flesh);
4:1,2,6. The **passions of the flesh** are not then just those sins

to which the body tempts, as if the physical nature of man were especially evil, but include every sin whether belonging only to the mind or expressed through the body. Gal. 5:19–21 shows the width of the conception (cf. N. W. Porteus and S. V. McCasland *I.D.B.*, II, pp. 276f; W. D. Stacey, *The Pauline View of Man*, London, 1956, pp. 154ff).

**wage war against your soul:** for man's inner conflict see Rom. 7:7ff; Jas 4:1; 1QS 3:17ff. Although the readers have been born anew (1:3,23) they do not escape temptation but must still struggle to overcome it. In Paul this contest is generally seen to lie between man's flesh and the Spirit of God (Rom. 8:1–14; Gal. 5:16–25), though sometimes it is a contest within man (Rom. 7:23) as in our verse.

**soul:** see on 1:9. In our present passage the writer approaches a more Hellenistic usage of the word than elsewhere in that he appears to set a higher part (soul) of man in conflict with a lower (flesh); but because the Christian has been reborn his soul has been reborn and it is his redeemed soul, not some pre-existing divine spark, which is here set in contrast with his flesh.

12. **good:** the Greek word (*kalos*), used twice in this verse, implies that their behaviour should not only be good but also be seen to be good.

**Gentiles:** the same Greek word is rendered 'heathen' in 1 Cor. 12:2; 1 Th. 4:5 (cf. 'pagans' in 1 Cor. 5:1) and should probably be translated similarly here. Jews used the word to denote non-Jews, but this can hardly be the primary significance here; it means non-Christian. Since Christians are the people of God (2:9f) it was easy to transfer the term to denote non-Christians.

**wrongdoers:** this could be used in the narrow sense 'criminals', indicating that Christians were accused of particular crimes (cf. Ac. 16:16ff; 19:23ff; from the second century onwards they were accused of incest, cannibalism and atheism), but may be used more widely indicating that Christians were slandered by the heathen (cf. Ac. 13:45; 18:6; Mt. 5:11; 1 Cor. 4:12f; Rev. 2:9, and from the non-Christian side, Tacitus *Annales* 15:44; Suetonius, *Nero* 16:2; Pliny, *Epistles* 10:96). At 2:14 the phrase definitely suggests criminal activity; at 3:17 and 4:15 it can be taken in either way.

**they may see your good deeds:** when slandered or persecuted Christians are not to withdraw into a ghetto (cf. 1 Th. 4:12; Col. 4:5) but to answer their opponents, not with verbal argument, but with positive loving behaviour (cf. Preisker), and to do this not for their own peace and safety but for the good of their tormentors. On 'good deeds' see W. C. van Unnik, 'The Teaching of Good Works in 1 Peter', *N.T.S.* 1 (1954) 92–110. 'good deeds' is not the direct object of 'see'; the literal rendering is 'see out of your good deeds', i.e. they are to observe and then come to a conclusion, viz., to glorify God. The whole of 12b is closely similar to the saying of Mt. 5:16 (cf. *Testament of Naphtali* 8:4) and almost certainly depends on it.

**the day of visitation:** God visits men either to judge and punish (Isa. 10:3; Jer. 6:15; Lk 19:44; N.B., the RSV often translates the word out of its neutral sense 'visit' into the appropriate meaning) or to bless and save (Gen. 50:24f; Job 10:12; 1 Sam. 2:21; Lk 1:68,78; Ac. 15:14). The phrase may then refer either to the final day of judgement, as van Unnik strongly urges (*op. cit.*, pp. 103ff), or to the time of the conversion of those who see and understand the good deeds of Christians. The former interpretation fits the general eschatological tone of the letter and is to be preferred.


THE CHRISTIAN AND CIVIL AUTHORITY 2:13–17

This is the first item in the code of duties guiding members of the church in their relations with the pagan world. The guidance given is generally similar to that of Rom. 13:1–7, though there is probably no literary dependence (see p. 33). 'The Christian and civil authority' is an obvious problem once the church has been described in the terms of 2:9; if it is the true nation and race why should it owe allegiance to earthly powers? At the very beginning of its existence the church came into conflict with the Jewish authorities (Ac. 3–8); for a time it was well treated by the Romans (e.g. Ac. 18:12–17), but was later persecuted under Nero and from then on increasingly drew the inimical attention of rulers (cf. pp. 39ff). As in Rom. 13:1–7; 1 Tim. 2:1–3; Tit. 3:1–3,8 (the two latter epistles are not by Paul but date from about the close of the first century); 1 Clement 60:4–61:2; 63:1 (probably from the final decade of the first century), so in 1 Peter respect and obedience for the Roman authorities is inculcated, despite, by the time of the later writings, the known fact of persecution. Two factors combined to further this respect: (i) the belief that civil authority was God's creation; (ii) the belief that the end of all things was at hand (4:7) and therefore the social situation might be accepted as it was (the latent factors within Christianity which have made it at times a revolutionary force had not then appeared). We may contrast the attitude revealed towards the state in 1 Pet. 2:13–17 etc. with that of Revelation (cf. 13:1; 18) where the state is regarded as satanic in origin; whether such a view is also implied in the reference to Rome as Babylon in 1 Pet. 5:13 we leave for discussion there.

13. **Be subject:** this is the theme of the social code, cf. 2:18; 3:1 (where 'submissive' is from the same Greek word); 5:5; Eph. 5:21; 6:1,5; Col. 3:18,20,22; Tit. 2:5,9. The conception has an even wider use in the NT, cf. 1 Cor. 14:34; 15:27–8; Eph. 5:22; 1 Pet. 3:22; God has ordered creation in such a way that for its harmony some are always subject to others.

**every human institution:** the RSVmg renders 'every institution ordained for men' and this is to be preferred. The difficult word is that translated 'institution' (Greek, *ktisis*). There is no real evidence that it can mean a human social institution like the state; the nearest to this is its use to denote the founding of a city. When the word and its cognate forms appear in the LXX they almost always denote something created by God, e.g. man (Dt. 4:32), the universe (Gen. 14:19,22), agriculture (Sir. 7:15; 40:1), wisdom (Sir. 1:4); see W. Foerster, *T.D.N.T.*, III, pp. 1023–8. Sir. 39:30 says that God created 'the sword that punishes the ungodly with destruction' (cf. 40:9f), and this is very similar to the conception of 1 Pet. 2:14. The principle objection to this view is the adjective 'human' attached to 'institution'; it suggests that man creates the state, but it can be taken as in the RSVmg in the sense that God (not mentioned but understood) creates in the sphere of human affairs; thus civil authority may be considered as instituted by God. This is similar to Paul's teaching in Rom. 13:1–7, and to that of the OT (Isa. 5:25–30; 45:1) which became more explicit in Judaism (Dan. 2:21,37f; 4:17,32; Wisd. 6:3); in the Jerusalem temple sacrifices were offered for the Roman emperor. Consequently the state is viewed as deriving from God's appointment. The Zealots in Judaism, who advocated violence against their nation's oppressors, never accepted this conception. To return to 1 Pet. 2:13, it is doubtful if there would be sufficient grounds in a view of the state as a human institution to make the claim for submission to it which Peter makes in the passage.

It is possible that on the RSVmg translation of 2:13a this phrase should be taken as a title for the whole of the social code; submission is then itemized in three areas, each of which, the state, the master and slave relationship, the family, is an institution created by God.

**for the Lord's sake:** is 'Lord' here God or Christ? Generally in the NT it denotes Christ and only means God in quotations from the OT or in thought dependent on the OT (see W. Foerster, *T.D.N.T.*, III, pp. 1086ff). This suggests we take it as Christ here. On the other hand the meaning 'God' is very appropriate to the RSVmg understanding of the earlier words—because God has created civil authorities we should be obedient to them—and this could be said to derive from OT thought. If it is understood of Christ then the phrase probably means 'so as not to bring dishonour on Christ'. Thus Christians are summoned to submission, not so that they may have an easy time in relation to the state, but as part of their service to the Lord.

14. **governors as sent by him:** though the Roman constitution distinguished between governors appointed by the Emperor and those appointed by the Senate our author was probably not aware of this distinction and assumes that all are sent by the emperor.

**by him:** *lit.* 'through him'. If we accept the RSVmg in verse 13a then this is probably a reference to God as the ultimate source of the power which comes to governors through the emperor.

**to punish those . . . :** it is the duty of the state to maintain law and order and preserve society from anarchy; this had already been taught by Paul (Rom. 13:3f) who derived it from his upbringing in Pharisaical Judaism. Roman justice was rightly famed in this respect, and Christians had already benefited from it (Ac. 18:12-16).

**to praise those who do right:** 'the rewards which were bestowed from time to time upon public benefactors, at the instance of the governor', e.g. 'laudatory inscriptions . . . the award of crowns, or of citizenship' (Beare). This was a very common custom in Asia Minor to which surviving inscriptions and statues testify. But few Christians would be of the social standing to receive such awards; it may be that the writer is thinking more generally of 'praise' as acquittal in the law court (cf. Schelkle); such a reference would balance the first half of the verse which certainly deals with legal proceedings.

15. **it is God's will:** this may refer back to verse 13 as well as forward to the remainder of verse 15, i.e. it is God's will that they should be subject to civil authority and that their good deeds should silence those who oppose them.

**the ignorance of foolish men:** the word used for ignorance, *agnōsia*, suggests culpable ignorance rather than mere lack of knowledge.

**foolish** is used frequently in Proverbs to denote men who are not just wayward but are opposed to God; thus the whole phrase is much stronger than the English would suggest. Perhaps the writer is a little optimistic in believing that the good deeds of Christians will end the calumnies and attacks of those who do not think of them as God's people.

16. **Live as free men:** to describe the ideal life in terms of freedom meant much for the ancient world because of its clear distinction between the slave and the free man. The freedom of the Christian does not lie in his superiority to outward circumstances, as many Greek philosophers would have thought it did, but in his willingness to accept obedience. His claim to freedom cannot be a **pretext** for behaviour which would bring him into conflict with the law, for the law rightly punishes the evil-doer (verse 14); freedom is not licence (cf. Gal. 5:13; Rom. 6:15; Eph. 6:5–7). The case is not considered where the Christian may have to be disobedient because the law makes demands contrary to Christian faith, e.g. the burning of incense to express allegiance to the emperor; this may be because the social code was formulated in a period prior to when this became a possibility and in a situation different from emperor worship; the code is not altered but the changed behaviour that may be required from Christians is considered in the passages which refer to persecution. The reference to Christian freedom is brief because it was already an accepted part of the instruction of Christians.

**servants of God** (cf. 1 Cor. 7:22; Rom. 6:22): the Christian can be free to obey the state because he is already God's servant. Early Christianity would never have regarded the Christian as the servant of the state; the latter conception was acceptable to much oriental life though alien to many Greek thinkers.

17. With four short imperatival clauses the section is rounded off.

**Honour all men. Love the brotherhood:** in Tit. 3:1f we likewise move from an attitude of submission to the authorities

to an attitude of respect for all men; in Rom. 13:1–10 we go
from the attribution of honour to the authorities to love of the
neighbour. In 1 Peter a distinction is drawn between the Christian's
attitude to the world and to the church; does our writer envisage
love as only being possible where it is reciprocated (within the
Christian community), whereas honour is possible without
reciprocation, or does he regard 'honour' as similar to but less
emotional than 'love'? In any case to 'honour' men is not necessarily a lessening of Jesus' demand to love one's neighbour (Mk
12:31); see also notes on 1:22.

**brotherhood:** the conception of Christians as brothers is here
made concrete in a rather uncommon use of the underlying word
to denote the church as a whole.

**Fear God. Honour the emperor:** amended from Prov. 24:21
(LXX) 'fear God and the emperor'. (In both 1 Pet. 2:17 and
Prov. 24:21 'emperor' is literally 'king'.) The amendment serves
to distinguish the attitude of the Christian to God from that to the
emperor (cf. Mk 12:17). 'Fear' is used regularly in the OT to
describe the true attitude of the pious to God (see on 1:17); it
would be misunderstood if applied to his relationship to the
emperor. The Christian needs fear no man, though he ought to
render him willing obedience and respect according to his position,
for man cannot do him ultimate injury (Mt. 10:28). The distinction implies that the emperor cannot be put on the same plane as
God—which was the tendency in Asia Minor.

THE CHRISTIAN SLAVE AND HIS OWNER 2:18–25

Sections dealing with slaves and their masters are found in the
other social codes in the NT, viz., Eph. 6:5–8; Col. 3:22–5;
1 Tim. 6:1f; Tit. 2:9f (cf. also 1 Cor. 7:21–3). Since many of the
first Christians were slaves this section is very relevant for the
communities to which the letter is written. Most of these slaves
were owned by pagan masters. Our author does not deal with the
duties of masters (contrast Eph. 6:9; Col. 4:1; Philemon 16;
*Didache* 4:10; Ignatius, *Polycarp* 4:3; *Barnabas* 19:7); it is extremely
unlikely that there were no Christian masters in the wide area to
which he wrote; why is there then no reference to them? Although
in 2:13–3:12 the letter seems concerned only with the strains that
arise when Christians live in relationship with non-Christians
(3:7 is the only possible exception) we might have expected a

discussion of the attitude of the Christian master to the non-Christian slave. Such a situation may, however, never have arisen if whole households were baptized and became Christian at the time of the master's conversion (cf. Ac. 16:15, 32–4). Perhaps the writer trusted hopefully that Christian masters would automatically treat their slaves correctly. The slave was a chattel, owned by his master, wholly at his disposal and without legal rights should he think that he had been misused. The NT accepts this situation and never suggests its abolition (cf. 1 Cor. 7:21); to do otherwise would have required a social revolution wholly out of keeping with the attitude to authority taught in 2:13–17; moreover a rebellion by slaves against authority would have been crushed with terrible cruelty, as had happened more than once in the past. But within the Christian community the slave was given a new dignity since he was no longer treated as a chattel or possession but as a person (Gal. 3:28; Col. 3:11); this is shown by the very fact of the presence of a section on the behaviour of slaves in the Christian social codes; pre-Christian codes did not think them worthy of mention. This recognition of the slave as a person could have created tension and the slave have begun to imagine he ought to be free but for the stress on subjection in these sections. The social code in 1 Peter is unique among those in the NT because it bases its instructions to slaves on the example of Christ who took the form of a slave (Phil. 2:7) and bore the punishments, reviling, beating, crucifixion, of a slave.

On the place of slaves in the ancient world see J. Carcopino, *Daily Life in Ancient Rome*, London, 1941, pp. 52–75; R. Flacelière, *Daily Life in Greece*, London, 1959, pp. 45–54; M. Grant, *op. cit.*, pp. 100–125.

18. **Servants,** i.e. slaves: not those working for a wage but those owned by others. The Greek word (*oiketai*) denotes household slaves, many of whom might be well educated and hold responsible positions in their households; there were also large slave gangs employed in agriculture for whom a different word would have been used; the church was an urban phenomenon at this time, and the latter type of slave is not addressed.

**be submissive:** see on 2:13.

**respect:** the same word as that translated 'fear' at 1:17; 2:17; 3:14 and 'reverent' at 3:2 (see on 1:17). It probably refers to the attitude of the pious to God (cf. 1:17; 2:17) rather than to his master; the whole exhortation receives its strength from the slave's relationship to God (cf. 'mindful-of God', 'God's approval', verses 19,20, and the similar reference to 'fear of God' in the social codes of Col. 3:22; Eph. 6:5), and not from his attitude to man (cf. 3:14f). Because he fears God he will be as patient under the threats and beatings of a cruel master as under the more gentle treatment of a good master. Most masters were good, for a maimed slave was a financial loss.

19. **one is approved:** the underlying word is *charis* which is normally rendered 'grace' in the NT (see on 1:2); it can hardly here have its full theological meaning, 'God's favour towards one who does not merit it'; it might possibly mean 'it is by God's grace you are able to endure', but to take 'grace' as 'power' tends towards a very depersonalised view of grace; more probably it has the meaning 'good' or 'excellent' (at Lk. 6:32–4 it is rendered 'credit'). Verse 20 makes it clear that it is the slave's conduct which is approved, and approved by God rather than by the master.

**mindful of God:** the word rendered 'mindful' possesses almost everywhere else in the NT a meaning roughly equivalent to our word 'conscience' (cf. 3:16,21). Because of the genitive 'of God' it is very difficult to give it this sense here; it cannot be God's conscience, and to understand it as 'a conscience responsive to God' (Beare) reads more into the phrase than it will bear. The word has also a non-ethical meaning, 'awareness', and if it is taken in this way the phrase means 'because you are Christians and as such share in the Church's sure knowledge of God' (C. A. Pierce, *Conscience in the New Testament*, S.B.T. No. 15, London, 1955, p. 108; cf. pp. 105–8).

**endures:** approval follows not just on the experience of pain but on its patient and complete endurance.

**suffering unjustly:** it would have been impossible for a Greek to conceive of a slave suffering unjustly at the hands of his master; what is owned cannot be treated unjustly (cf. Aristole, *Nicomachean Ethics* V. 6:8–9).

20. **do wrong:** this verb re-appears in verses 22,24 as a noun in the sense of 'sin'. Because the whole verse is set in terms of God ('credit', 'God's approval') we should therefore understand 'do wrong' as wrong before God and not just as a mistake in the eyes of a master. Generally the two would have coincided—disregarding the master's instruction will have been sin—but there may have been occasions when the slave would have been asked to perform

a religious duty or an immoral action which would have con-
flicted with his conscience as a Christian.

**do right:** this will likewise have a double meaning (cf. van
Unnik, *N.T.S.* 1 (1954) 99f); behaviour in conformity with the
master's commands would normally coincide with conformity to
God's will; when it does not the slave may have to suffer unjustly.
He might also suffer unjustly from a capricious and vindictive
master whose command he had actually obeyed.

21. **to this,** i.e. to suffering.

**called,** i.e. by God. They have been chosen by him and are
members of his people (1:2; 2:9; 5:10); thus they are given a
new dignity and a new destiny, viz., to suffer, and not just to
suffer but as the sequel shows to suffer as Christ suffered.

**Christ also suffered for you:** the nature and meaning of
Christ's sufferings are expounded in the verses that follow.

**example:** as the teacher writes a line which the scholar is to
copy so Christ provides an example; he took the form of a slave
(Phil. 2:7); thus the sufferings of the slave who was considered
in that period to be little different from an animal are linked to
those of his Lord (cf. Jn 15:20).

**follow in his steps:** written deeply into the Gospel tradition is
Jesus' call to men to come after him (Mk 8:34; Mt. 10:38;
Lk. 14:27; Jn 13:15; cf. Rom. 8:17; Phil. 2:5–11; 1 Th. 1:6;
Heb. 12:2; 13:13). To follow in his steps is however more than
to take him as an example; without him there would be no way
in which to go; it is easier to come second than to pioneer.
In creating the way Christ is saviour as well as example; thus in
verse 24 we pass quite easily from the example of Jesus' sufferings
to their redemptive value.

22–5. The writer expands his reference to the sufferings of
Christ by a subtle interlacing of his own words with words
drawn from Isa. 53 and adapted to his purpose (cf. pp. 28f). All the
NT descriptions of the Passion depend heavily on OT phrases
and allusions for the early church was firmly convinced that the
death of Jesus fulfilled the OT. The dependence on the OT in
1 Peter argues against authorship by an eye-witness or dependence
on an eye-witness (cf. pp. 51ff). In particular if the story in Mark
and that in Peter are supposed to come from the same eye-witness
then we need to note that the passion account in Mk 15:21–39
depends on allusions to the Psalms rather than to Isa. 53. Much
discussion has taken place whether the application to Jesus'

death of Isa. 53 and related OT passages goes back to Jesus himself
or not; we do not need to determine an answer. It is however
certain that the conception of vicarious suffering was current in
this period (cf. 2 Mac. 7:37f; 4 Mac. 6:27ff; 17:22; 18:4; cf.
G. F. Moore, *Judaism*, I, Cambridge, Mass., 1927, pp. 546ff), and
the statements of Isa. 53 were bound to be attached very speedily
to Jesus. This is carried out more explicitly in our present passage
than in any other part of the NT. The inner logic of the passages
cited draws the argument beyond Christ as the example (verses
22f) to Christ as the Saviour (verse 24f); once the writer has
mentioned the cross he is driven on to speak of its atoning power.

Boismard, following Bultmann ('Bekenntnis- und Liedfrag-
mente im ersten Petrusbrief', *Coniectanea Neotestamentica* 11 (1947)
1–14) and Windisch, argues that verses 22–5 are a quotation from
a Christian hymn. He points to the four relative pronouns in the
passage (their use is a characteristic of ancient hymnic style;
unfortunately they have disappeared in the English translation).
The hymn was originally in the first plural, and this is still found
in verse 24; elsewhere it has been changed to the second plural
for homiletic purposes. At this stage the argument only requires a
simple reference to the innocent suffering of Christ; it is the use of
the hymn which introduces the atonement. Boismard also draws
attention to certain parallels of thought with Paul and 1 John.
Unfortunately these parallels are those which would emerge
naturally from a common indebtedness of the three writers to
either Isa. 53 or the primitive Christian catechesis on the death of
Christ; at no point is there a clear verbal quotation from the
supposed hymn in Paul or 1 John to enable us to check on its
existence and form. Further, the way in which the OT is used in
verses 22–5 is wholly in keeping with the way it is used elsewhere
in the letter in that the writer adopts and adapts its words and
intermingles them with his own. These objections are not sufficient
to dispel completely the possibility that there may be dependence
on a Christian hymn, but lacking confirmatory quotation elsewhere there can be no assurance of this; certainly there is dependence on primitive Christian tradition. If a hymn has been used,
then no claim can be made that the writer of the epistle was an
eye-witness of the passion.

22. This verse is drawn from the LXX of Isa. 53:9 with
variations some of which may have been already current in the
early church (cf. 1 Clem. 16:10). Our author himself appears to

have changed 'iniquity' (*anomia*) to 'sin' (*hamartia*) and so linked
verses 20 and 24 with this present verse and indicated that he is
drawing attention not only to the innocence of Jesus in respect of
any particular crime for which he was executed but also to his
general sinlessness, an idea found widely in the NT (1:19;
2 Cor. 5:21; Heb. 7:26; Jn 8:46; 1 Jn 3:5).

23. Verse 23a enlarges on verse 22 showing one way in which
Jesus was sinless in his passion; when reviled he did not retaliate
(cf. Mk 15:29-32; 14:65; 15:16-20; Lk. 23:11,36f; Jn 19:1-5); he
thus followed the principle of non-retaliation which he himself
had taught (Mt. 5:38-44). His conduct contrasts with that of
some of his followers who threatened their persecutors with eternal
punishment (cf. Paul before the Sanhedrin, Ac. 23:3). Jesus'
silence under rebuke, while perhaps historical, also reflects
Isa. 53:7.

**he trusted to him:** *lit.* 'he handed (himself) over to him';
this reflects Isa. 53:12 (LXX) where the same verb occurs; it was
also frequently used in the NT in relation to the redemptive
significance of Jesus' death; cf. Rom. 4:25 (='put to death');
1 Cor. 11:23 (='betray'); Gal. 2:20 (='gave himself'); its use
here facilitates the transition which comes with verse 24 from
Christ as example to Christ as redeemer.

24. The writer changes from the second plural to the first
plural because, while Jesus in certain aspects of behaviour is an
example to slaves, he is the redeemer of all men. Underlying the
passage of thought from Christ as example to Christ as redeemer is
the assumption that only the redeemed can follow his example.
**the tree,** i.e., the cross (cf. Ac. 5:30; 10:39; 13:29; Gal. 3:13
which quotes Dt. 21:22f). 'Tree' was used in secular Greek for the
scaffold and passed into Christian usage as a synonym for the
cross. Since in Acts it is used without the associations relating to
the curse on the one who hangs from a tree which we find in Gal.
3:13, we should probably not read those associations into its use
here.
**bore our sins:** cf. Isa. 53:4,11,12; Heb. 9:28; Jn 1:29. The
writer has probably no precise OT rite (e.g. the sin-offering, the
scape-goat) in mind, but is content to stress the redemptive
significance of Jesus' death by his use of OT sacrificial language;
in sacrificial death men's sins are taken away. The RSVmg
renders 'carried up our sins . . . to the tree'; this depends on an
alternative translation of the word 'bore'. So long as the tree is

not understood as the altar, for sins were never laid on the altar, it is a possible rendering; sins are then regarded as a burden which Christ lifts up from men. The RSV text is to be preferred because it fits more appropriately the ideas of Isa. 53 and the common Christian tradition about the death of Jesus.

Our author makes frequent reference to the sufferings and death of Jesus in relation to the salvation of men but he does not advance any clear theory of the atonement. His emphasis in the present passage began with the suffering of Christ as an example for slaves and passed over (and we must presume that if he is quoting a hymn he agrees with it for he did not need to use verses 24f) to its redemptive value as seen in the light of the suffering of the servant of Isa. 53. In his other references he is equally dependent on the OT (see notes on the different passages): 1:2 utilizes the ceremony of covenant inauguration (Exod. 24: 3–8); 1:18f regards Christ's death as 'ransom' with overtones of the Passover lamb and the Exodus deliverance; 3:18 may refer to the sin-offering. These passages clarify the purpose of Christ's death: 1:2 suggests the inauguration of the new covenant from which all men benefit; 1:19 through its Exodus overtones suggests deliverance from sin and the ransom concept equally implies freedom from it; 2:24 implies the taking away of sin from men, 'healing' through Christ's sufferings and the call to, and ability for, a life of righteousness; 3:18, 'that he might bring us to God', indicates an access to God which those whose sins have not been atoned for do not possess. None of this is out of keeping with the main lines of NT thought; this makes man's redemption hinge on the death and resurrection of Christ, though it expresses how this takes place in various ways, some of which are reflected in our letter. For a fuller discussion see V. Taylor, *The Atonement in New Testament Teaching*, 2nd edn., London, 1945, pp. 25–34; L. Morris, *The Cross in the New Testament*, Exeter, 1965, pp. 316–333; E. Lohse, *Märtyrer und Gottesknecht*, 2nd edn., Göttingen, 1963, pp. 182–7.

**his body:** cf. Rom. 7:4; Col. 1:22; the phrase ties redemption firmly down to the historical life of Jesus. There is a possible allusion to teaching similar to that of Heb. 9–10, where Christ unlike the OT priests offers himself (cf. Windisch).

**die to sin and live to righteousness:** there is a superficial resemblance to Rom. 6:11 (cf. pp. 32f) but the word rendered 'die' is not the same as the word Paul used; the phrase might be rendered 'cease from sin and live to righteousness'. As in Paul the Christian is to live a new life because of Christ's redemption, but the conception of a death and resurrection with Christ is muted (cf. Rom. 6:3–11; Gal. 2:19f; Col. 2:11–3:4).

**wounds . . . healed:** drawn from Isa. 53:5. We return to the second plural because the reference to slaves has become more direct; they would suffer 'wounds' (*lit.* 'weals') in the frequent beatings received from good as well as bad masters. The metaphor is of obvious application to Jesus who healed the sick, and is in keeping with the Jewish and primitive Christian conception of vicarious suffering.

25. **straying like sheep:** adapted from Isa. 53:6.

**returned:** the word is used frequently in the LXX to denote the turning of men to, or away from God. It reads too much into it here to take it as suggesting that the readers had once been with the shepherd, had strayed from him and were now coming back. It implies rather that the natural place for the sheep is in the flock with the shepherd and that the readers by their conversion and baptism have found this place.

**Shepherd,** i.e. Christ rather than God. The image of sheep draws in that of shepherd; this is used regularly in the OT of God (Ps. 23; Isa. 40:11; Jer. 23:1–4; 50:6; Ezek. 34; Zech. 11:4–17) and in the NT of Jesus (5:4; Jn 10:11ff; Heb. 13:20; Rev. 7:17; cf. Mk 6:34; 14:27; Lk. 12:32).

**Guardian:** this is the word (*episcopos*) from which the ecclesiastical title 'bishop' is derived. The rendering given here is one of its common meanings in Greek; possibly there is also an allusion to the ecclesiastical title which was already in partial, though probably not general, use at this time (Phil. 1:1; 1 Tim. 3:2; Tit. 1:7). The association of the images of Guardian and Shepherd is not unnatural (cf. Ac. 20:28; CD 13:9ff).

Christ is thus finally depicted not only as the one who through his death atones for sin but as the one who protects, feeds, oversees the life of his people: he is example (verse 22f), redeemer (verse 24) and Guardian (verse 25).

### The Duties of Wives and Husbands 3:1–7

The final item in the social code takes up behaviour within the family (cf. Col. 3:18–21; Eph. 5:22–6:4; 1 Tim. 2:9–15; Tit. 2:4f). In common with the passages from Colossians and Ephesians (but not those from 1 Timothy and Titus) there is instruction for husbands as well as wives, but unlike them there is no reference to children. Much more attention is given to wives (3:1–6) than to husbands (3:7). This may have been done because there were many more women in the Christian community than men but more probably because the position of the woman was much more difficult; her conversion would produce a greater strain in the family than that of her husband to whose religion she was normally expected to adhere (cf. Plutarch, *Praecepta Coniugalia*, 19). The wife depended completely on her husband for the necessities and luxuries of life and much pagan thought considered that her legal position was very little different from that of a slave (cf. Augustine, *Confessions*, 9:19). The problem was especially acute where, as envisaged here, the husband was not a Christian; already at Corinth Paul had encountered the strain which appeared in mixed marriages and he had advised their continuance if this was at all possible (1 Cor. 7:12–16); our author clearly accepts this since he nowhere suggests the possibility of divorce. The advice given to wives is closely similar to that in 1 Tim. 2:9–11. On the position and dress of women in the ancient world see J. Carcopino, *op. cit.*, pp. 76–100, 164–70; R. Flacelière, *op. cit.*, pp. 55–82, 156–66. The difficulties of wives in a mixed marriage are recounted in some detail by Tertullian, *Ad Uxorem*, II, 4–7.

1. **Likewise:** this introduces the next item in the social code (cf. verse 7); it does not mean that wives are to be submissive like slaves (2:18–25).

**be submissive:** for the early church the family was a divine institution; this takes up 2:13a (RSVmg). There was a strong strain in Judaism, later continued in Christianity, which traced the subordination of the wife to the divine decree of Gen. 3:16.

**your husbands:** the writer is not teaching about man/woman relationships in general but only those of husbands and wives.

**they do not obey the word,** i.e., they are non-Christian and the marriage is mixed. 'Word' is used here in the sense of Gospel (cf. 4:17). The husband may have heard the word when his wife in the first flush of enthusiasm told him of her new faith or entertained a Christian preacher or persuaded him to come to a Christian service.

**may be won,** i.e. may become Christian; cf. 1 Cor. 9:19–22 where the same word is used with the same meaning.

**without a word:** 'word' is now used in the sense 'speech'.

The Word does not need to be presented only in words; if the presentation by words has failed a new approach requires to be tried. This passage gives one of the relatively few glimpses into the conduct of its mission by the early church; it is surprising how rarely in the NT Christians are instructed in the method of carrying out this mission.

**behaviour:** this is the new approach: in this way Monnica, the mother of Augustine, won her husband (Augustine, *Confessions* 9:19).

2. **when they see:** see on 2:12; the early church understood the importance of behaviour which all men could recognize as good.

**reverent:** i.e. to God. The Greek word is literally 'fear'; see on 2:18 and 1:17.

**chaste:** not in the narrow sense of marital fidelity alone but of pure, simple and sincere behaviour generally. In the Greek the words 'reverent' and 'chaste' are not co-ordinate but it is implied chastity arises out of reverence to God.

3. **outward adorning:** the ostentatious and luxurious dress of women is a frequent subject of attack in the OT, in Judaism and the ancient world generally (e.g. Isa. 3:18–24; Philo, *De Virtutibus* 39; Plutarch, *Praecepta Coniugalia*, 26,48). In 1 Enoch 8 (cf. *Testament of Reuben* 5) the desire of women for ornament is attributed to the activities of fallen angels, a tradition which may well have been known to our author (see on 3:19 for his acquaintance with this apocalyptic writing). The luxury described in 1 Peter implies that there were women of wealth in the churches; slaves and women of inferior social class would never have been able to dress in this fashion. Restraint in dress features in only one other form of the social code in the NT (1 Tim. 2:9f).

4. **the hidden person of the heart:** the thought is somewhat similar to that in Paul's phrase 'inner nature' (2 Cor. 4:16; cf. Rom. 2:28f; 7:22; Eph. 3:16) but is verbally different, and is not therefore a direct borrowing: it is also used here of moral behaviour alone and thus much less profoundly than in Paul (cf. Selwyn).

**imperishable jewel:** 'jewel' is not found in the Greek but is supplied in the English as an equivalent of 'adorning' in verse 3. The adjective 'imperishable' can also be taken as a noun 'the incorruptibility'. Translated as in the RSV the human spirit is regarded as an adornment of the inner nature of man. Elsewhere 'spirit' in 1 Peter means the Spirit of God (1:2,11,12; 3:18;

4:6,14); if the reference at 3:18,19; 4:6 is to the human spirit (this is unlikely; see notes on the passages) it is as descriptive not of a part of man's make-up which might be distinguished from his 'heart' but of his whole or essential being; heart is used also in this latter way at 1:22; 3:15; in both cases this is normal NT usage. We prefer then to see here a reference to the Spirit of God which endows the Christian with a new being and to translate 'by means of the incorruptibility of the gentle and quiet Spirit' (cf. Schelkle). The human spirit of the Christian is not just a so-called spiritual part or faculty but man himself reborn by the Spirit of God.

**gentle and quiet spirit:** in the earlier parts of the OT God's Spirit is generally associated with mighty acts of power but in the later parts of the OT and certainly within the NT power is seen to lie in gentleness and quietness as much as in vigour (cf. Gal. 6:1; 1 Cor. 4:21).

**which** refers not to 'spirit' but to the whole preceding thought; true character is precious in God's sight.

5. **So once:** women of the OT people of God are now offered as an example to Peter's women readers. The Christian church was not yet itself long enough in existence to furnish examples.

**holy women:** they are holy, not because of their exemplary behaviour, but because they belonged to the holy people of God (cf. 'holy prophets', Lk. 1:70; Ac. 3:21; Eph. 3:5) as do the women readers of the letter.

**hoped in God:** since 'hope' is used so often in this epistle to describe the true attitude of members of God's people to him (1:3,13,21; 3:15) it would be wrong to see here any specific reference to the Jewish messianic hope.

**were submissive:** the argument returns to the primary theme of the section.

6. **Sarah:** an individual example for this primary theme is now provided. As Jesus had been an example to the slave (2:18–25) so is Sarah to the wife; there are limitations to the conception of the *imitatio Christi*! But as we shall see Sarah is more than an example and like Jesus occupies a theological position. In Eph. 5:22–33 a christological basis is given to marriage.

**obeyed Abraham:** the tense of the verb (aorist) suggests that the writer has one particular incident in mind and because of the reference to 'lord' this must be Gen. 18:1–15; it is however difficult to discover a reference to Sarah's obedience in that passage. As in Jewish thought so in I Peter Sarah is obviously idealized.

**calling him lord:** the only occasion when Sarah uses 'lord' of Abraham is Gen. 18:12 where the English has 'husband' but the Hebrew and the LXX translation could be taken in the sense 'lord'; there is however no special act of submission on her part and the English is a correct rendering of the original. There is here a somewhat arbitrary use of the OT.

**you are now her children:** just as believers in general are regarded as the children of Abraham (Rom. 4:11f; Gal. 3:7,16,29; Heb. 2:16 etc.) so believing women are taken to be the children of Sarah. Sarah and Abraham appear together as the progenitors of the people of God in Isa. 51:1f and this thought underlies the present reference to Sarah; she is thus much more than an example of behaviour to Christian women readers; without her there would have been no people of God.

**if you do right . . . :** this clause is probably not conditional; if it were it would imply that the readers were believing women through their good works. The two verbs 'do right' and 'terrify' are participles and should probably be taken as imperatives (see p. 30) and the whole clause read as an independent sentence, 'Do right and let nothing terrify you' (cf. van Unnik, *N.T.S.*, 1 (1954), 100f).

**let nothing terrify you:** probably a reminiscence of Prov. 3:25. Many women would have husbands to fear if they took an independent line in religion.

7. A brief exhortation is now given to husbands. Since these are described as 'joint heirs' of the grace of life it may be assumed that mixed marriages are not in view. Even in a mixed marriage the position of the Christian husband was not in any way as difficult as that of the Christian wife (verses 1–6). The husband would expect his wife to follow his religion. In Acts (16:14f, 32f) we read of the baptism of households when the head of the family has become a Christian and probably in our present passage the wives of Christian husbands are assumed to be Christian.

**considerately:** the husband is to act with understanding love toward his wife, not considering his rights and privileges but his duties (cf. 1 Th. 4:4f; Eph. 5:25).

**weaker sex:** it is not specified whether they are to be regarded as physically, intellectually or morally weaker or taken as weaker

because the husband is the directing head of the family; probably
these different aspects should not be clearly distinguished.
It is because the wife is weaker and not because she is one of the
mighty of the world (cf. 2:17) that the husband is to **bestow
honour** on her: a practical application of 1 Cor. 12:22ff.

**sex:** an unusual word (*skeuos*) is used; it literally means 'thing,
vessel, tool', but it had already come to be used of people (Ac.
9:15; 2 Tim. 2:21; cf. Rom. 9:21–3) and of women in particular
(1 Th. 4:4); its use here is not intended as an insult to women
suggesting that they are for men's use, for the comparative
'weaker' implies its application also to men.

**joint heirs:** though husbands and wives are regarded here as
complementary in marriage to one another, there is no distinction
between them in the sphere of salvation (cf. Gal. 3:28; Mk 12:25);
from this latter fact a new conception of marriage has emerged
gradually in Christianity.

**the grace of life:** the gift which God in his grace gives consists of
eternal life. For 'grace' see notes on 1:2.

**your prayers:** it is not clear whether the reference is to the
prayers of the man alone or to the prayers of both (cf. 1 Cor. 7:5),
though even then not necessarily to their prayers offered jointly.
The underlying principle that a man's relation to God is not
independent of his relation to his fellows is clear elsewhere in the
NT; cf. 1 Jn 4:19–21; Mt. 5:23; 25:31–46; 1 Cor. 11:20–9;
Jas 4:1–4.

When we look back over the use in our letter of the social code
we observe the stress on the duty of the citizen, the wealthier wife
and the slave, and the absence of reference to the duties of
masters and children. A community is envisaged in which there
are both rich and poor and an attitude adopted somewhat similar
to that upheld by some sections of non-conformity in the nine-
teenth century: control by the wealthy is assumed and left
unrestricted, but they themselves are expected, as we learn from
other parts of the letter, to be personally puritanical.

## EXHORTATION 3:8–12

This is not a summary of the preceding instructions but a final
exhortation addressed to all Christians and confirmed by an
appeal to the OT. Since the other examples in the NT of the

social code do not end in any similar general exhortation, this is
probably not part of the social code. The injunctions of verses 8,9
are however part of the general ethical teaching of the church
and probably belonged to its catechetical instruction (cf. Col.
3:8–15; Rom. 12:9–12, and especially 1 Th. 5:13–22; see Selwyn,
pp. 407–15). The exhortation is carefully constructed; the themes
of verses 8,9 re-appear in reverse order in verses 10–11 in the
quotation from Ps. 34:12–16 (cf. Schweizer).

8. **unity of spirit . . . humble mind:** these five phrases
reproduce five adjectives in the original. The first three and the
noun associated with the fifth are all found in good literary Greek;
the fourth is frequent in medical Greek (naturally with another
meaning!). None of the first four is common in the LXX but they
occur, partly in cognate forms, in the NT and the ideas they
represent are frequent therein (cf. Beare).

**unity of spirit:** cf. Rom. 15:5; Phil. 2:2.

**sympathy:** cf. Rom. 12:15; Heb. 10:34; 1 Cor. 12:26.

**love of the brethren:** cf. 1 Pet. 1:22; Rom. 12:10; Jn 15:12.

**a tender heart:** cf. Eph. 4:32; Col. 3:12.

**a humble mind:** cf. 5:5f; Eph. 4:2; Phil. 2:3ff. This represents a
new quality of life which was introduced by Christianity into the
Hellenistic world. In classical Greek the underlying word possessed the sense 'base, mean'; in the Christian faith it obtained a
new meaning and signified a new virtue 'humility'.

Unlike the preceding social code the virtues listed here relate to
the inner life of the church, to the intercourse of Christians with
one another, and not to their attitude to those outside their body.
The latter attitude re-appears in verse 9 and can also be taken to
be present in the last two phrases of verse 8; the first three however
definitely speak of harmony within the church. Of course harmony within the church will speak to the world outside of peace
with Christ.

9. The thought of this verse is akin to sayings of Jesus recorded
in Lk. 6:27f (cf. Mt. 5:43f) but the words are closer to expressions
in the paraenetic sections of other epistles (Rom. 12:14; 1 Th.
5:15, cf. 1 Cor. 4:12) and probably come from the common
instruction of the church rather than directly from the words of
Jesus (the latter may indeed have been affected in their trans-
mission by the common instruction). In the epistles the thought is
nowhere ascribed to Jesus; at this stage in the life of the church he
had not apparently become a moral authority for it. Judaism

E

contains statements which are very contrary to the advice given here, e.g., 'that they (the members of the Qumran community) may love all the sons of light, each according to his lot in God's design, and hate all the sons of darkness, each according to his guilt in God's vengeance' (1QS 1:4 Vermes, *op. cit.*, p. 73; cf. 1QS 9:21f); but there are also in Judaism many passages which teach sentiments very similar to what we have in 1 Peter, e.g. 'If ill-requitals befall you, return them not either to neighbour or enemy, because the Lord will return them for you and be your avenger on the day of great judgement, that there be no avenging here among men' (2 Enoch 50:4; translation as in R. H. Charles, *Pseudepigrapha*, Oxford, 1913). Greek moral instruction can also be very unlike what we have in 1 Peter yet at times some writers approximate to it. Jesus has already been presented as an example of one who did not revile (2:23); his life can serve equally as an example of the other aspects of an unwillingness to return evil; in the light of his example Prov. 17:13 could have led to the formation of the teaching of the church on this matter.

**bless:** this means much more than 'speak well of' (the earlier secular meaning of the word). In biblical idiom 'to bless' is to invoke God's graciousness on a person. In the OT it was the function of the priests to bless (cf. Num. 6:22-7); our writer has already taught that all Christians are priests (2:5,9); this may be the reason he exhorts them to bless. Blessing leads naturally to the thought of inheritance (this is the literal meaning of the word rendered **obtain**); the OT patriarchs handed on their inheritance by blessing their descendants (Gen. 27; 48:15f). An inheritance is never earned; it is received as a gift. The inheritance which our writer has in mind is salvation, final salvation rather than its present enjoyment (cf. 1:4).

**to this** may refer either forwards (they are called to obtain the blessing) or backwards (they are called to bless and not to return evil for evil); the quotation from Ps. 34 in verses 10-12 definitely suggests the second; the readers are summoned to the moral life so that ultimately they **may obtain a blessing.** This view appears elsewhere in the NT (Mt. 5:12; 25:31-46); it would appear to clash here with the conception of the inheritance as a gift (see also on 4:13. On the place of 'reward' in the NT in relation to its ethical teaching, cf. Kirk, *op. cit.*, pp. 140-6; R. Schnackenburg, *The Moral Teaching of the New Testament*, London and Freiburg, 1965, pp. 144-67).

**called:** cf. 1:15; 2:9,21.

10–12. The quotation comes from the LXX of Ps. 34:12–16 with some variations; most of these are to be accounted for by our writer's desire to make the passage fit smoothly into his context. The principal variation is the omission of the concluding line of Ps. 34:16, 'to destroy their remembrance from the earth'; it perhaps goes farther than our writer would wish in its rejection of evil-doers.

10. **life, good days:** in the context of Ps. 34 these refer to the present life; in line with the reference to blessing in verse 9 they have been re-interpreted of eschatological salvation.

11a. This line is apposite in view of the frequent reference in the letter to doing right or good and doing evil or wrong (2:12,14f,20; 3:6,9).

11b. cf. Mt. 5:9.

12. This gives the basis for the preceding statements about conduct: the realisation that all life is lived in the presence of God will produce true behaviour and therefore ultimately eternal life.

## PERSECUTION THREATENS 3:13–4:19

The church as a whole is again addressed and the individual groups with their special needs (2:13–3:7) forgotten, for persecution threatens the very existence of the people of God and they must learn both how to suffer and the place of their sufferings in the purposes of God.

### Suffering for Righteousness' Sake 3:13–17

The behaviour of Christians under unjust suffering is discussed and they are assured that if they endure it successfully they will ultimately be blessed.

13. **harm:** this word is the verbal form (in Greek) of 'evil' in verse 12 making the transition to the new theme of persecution more natural than appears in English: 'The face of the Lord is against those that do evil, but in fact is there anyone who can really do evil to you?' The answer 'No one!' is obviously intended, but is this true? At first sight it would appear to imply that those who do what is right will not have to suffer persecution. But the possibility of unjust suffering is recognized at 1:6; 2:19; 4:12–19 and probably in 3:14; the church had already been long enough in existence to have experienced sufficient opposition to realise that

sheer goodness will not quell persecution (and if the letter is by
Peter he would have learnt this from what happened to him in
Ac. 3, 4, 12). We must therefore understand 'harm' in the sense of
damage to the true life of the Christian (cf. Schelkle, Knopf, Bigg,
Selwyn, Wand etc.); he will neither be corrupted to hate his
persecutors nor will he lose his inheritance (1:4; 3:9; cf. Rom.
8:31; Mt. 10:28; Lk. 12:4). Verse 13a may be derived from
Isa. 50:9 (LXX).

**zealous:** this word has an interesting background. Phinehas
slew an Israelite who had married a Midianite woman (Num.
25:6-9) and his zeal is emphasised (25:11-13); thereafter he was
held up as an ideal of behaviour, especially from the time of the
Maccabean revolt onwards; one Jewish party which opposed the
Romans by force in the first century A.D. was known as the
Zealots. The word is an odd choice here since excessive zeal is
associated with a tendency to annoy and irritate others rather
than with the gentleness and reverence desired in verse 15.
It must be taken to stress the active nature of right behaviour and
we find it associated with goodness elsewhere in the NT (Tit. 2:14;
1 Cor. 14:12; cf. 1 Cor. 12:31; 14:1; Ac. 21:20; Gal. 1:14).
Reicke, who dates our letter prior to the fall of Jerusalem when the
Zealots were very active, suggests that this explains the choice of
the word; Christians ought not to be carried away by revolutionary
activity but be zealous for what is good. This may explain the
introduction of the word among the Christians but cannot be
used to date 1 Peter prior to the fall of Jerusalem; the word once
introduced would continue in use.

14a. **suffer:** this is one of the few places in the NT where the
optative mood is used. In a conditional clause, as here, it implies
that there is no certainty of fulfilment of the condition, but it
goes too far to speak of it as an unlikely contingency; it may
happen or it may not. 'St. Peter well knows that in fact such
sufferings are eminently probable in the Christian life, and
indeed perhaps already a reality for his readers. His tact, however,
leads him, when speaking of sufferings to those who are seeking
to avoid them, to put the matter on the theoretical plane' (M.
Zerwick, *Biblical Greek*, English edn. by J. Smith, Rome, 1963,
p. 111). On the relationship of this passage to 4:12-19 and 5:9
and the question of the unity of the epistle and the nature of the
persecutions, see pp. 20ff, 36ff.

**for righteousness sake:** their suffering is not suffering in

general but that which comes because they are Christians, i.e.,
because they have the gift of righteousness (Rom. 3:20–5:21) and
therefore strive after righteous living.

**blessed:** the beatitude is a biblical figure of speech, cf. Ps. 1:1;
2:12; Mt. 5:3–12; Lk. 6:20–3; Jas 1:12; Rev. 14:13. The 'blessed'
is not just someone who is happy but someone on whom God's
blessing rests. The RSV rendering 'you will be' is perhaps mis-
leading; the Greek lacks a verb and it might equally be translated
with the present tense, 'you are blessed'; the blessing of God which
will accompany their persecution is not limited to the thought of a
reward in the next life. But if it is a present reality it is not just an
interior joy; it is much more objective. The beatitude here recalls
that of Mt. 5:10; this saying of Jesus had passed into the thought
of the early church and there is no need to suppose that we have
here an actual quotation from Jesus' words made by someone
who had heard them (cf. pp. 31, 51ff).

14b. **Have no fear of them:** a quotation from Isa. 8:12
(LXX). In Isaiah the prophet is told not to fear the king of
Assyria as the Israelites do; here the meaning has been changed;
when the words are isolated from their context they can be
translated as in 1 Peter; the original meaning 'do not fear with
their fear' would be impossible in the context of 1 Peter. The
readers can be fearless before their persecutors because they fear
God (2:17; cf. Schweizer).

15. **reverence Christ as Lord:** this continues the quotation
from Isa. 8:13 (Note that 8:14 was quoted at 2:8). Our writer
replaces the 'him', referring to God, of the original with 'Christ':
the early church regularly saw in OT passages about God as
'Lord' a reference to Jesus, cf. 2:3. In our translation 'Christ' is
understood predicatively; it might also be taken in apposition to
'Lord' and rendered 'reverence the Lord who is Christ' (cf. Bigg).
The word 'reverence' is the same as that in the Lord's Prayer,
'Hallowed be thy name' (Mt. 6:9; Lk. 11:2); it means 'acknowledge as holy'. The readers of the epistle are to do this in their
**hearts,** where they would normally feel fear of their persecutors
(cf. Selwyn). As the continuance of the verse shows it is not a
suggestion that they are to keep their confession of Christ to
themselves; there must be both inner and outer confession
(cf. Rom. 10:9f).

**defence:** this may suggest that the Christian will be brought
before a court of law, for the underlying word *apologia* is the

technical word for the defendant's rebuttal of charges, but it can also be used of a rejection of private accusations (e.g. 2 Cor. 7:11); because of the indefinite 'any one' it should be taken in the latter sense here; as Wand suggests, 'officious neighbours' may well have brought many trials to Christians. In all such circumstances what is required is a reasoned defence (and this the word implies) rather than a censorious sermon (cf. 3:1–6).

**the hope that is in you:** in this letter 'hope' is used almost as an equivalent for 'faith' (cf. 1:13,21; 3:5); the Christians have thus to explain their faith ('in you' probably means 'among you Christians') rather than tell about their hope of a future life, though this would be part of their faith.

**with gentleness and reverence:** reverence towards God (the word is the same as 'fear' in 1:17, 2:17 etc.; see notes there) should determine the attitude of the readers to others; if before him they are genuinely humble they will not be aggressive towards others; sometimes martyrs have tended to pity their ignorant and erring accusers, being proudly certain that they and they alone possess the truth.

16. **conscience:** this denotes an attitude towards God from which a true attitude toward man will emerge (cf. notes on 2:19). **those who revile your good behaviour in Christ may be put to shame:** it is equally possible and preferable in the context to render this 'those who revile you may be put to shame by your good behaviour in Christ' (so Selwyn). Accusations against the Christians must be dispelled by their conduct. That persecutors are put to shame does not mean that they are envisaged as being converted, the time of their shame may be the day of judgement (2:12).

**in Christ:** this phrase was used extensively by Paul who probably coined it; he used it both to denote the action of God in redeeming men through Christ and to denote Christians as joined together in fellowship with Christ; when the Christian is united to Christ in fellowship on the basis of what God has done for him in the death and resurrection of Christ then his 'behaviour' is 'good' and will be his defence against his accusers.

17. **For it is better to suffer for doing right:** unfortunately persecutors are often incensed by those they persecute and not won over by their good behaviour, so this verse qualifies verse 16b. There are two ways of understanding our verse: (i) It may be taken as parallel to 2:20; if the Christian is to suffer it is important

that he does so, not as a criminal, but as one who can be clearly seen only to have done good. (ii) It may be taken in the sense 'it is better to suffer now for doing right than to suffer later (in the judgement) for doing wrong (i.e. betraying the Christian cause)' (cf. J. R. Michaels, 'Eschatology in 1 Peter iii. 17', *N.T.S.*, 13 (1967) 394–401): this fits the general eschatological tone of the letter. In this second rendering the meaning of 'better' is at once obvious; in the first it presumably means that it is morally preferable rather than that it is more advantageous to the persecuted.

**if that should be God's will:** as in verse 14 there is a certain indefiniteness in regard to the occurrence of persecution (again expressed by the optative mood). Suffering can lie within the will of God; cf. Jesus' words at Gethsemane, 'yet not what I will, but what thou wilt' (Mk 14:36). This will be all the more true if the suffering lying before these Christians is that which will introduce the parousia; see on 4:13.

Verse 17 not only qualifies verse 16 and sums up verses 13–17 but also prepares for verses 18–22 (compare the flow of thought from 2:20 to 2:21); we move from the suffering of the Christian to the suffering of Christ which was for the sin of men.

### The Example and Victory of Christ 3:18–22

This is a very difficult passage of which many special studies have been published, e.g. J. A. MacCulloch, *The Harrowing of Hell*, Edinburgh, 1930; B. Reicke, *The Disobedient Spirits and Christian Baptism*, Copenhagen, 1946; W. J. Dalton, *Christ's Proclamation to the Spirits* (Analecta Biblica 23), Rome, 1965. A number of attempts have been made to discover in it the fragment of a primitive hymn or creed. Windisch regarded the whole as a hymn in four strophes but it is impossible to work it out into such a literary structure (cf. Selwyn, p. 195; Dalton, *op. cit.*, p. 87). Bultmann (*op. cit.*) found a confessional hymn whose beginning lay in 1:20 and which consisted of 3:18,19,22; his reconstruction seems too hypothetical to carry conviction (cf. J. Jeremias, 'Zwischen Karfreitag und Ostern', *Z.N.W.*, 42 (1949) 194–201; Dalton, pp. 92–5). More recently Boismard (*Quatre Hymnes baptismales*, pp. 57–109), using Bultmann's suggestion, has evolved an amended version which resembles more closely the possible form of a hymn since each line in it begins in Greek with an

aorist passive participle; we reproduce it in a form approximating
to the RSV translation; the subject is Christ:

> Destined before the foundation of the world
>   manifest at the end of times
> Put to death in the flesh
>   made alive in the spirit
> Evangelised to the dead
>   gone into heaven
> Made subject to him: angels and authorities and powers.

Boismard finds a close structural resemblance between this and
the hymn of 1 Tim. 3:16 and also a certain parallelism of thought;
he believes that traces of the hymn are also to be found in 2 Tim.
1:9f. It will be observed that in order to maintain the required
form he has substituted the reference to the preaching to the dead
from 4:6 for that of the preaching to the spirits of 3:19. Given
such a closely woven hymn it is difficult to see how anyone should
have been so insensitive to it as to break it up and leave it in the
way it now supposedly appears in 1 Peter.

Cullmann (*The Earliest Christian Confessions*, London, 1949,
p. 20; cf. Schelkle) has stressed the credal character of elements in
our passage, viz., 'Christ died for us, descended to the spirits in
prison, was raised, ascended into heaven, sits at the right hand of
God'. Our exegesis will show that many of the phrases of the
passage echo those found elsewhere in the NT and other early
Christian writings and there is no reason to doubt that our writer
is drawing on the common forms of Christian belief. It is doubtful
whether 'descended to the spirits in prison' was at the time of this
letter part of the common formulation of belief; 3:19 may have
helped to make it such but there is no contemporary evidence for
its acceptance as with the other elements to which Cullmann
points.

We cannot then disagree that liturgical elements, whether
credal or hymnic (and it is difficult always to distinguish them
precisely), are found in verses 18 and 22. However, verses 19–21
read much more like an independent construction of the writer;
there is really nothing poetic about their form and nothing in
their content pertaining to the fundamentals of Christian thought
as we know it towards the end of the first century, or even the
early second. It is hazardous to isolate with any precision underlying elements but we can probably accept with some degree of

certainty those that Cullmann suggests apart from the reference to the spirits in prison but probably adding to them some others, resulting in the following: 'Christ died for sins (once for all?)', 'the righteous for the unrighteous', 'that he might bring us to God', 'being put to death in the flesh, made alive in the spirit', 'through the resurrection of Jesus Christ (perhaps in the original creed this was a simple verb 'raised'), 'who has gone into heaven' (or 'ascended'), 'at the right hand of God(?)'.

18. As in 2:21 the thought of the suffering of believers leads to that of Jesus' redemptive suffering; he is the supreme example of one who suffered 'for doing right' (verse 17). But we are carried further than in 2:21–5 for we go beyond the death of Christ to his resurrection and ascension (verses 18b–22); here Christ can no longer serve as example, but what he has accomplished through his victory can assure Christians of their own eventual victory and so sustain them in their present sufferings.

**died:** the RSVmg gives the alternative 'suffered'; this is favoured by one of the best manuscripts (Codex Vaticanus) yet the majority including the recently discovered **P**[72] support the reading 'died'. This is the normal word in the NT to describe the death of Jesus, but 'suffered' is sometimes used in the same way, e.g. Lk. 22:15; Ac. 17:3 (cf. 'suffered under Pontius Pilate'). The meaning is consequently the same whichever we choose. The theme of the passage is 'suffering' (3:17; 4:1), and it is easy to see that 'died' could have been altered to 'suffered', the prevailing word in the letter; this would also bring it into line with the similar wording of 2:21. But equally 'suffered' could have been changed by a copyist into 'died', the normal word in the early church for the death of Jesus. If we suspect an early credal or liturgical foundation to the passage then it is more probable that 'died' is original. We accept 'died' as being what the author wrote. It should not be taken to imply that Christians are to die as Christ died ('Christ *also* died'; there is some evidence that 'also' should be omitted), i.e. a redemptive death. The RSVmg gives a second place in this verse where the text shows variation in some manuscripts, viz., the addition of 'for us (you)' after died. Kubo (*op. cit.* pp. 39f) thinks that this may be correct in that 'the righteous for the unrighteous' requires an earlier identification of the unrighteous.

**for sins:** Christ, introduced as an example of one who suffered 'for righteousness' sake', is immediately seen to be more than an example; his death is related to sin as his followers' deaths cannot be. Its redemptive nature has already been set out in 1:18f; 2:24f; it was part of the tradition of the church from a very early period cf. 1 Cor. 15:3; Heb. 10:12; Gal. 1:4.

**once for all:** this word (*hapax*) cannot be reduced to 'once upon a time'; it must either be taken in the sense 'once only', so that death has no more dominion over Christ (so Beare, cf. Rom. 6:9f), or more probably as in Heb. 9:26,28 'once for all time', so that no other sacrifices for sin are ever again necessary.

**the righteous for the unrighteous:** for the innocence of Christ cf. 1:19; 2:22ff; it was again a common theme in early Christianity (Lk. 23:22,47; Mt. 27:19; Ac. 3:14; 2 Cor. 5:21).

**the righteous:** probably a title used of Jesus in the early church, cf. Ac. 7:52; 3:14; 1 Jn 2:1,29; 3:7 (see G. Schrenk, *T.D.N.T.* II, pp. 186–9).

**that he might bring us to God:** this is the consequence of the death of the righteous one. With the possible exception of the RSVmg addition, 'for us', to 'died' (see abcve) the whole passage has been in the second person plural; the unexpected change to the first person plural probably indicates the use of another piece of liturgical tradition. (Some manuscripts do read 'you' here instead of 'us' but as it is much more likely that the first person would be changed to the prevailing second than vice versa, we may assume that 'us' is original.) The death of Christ gives men access to God, cf. Rom. 5:2; Eph. 2:18; 3:12 (where the cognate noun is used). While it is true that the word is used in the OT to denote the presentation of cultic persons to God (Exod. 29:4,8; 40:12; Lev. 8:24; Num. 8:9f) it reads too much into its present usage to give it this cultic meaning in relation to Christians as priests (2:5,9) as Schelkle does; the context does not require such an overtone.

Reicke (*The Disobedient Spirits and Christian Baptism*, pp. 213ff) argues that this verse means that as Christ died for the sake of others so Christians ought to suffer for their sake in order that they might be led to God (cf. Bigg); the Christian cannot atone for the sins of others but by his patience under suffering and the defence he puts up for his faith (3:13–16) he may turn them to God. Reicke links this with 3:19 where Christ is viewed as preaching to beings inimical to him. It is however difficult to trace this line of thought consistently through the passage: 3:13–17 does not deal with the effect of the suffering of Christians on others but on themselves; to accept Reicke's interpretation means that the traditional language of verse 18 in regard to Christ's atoning death has to be minimized at each point so that the element of atonement practically disappears. This interpretation is unacceptable.

**being put to death in the flesh but made alive in the spirit** is again traditional language; a similar contrast of flesh and spirit is found in Rom. 1:3f; 1 Tim. 3:16. The contrast is not between two parts of man's nature, his flesh and his spirit (a contrast which is on the whole foreign to the NT), nor between two parts in Christ, a human and a divine (his divine nature could not be said to be made alive in his death), nor is it possible to take 'spirit' to mean that Christ went in a bodiless fashion to preach to the 'spirits' (verse 19). When spirit is opposed to flesh in the NT the opposition of divine Spirit to human existence is intended; cf. Gal. 5:16ff; Rom. 8:1ff and see W. D. Stacey, *op. cit.*, pp. 128ff; 154ff; cf. the articles by E. Schweizer and others on *sarx T.W.N.T.*, VII, pp. 98ff and *pneuma, T.D.N.T.* VI, pp. 332ff; the latter is translated as *Spirit of God* in the series *Bible Key Words*, London, 1960. Both 'flesh' and 'spirit', datives without a preposition, are best taken as datives of reference (so Selwyn, Dalton, *op. cit.* p. 134); this is also the way in which they need to be taken in 1 Tim. 3:16; they certainly cannot be taken as datives of the instrument, for while Christ may have been made alive by the Spirit he did not die by means of the flesh. The phrase then means that Christ died in the human sphere but was made alive and continues alive in the sphere of the Spirit.

**made alive:** the underlying word (*zōopoiein*) normally refers to the resurrection in the NT (Jn 5:21; 6:63; Rom. 4:17; 8:11) and this is the reference here.

19. It has been argued that the word 'Enoch' has been omitted from this verse and should be its subject, for the first three Greek words (*en hō kai*) are of similar sound to Enoch and this led an early copyist to omit the name; Moffatt and Goodspeed adopted this suggestion and insert the word Enoch in their translations. It can be supported with the argument that Enoch was believed to have preached to fallen angels. However there is no textual evidence in any manuscript of 1 Peter to sustain this emendation and conjectural emendations are exceptionally hazardous; Christ is the subject of verse 18 and again of verse 22 and a sudden transference of attention to Enoch does not suit the

stream of thought; the insertion of Enoch also renders very difficult the meaning of 'in which'. The RSV has wisely ignored the suggestion.

There are six difficult questions which face any interpreter of our verse: (i) What is the antecedent of 'in which'? (ii) When did Christ go to preach to the spirits? (iii) Who are the spirits in prison? (iv) Where is their prison? (v) What did Christ preach to them? (vi) Do 3:19 and 4:6 refer to the same event?

These questions are inter-related and to assist their understanding we shall briefly summarise the conclusions we reach: in the period between his death and resurrection Christ descended into the underworld where supernatural evil powers, the spirits, were held imprisoned; these powers were those who had enticed women to sin before the flood (Gen. 6:1-4); to them Christ offered salvation, but we do not learn whether they accepted it or not; it was also at this time that Christ preached to the dead (4:6), i.e., all who had died prior to his time; the dead are, however, a separate group from the spirits.

(i) **in which**: some interpreters have taken this to refer to 'spirit' in verse 18. As we have seen, a true understanding of 'spirit' means that this cannot be explained as 'Christ went as a spirit to preach to the spirits'; it is also unlikely that 'spirits' refers to 'dead people', which is required if the parallel is to be complete. Dalton (*op. cit.*, pp. 137-43) argues that it means 'in this sphere (of the Spirit)' or 'under this influence'; this is the simplest way to take it, but Selwyn has argued 'that there is no example in the NT of this dative of reference . . . serving as antecedent to a relative pronoun' (we have argued that 'in the spirit' is such a dative of reference). Where 'in which' (*en hō*) occurs elsewhere in 1 Peter it refers back to a phrase rather than to an individual word (1:6, see the notes there) or is a conjunction (2:12, 'in case'; 3:16, 'when'; 4:4, where the RSV has treated it as a conjunction and created a co-ordinate clause; the literal rendering would be 'in which they are surprised . . . profligacy, they blaspheme you'). Probably it should therefore be taken either as a relative (Selwyn) referring to the whole of the preceding phrase ('in which state', i.e. that of being made alive in the Spirit) or even to more of verse 18 ('in the course of which', referring to Christ's passion and resurrection generally), or as a conjunction (Reicke, *Disobedient Spirits and Christian Baptism*, p. 113; 'on which occasion', i.e. the occasion of Christ's death or resurrection). It will be noted that the RSV translators have excluded the reference to 'the spirit' by the insertion of a semi-colon and not a comma between the verses.

(ii) When did Christ go to the spirits in prison? We note first that if Boismard's reconstruction of the hymn (see pp. 135f) is accepted any journey of Christ to these spirits is excluded and so for the hymn the question is irrelevant; the reference however is to be found in I Peter and we have to ask after its meaning therein. Three solutions have been offered (a) before his incarnation; (b) between his death and resurrection; (c) at the time of his ascension. (a) goes back at least as far as Augustine (*Epistles* 164:15ff). Appearances of Christ on earth before his incarnation are mentioned in the NT, e.g. I Cor. 10:3f, and perhaps I Pet. 1:11 (see notes there). Such an interpretation is out of touch with the sequence of thought in 3:18–22 which moves from Christ's death to his heavenly session, and it contradicts the more probable explanations of 'in which'. This solution may therefore be set aside.

**he went** represents an aorist participle and describes a single action; does this action precede or follow that of the similar aorist participle 'made alive' (verse 18)? Certainly in the succession of actions in these verses it follows it, and the Greek for 'has gone' in verse 22 and 'he went' here are identical. Dalton (*op. cit.*, pp. 159–61) therefore argues that since the word in verse 22 refers to the ascension it must do so here also; the material between 'he went' and 'has gone' was not drawn from the tradition and the last word of the tradition 'he went' was repeated in verse 22 to indicate its resumption. In Bultmann's reconstruction of the underlying hymn the preaching to the spirits is clearly set after the resurrection. Over against these arguments we may note that 'he went' is quite neutral and refers in itself neither to upward nor downward movement; it is used of the ascension in verse 22, but this is indicated by the addition 'into heaven' (cf. Ac. 1:10). If 'being put to death . . . the spirit' was a fixed liturgical phrase then its sequence could not be broken by the insertion of the reference to a movement of Jesus during the interval which it covers (Schelkle) and the reference would have to follow it. If 'he went' refers to the ascension then we should more correctly expect a present participle rather than an aorist, 'on his way (to heaven) he preached' (Reicke, *op. cit.*, p. 65). There is other evidence in the NT for a journey by Jesus during the interval between his death and resurrection, cf. Ac. 2:25ff (the quotation of Ps. 16:8–11); 13:35; Rom. 10:7; Mt. 12:40; in Heb. 9:1–10:14 Jesus offers his blood on the heavenly altar; Lk. 23:43 may indicate a journey for both Jesus and the penitent thief; the Johannine usage of the word 'lift up' (*hupsoun*) to denote Jesus' death and exaltation suggests the same (cf. Jeremias, *op.cit.*). We conclude that the reference in 'he went' is to a journey prior to the resurrection.

(iii) Who are **the spirits**? They are either supernatural beings or men who have died; the rejection of a pre-incarnate journey by Jesus excludes the possibility that they were the generation of the flood. If our author used the hymn which Boismard reconstructs, then since he substituted a reference to 'spirits' for 'the dead' he may be assumed to have identified the two, i.e., the spirits are men who have died. There is no adequate proof that this hymn lies behind 1 Peter. We speak loosely of the survival of a man's spirit after death but it was unusual in either Greek (*pneuma*) or Hebrew (*ruah*) for 'spirit' to be so used. On the whole in Hebrew 'spirit' came to represent the higher strata of the functions of man rather than a part of man, let alone an immortal part (cf. N.H. Snaith, *op. cit.*, London, 1944, pp. 146ff). In Greek 'spirit' is a substantial term, the soul is composed of the superfine substance 'spirit', rather than an individualizing term, there is *a* spirit in man (E. de W. Burton, *Spirit, Soul, and Flesh*, Chicago, 1918, p. 121). However by the NT period 'spirit' is beginning to be used of a part of man (Wis. 15:16), almost equivalent to the soul which is the usual name for that part which survives death (Wis. 3:1; 4:14), and so can be thought of as surviving; this new meaning of the word could appear easily because the word also means 'breath'; a man's dying breath would be the departure of his spirit; this, however, does not necessarily imply survival as spirit (Wis. 2:3; Est. 16:12). In the NT there is only one clear instance of this usage of 'spirit' to designate the surviving part of man, viz., Heb. 12:23. Lk. 23:46 and Ac. 7:59 will accommodate themselves to this idea but they do not entail it; 'my spirit' is only a substitute in them for the personal pronoun; in Lk. 24:37,39 'spirit' means 'ghost'. Moreover even in Heb. 12:23 'spirits' is qualified so that there can be no doubt that human beings are intended, and these 'spirits' are not in Hades but with God, a natural conclusion if 'spirit' is the higher part of man which responds to God (Bar. 2:17 does not imply that the spirit is in

Hades). In 1 Enoch 22:3–13 we have the peculiar phrase, 'the spirits of the souls of the dead', but again 'spirit' is not used absolutely of the dead.

However 'spirits' is used regularly by itself to denote supernatural beings; the phrase 'unclean spirits' is frequent in the Gospels (Mk. 1:23,26,27; 3:11; 5:2,8, etc.); 'spirits' appear widely in the intertestamental literature (Tob. 6:6; 2 Mac. 3:24; *Jubilees* 15:31; 1 Enoch 60:11ff; *Testament of Dan* 1:7; 5:5; 1QS 3:17ff; 1QM 12:8f; 13:10) and according to the context those so designated are good or evil supernatural beings. In view of this widespread usage we are forced to accept this as the meaning in 1 Peter (cf. Dalton, Selwyn, Reicke etc.). As we shall see there is a parallel to our passage in 1 Enoch and there the reference is definitely to supernatural beings.

(iv) Where is the **prison** of these spirits? In Jude 6; 2 Pet. 2:4; 1 Enoch 10ff (cf. Rev. 18:2; 20:7) fallen angels are regarded as bound, and therefore presumably in prison. The precise location of their confinement is difficult to determine since the descriptions of it are not clear; it is in darkness (1 Enoch 10:4f), in the valleys of the earth (10:12), in the abyss (21:1–7); flame and fire are present (10:6,13); in 17–19 it is a place beyond heaven and earth, but not necessarily below the latter. In Rev. 20:3 (cf. 20:10) Satan is flung into the pit (termed 'prison' in 20:7); in *Jubilees* 5:6 the fallen angels are bound in the depths of the earth (cf. 1QH 3:17f); 2 Pet. 2:4, which says they are cast into Tartarus (rendered 'hell' in RSV), appears to imply that they are in the underworld. Over against this it may be argued (so Dalton) that evil supernatural beings were often considered to dwell in the heavens (e.g. Eph. 6:12); behind this lies the conception of multiple heavens; according to *Testament of Levi* 3:1ff; 2 Enoch 7:1–5; 18:3–6 the spirits inhabit the second heaven. From such a position they are able to exercise a malign influence over men. But in none of these passages is it clear that the angels are imprisoned; this is found in *Odes of Solomon* 22:1ff and in the Mandaean literature (cf. H. Schlier, *Christus und die Kirche im Epheserbrief*, Tübingen, 1930, pp. 13–15). The evidence indicates that it is much more probable that the spirits are considered to be imprisoned in the underworld than in the upper air or second heaven. Even if the latter is accepted as the true interpretation it would not imply that Christ preached to these spirits during his ascension: cf. (ii) above.

(v) What was it that Christ preached to the **spirits,** judgement or salvation? What was the result of his preaching? The Greek word for 'preach' is derived from the word for a herald and is normally a neutral word meaning 'proclaim publicly' without any indication of the content of what was proclaimed. This neutral meaning is occasionally retained in the NT (Rev. 5:2; cf. Lk. 12:3), but almost always it means 'preach salvation'; it is normally followed by a noun indicating what is preached, e.g. the gospel, Christ; even when it is used without any such qualification it still implies the preaching of salvation (Mk 1:38; 3:14; Mt. 11:1; Rom. 10:14; 1 Cor. 1:21; 9:27). There is no occasion when it is used absolutely to mean the preaching of judgement. Dalton however argues that we ought not to understand 'salvation' in 1 Pet. 3:19 on the grounds that; (a) what holds for 'preaching' to men cannot be regarded as holding for spirits (*op. cit.*, pp. 154f). This has no substance as an objection unless for dogmatic reasons it is argued that redemption cannot be offered to fallen angels; (b) it is repugnant to the context, for if it was believed that disobedient angels are finally saved then Christians might draw the conclusion that they need not resist persecution since they will in any case be saved (pp. 155ff). Dalton's first argument could be turned against him here; what is true of angels may not be true of men. More positively it should be noted that there are a few passages (e.g. Col. 1:20; Eph. 1:10) which imply a general restoration; the readers of these passages needed encouragement and were certainly not unacquainted with suffering. If 4:6 refers to the same event as 3:19 (it probably does not) it implies that salvation is preached. (c) 3:22 shows that the spirits were overcome by Jesus and not saved (p. 157). But 3:22 and 3:19 may not refer to the same event. It is important to realise that to say 'salvation was preached to angels' no more implies that all were saved than it does in the case of men; 1 Tim. 3:16 also does not state the result of Christ's being seen by the angels. There is thus no reason to reject the normal NT meaning of 'preach', i.e., that it relates to salvation. What is not clear is the result; if 3:22 refers to this preaching then the spirits do not accept the proffered salvation; 2 Enoch 18 may, however, imply the possibility of angelic repentance and conversion. Probably the matter is unclear to us because our author is not interested in describing what happened to the spirits but in what Christ did (cf. Schlatter).

(vi) 3:19 and 4:6 do not refer to the same event; 3:19 relates to

spirits, 4:6 to men; both, however, may have been preached to
on the same journey of Christ (see on 4:6).

If a journey of Christ to the underworld is pictured in I Pet.
3:19, what influences created it? The theme is well-known in
ancient literature (e.g. Orpheus), but the story of Orpheus and
those similar to it are far removed from the milieu of primitive
Christianity and can only have had indirect influence. I Enoch
is a probable source of much more direct influence; this apocalyptic
book was known to the early church; it is quoted in Jude 14;
most of it, if not all, and certainly the portion in which we are
interested, is pre-Christian. It recounts the story of a journey by
Enoch (Gen. 5:21–4) to the angels who had sinned with women
(Gen. 6:1–4) and produced giants. Enoch (1 Enoch 13:1ff)
preaches condemnation to them; they are ready to repent, but
he rejects their penitence (13:7; 14:1ff). In Jewish apocalyptic
tradition the story of Gen. 6:1–4 (the sin of the sons of God, who
were taken to be fallen angels) was closely connected with the
flood in the time of Noah (1 Enoch 6; 65; *Jubilees* 5; *Testament of
Naphtali* 3:5; CD 2:18–20). Since our author writes that the
disobedience of the spirits took place in the days of Noah (3:20)
we may assume he is referring to the disobedience of Gen. 6:1–4.
Enoch apparently made his journey not at the time of his ascent
to God (Gen. 5:24) but when raptured (cf. 1 Enoch 1:2; 12:1ff;
17:1).

The development of the doctrine of the descent into Hell in the
early church does not greatly assist the understanding of our
passage. The earliest certain reference is in Justin, *Dialogue with
Trypho* 72, who quotes from a passage which he found in his
copy (LXX) of Jeremiah, 'The Lord remembered his dead from
Israel who slept in the earth of the grave and he descended to
them to preach his salvation to them'; this must be considerably
earlier than 160 A.D. (the approximate date of Justin's writing).
A similar statement is found in the *Gospel of Peter* 10:41f (middle of
the second century) though the nature of the preaching is not
described. From the time of Irenaeus (*Against Heresies*, V. 31:1,
*c.* 180 A.D.) it became an increasingly common doctrine among
the fathers in the form of a descent to preach salvation to the
dead; Irenaeus himself knew I Peter but does not relate the
doctrine to our letter though he does relate it to other NT passages;
Clement of Alexandria (*Stromata* VI, 6. 38–9) is the first to make
this explicit connection. It may be that in the earlier part of the

second century the doctrine existed independently of 1 Peter and
was a more general belief of the church than its appearance in
1 Peter alone would suggest; perhaps Irenaeus and others did not
attach the doctrine to 1 Peter because they viewed the latter as
teaching a preaching, not to the dead, but to the spirits. We have
already seen that from a time much earlier than 1 Peter there
was a belief in some form of journey by Christ (e.g. Ac. 2:27;
Rom. 10:7; Eph. 4:9), though no indication is given of what he
did on this journey.

20. **who formerly did not obey:** as we have already seen the
apocalyptic writings on the basis of Gen. 6:1-6 depict a group of
angels (or spirits) who fell at the time of Noah; the first part of our
verse makes clear that it is these spirits and not just any spirits to
whom Christ preached.

**God's patience** derives in this context from Gen. 6:3 but is a
common theme in Judaism and the NT (*Pirque Aboth* 5:2; 1 Enoch
9:11; 60:5; 93:3; Rom. 2:4; 9:22; Ac. 14:16; 17:30; 2 Pet. 3:9);
it is a patience which precedes judgement. This is relevant to
Peter's readers, for God is soon to begin his judgement (cf. 4:7,13,
17 etc.). The flood often served as a parable of God's apocalyptic
judgement (Mt. 24:37-9; 2 Pet. 2:4-10; 3:6f); the generation of
the flood is regarded as a most sinful people and serves as a
warning example to the ungodly (2 Pet. 2:6; cf. Wis. 10:4; 3 Mac.
2:4; *Testament of Naphtali* 3:5).

**were saved:** as Noah and his family (eight persons) were
delivered from the flood so Christians will be delivered from the
coming judgement. Having made the transition from the spirits to
Noah it is natural to make the further transition to the thought of
those who were saved through the ark and represent the church
as saved.

**Noah** features in Jewish literature as a great figure of the past
(Ezek. 14:14,20; Wis. 10:4; Sir. 44:17) and in the NT as an
example to Christians (Mt. 24:37f; Heb. 11:7; 2 Pet. 2:5).

**eight persons:** the number is mentioned to emphasise the few
who were saved; likewise the Christian community is small
compared to the many who oppose it or are indifferent to it.
There is insufficient evidence for taking 'eight' as a symbolic
number.

**through water:** in verse 21 this is taken up as a reference to
baptism through which Christians are saved. 'through' can be
given:

(a) a local sense: (i) Noah was saved by going through water into the ark; there is a rabbinic legend that he only entered the ark when the water reached his knees and forced him to go through it to the ark; or (ii) he passed through water while in the ark until he reached dry land (cf. Wis. 14:5).

(b) (preferably) an instrumental sense, by means of water; strictly Noah was saved from water but the baptismal reference which follows has forced our writer into the strange statement 'through water' in relation to Noah. 'Water' in the context stands for the whole action of baptism and not just for the material substance used in it. We note finally that whereas the verse began with judgement (the flood) it ends with salvation; what is to unbelievers their judgement, is to believers their hope and trust.

21. **Baptism, which corresponds to this:** the transition from water to baptism is natural. (The grammar of the first few words of verse 21 is very complex.) To what does baptism correspond, i.e., to what does 'this' refer? It may refer either to 'water' alone, or, more probably, to the whole action of the building of the ark and the salvation of Noah and his family. Selwyn takes 'correspond' in a different way and considers those who are saved now as corresponding to those who were saved then, but the connection does not run as naturally; we move from verse 20 to verse 21 through 'water' in relation to the ark and then baptism and not through 'corresponding' people. The correspondence of events and people in the OT with those of the NT is found repeatedly in the latter, e.g. 1 Cor. 10:1-11 (again with reference to baptism), Melchizedek in Hebrews, Elijah and John the Baptist (Mt. 11:14; 17:12), Jonah and Christ (Lk. 11:29-32), Adam and Christ (Rom. 5:12ff). The underlying assumption is the regularity of God's behaviour under both covenants. Often, however, the correspondence rests on somewhat slender grounds (e.g. Gal. 4:21-31). The event in the OT may be said to prefigure imperfectly that which corresponds to it in the NT.

**now:** see p. 25.

**not as a removal of dirt from the body:** the nature of baptism is now explained negatively, and in the following phrase positively. Whatever baptism removes is not removed from the body alone; cleansing from sin is a much deeper process. In the background may lie a contrast with Jewish circumcision and pagan lustration rites which were sometimes conceived as dealing only with outward faults.

**an appeal to God for a clear conscience:** this is one possible
rendering of the Greek word (*eperōtēma*); generally it means
'question, inquiry', but this does not give a good sense here since
we would expect the nature of the question to be indicated; it can
mean 'appeal' and also 'pledge'; this last is preferable (cf. G. C.
Richards, '1 Peter iii:21', *J.T.S.*, 32 (1931) 77) and has been
accepted by most recent commentators (Selwyn, Reicke, Dalton,
Boismard). It is probable that in baptism in the early church the
candidate responded with an oral pledge, a statement of his
belief, to the invitation to be baptized; this pledge would have
been not merely an asseveration of faith in Christ but also a
promise to maintain his loyalty to God. We would therefore
translate (with Dalton, *op. cit.*, pp. 224–8), 'a pledge made to
God to maintain a clear conscience', or 'a pledge made to God
proceeding from a clear conscience'. Note the contrast of 'pledge'
here with 'not obey' (verse 20).
**conscience:** cf. 3:16.
**through the resurrection of Jesus Christ:** baptism does not
save either because of its washing effect or because of the loyalty
of the candidate but because of the resurrection of Jesus Christ;
here we approach the conception of Rom. 6.

22. **angels, authorities and powers:** terms for superhuman
powers which were believed to affect the lives of men; they are
frequently referred to in the NT under these and other names
(cf. Rom. 8:38; 1 Cor. 2:6–8; 15:24; Gal. 4:3,9; Col. 1:16; 2:8;
Eph. 1:21; 6:12). They were closely associated in Jewish thought
with 'folk-angels', i.e. angelic powers who were believed to
govern the nations, and in both Jewish and Hellenistic thought
with the stars (cf. C. D. Morrison, *The Powers That Be*, S.B.T. 29,
London, 1960; G. B. Caird, *Principalities and Powers*, Oxford, 1956);
in the period prior to the NT there had been a great growth in
belief in astral influence on the lives of men. In Judaism and
Christianity the powers were regarded as behind idolatry
(1 Cor. 10:19ff; Rev. 9:20; 1 Enoch 99:6f; *Jubilees* 1:11; 22:17);
Satan is the god of this world (Jn 12:31; 14:30; 16:11; 2 Cor. 4:4).
The readers of the epistle would thus consider them to be the real
powers which lay behind their persecution. The letter has now
returned from its theorising about the flood to its central concern,
the persecution of the church.
**subject to him:** the NT tradition associates the Christ event
with a victory over these angelic powers. This victory may be

depicted as future (1 Cor. 15:24), connected to the ascension as
here (cf. Eph. 1:21), or related to the death of Jesus (Col. 2:15);
sometimes Christ's superiority is expressed or implied without any
reference to the time factor (Rom. 8:38f; Phil. 2:10; Col. 2:10).
Once it is said that the powers were created by Christ (Col. 1:16).
The church makes known to them God's wisdom in the Christ-
event (Eph. 3:10) and its members are still engaged in a struggle
with them (Eph. 6:12; Gal. 4:3,9). In 1 Pet. 3:22 it is to be
assumed that their subjection took place as Christ went to heaven,
for they were believed to inhabit the region between earth and the
highest heaven (cf. Eph. 2:2; 6:12; *Testament of Levi* 3:1ff; 2 Enoch
7:1–5; 18:3–6).

Are the angelic powers evil and did they fall in the time of
Noah (Gen. 6:1–4), i.e., are they identical with the spirits of 3:19?
The tradition underlying 3:19 is Jewish but that underlying 3:22
is Hellenistic as well as Jewish. 3:19 was not at the end of the first
century part of the common Christian tradition whereas the
subjection of the angelic powers was. 3:22 gives Christ's victory
over these powers, a victory which would have been unnecessary
if they lay bound in prison before his ascension. (In the apocalyptic
literature they are sometimes viewed as released from prison, but
this leads to their destruction or their confinement in eternal fire,
and this is taken to be a punishment rather than a victory.)
There is no uniform conception that all angels fell in the events of
Gen. 6:1–4; in one branch of the tradition the fall of Satan and
other spiritual powers took place earlier (cf. E. Langton, *Essentials
of Demonology*, London, 1949, pp. 107ff); Milton's idea of a
Satanic fall in heaven prior to the creation of man goes back to
this strand of belief. We conclude that 3:19 and 3:22 are divergent
conceptions which have come together in this passage but are not
intended to refer to the same event.

The resurrection, ascension, and session of Christ at God's right
hand are common elements in the faith of the early church; so
with the reference to the resurrection in verse 21 we have returned
after a parenthesis to the creed underlying this section.

Looking back over the development of thought we see that
3:18–22 continues the argument of 3:13–17, the suffering of
Christians; Christ is introduced as example and, once introduced,
controls the thought; we move from his atoning death to his
resurrection and victory over the evil powers; this victory serves

to assure his followers that there is nothing to harm them if they stand firm for what is right (3:13). By way of parenthesis the writer has dealt with the period between Christ's death and resurrection, answering the question which must surely have been asked many times, What happened then? The precise significance of verse 19 will probably always elude us. It depends on the tradition about Enoch; what he did, Christ also did; but Christ went further because his concern for the spirits led him to tell them of salvation. However we cannot deduce from this that there is a 'second chance' for men after death or that all men and all spirits will eventually be reconciled to God (cf. Col. 1:20); the former does not follow, because 3:19 deals with spirits and not men, the latter, because we do not know the result of Christ's preaching; 3:22 would suggest that some angelic powers are regarded as continuing hostile to men and therefore unreconciled.

## ABSTAIN FROM EVIL 4:1–6

This section continues the theme of persecution and 4:1a links back to 3:18a. The temptation to assimilate to non-Christian ways and so escape suffering must be resisted.

1. **Christ suffered:** is this to be understood in the general sense that Jesus endured suffering throughout his life or in a more particular sense as referring to his death alone? The RSVmg which adds the words 'for us (you)' implies that 'suffered' must be understood redemptively and therefore means 'died'. The addition of the RSVmg, which is not found in $P^{72}$, is one that would have been easily made under confessional and liturgical pressures and would harmonise the present passage with 2:21 and possibly 3:18. But even if we omit the words Christ's suffering cannot exclude his death; 'suffered' may in fact have been chosen instead of 'died' because it permits an easier transference to the suffering of Christians.

**arm yourselves:** the Christian is instructed to prepare himself for persecution. The military metaphor is common in early Christian writing (1 Th. 5:8; Rom. 6:13; 13:12; Eph. 6:11–17; 2 Cor. 10:4) and is found both in the OT (Isa. 59:17f; cf. Wis. 5:17–23) and secular Greek literature. Selwyn considers it may be possibly related to the baptismal conception of the putting on of clothes, and therefore part of the early Christian baptismal catechism (pp. 396f, 456–8).

**the same thought:** does this refer backwards to 'Christ suffered in the flesh' or forwards to 'whoever has suffered . . . sin' (the word rendered 'for' by the RSV also means 'that' and if so rendered verse 1b would give the content of 'the same thought')? Our discussion of verse 1b will show that the translation of the RSV is probably correct.

**whoever has suffered . . . sin:** this seems to be a proverbial expression related to Rom. 6:7. It has been understood in a number of different ways:

(a) In common with a strand of Jewish thought (cf. 1 Enoch 67:9; 2 Mac. 6:12–16; 2 Baruch 13:10; 78:6; Sir. 2:11; cf. Moore, *Judaism*, Cambridge, Mass., 1927–30, II, pp. 248–56) it is taken to mean that suffering if rightly borne purifies the sufferer from sin; the flesh as the seat of sin requires to be purified (e.g. Selwyn, Bennett, Wand).

(b) Suffering is felt in the flesh; the flesh, the seat of sin, is thereby disciplined and unable to exert its desires; therefore sin is conquered (e.g. Bigg, Knopf).

(c) Martyrdom itself might be considered to atone for sin, as sometimes in the later church; this view may be dismissed because suffering in our context cannot be restricted to death.

(d) 'Suffering' is taken to mean 'dying', but not in the literal sense; the resemblance of the whole phrase to Rom. 6:7 combined with the mention of baptism in 3:21 suggests that we have here the Pauline conception of a death with Christ to sin in baptism (e.g. Dalton, Cranfield, Walls-Stibbs).

In favour of this fourth interpretation are its general affinity to Pauline thought (and we have seen that our author probably knew the ideas of Romans, cf. pp. 32ff), the presence of the baptismal reference in the context (3:21), and the attribution to 'suffered' (an aorist participle implying one past action) of its past sense with the consequent avoidance of a present reference in it. There are, however, serious objections to it: (i) The Pauline conception of the believer's death with Christ is not elsewhere present in the epistle and 4:1b is an exceedingly tortuous way to introduce it without preparation; more generally the so-called Pauline mysticism is lacking in our letter (see p. 34). (ii) The introduction of the idea seems unnecessary in a section devoted to the encouragement of the Christian in a period of persecution. (iii) It is more natural to take 'suffered' in 4:1a to refer to the suffering of Christ than to his death. (iv) The Pauline teaching

speaks of 'dying' with Christ in baptism and not of 'suffering'.
(v) Elsewhere in our letter 'sin' is used in the concrete sense
'acts of sin', whereas in Pauline teaching it means the state of sin
or is a power opposed to man.

Both the interpretations (a) and (b) take sin in the sense of
concrete actions; combined with the aorist 'suffered' they would
appear to mean respectively (a) individual acts of suffering purify
from actual concrete sins and (b) individual acts of suffering lead
to the conquest of actual concrete sins. It would be more normal
to have the present participle suggesting that the process of
suffering led either to gradual purification from sin or to gradual
conquest of it but there is a peculiar tendency in 1 Peter to use the
aorist in preference to the present (cf. p. 26). This explanation
also means that 'flesh' must be taken in a slightly different sense
in verse 1b from its sense in verses 1a, 2; but the flesh is widely
used in Paul and in the Qumran writings to denote the seat of sin.
If purification is clearly distinguished from forgiveness and any
idea of reconciliation to God through suffering is excluded, as it
must be in the light of 2:24; 3:18, then the conceptions of purification from and conquest over sin do not differ widely. But the
question will remain whether it is true that suffering borne in the
spirit of humility does lead to purification or conquest in any way
different from what would have taken place provided only that the
proper spirit of humility was present. However the idea is one
that has frequently recurred in Christian thought (cf. the quotations given by Selwyn and Moffatt); for this reason, and because
of the difficulties of fitting (d) to the context and thought, a
combination of (a) and (b) is the preferable solution. 1 Cor. 5:5
may possibly represent a similar thought. We may not extend the
idea to suppose that suffering frees the Christian from all sin for
ever. It can now be seen that 'the same thought' refers backwards,
for if it refers forwards it would imply that Christ purified himself
from sin by his suffering, an intolerable view to our author since
he holds that Christ was free of sin (1:19; 2:22; 3:18).

2. This verse gives the reason why Christians should arm
themselves with the thought that Christ suffered, viz., so that they
may live pure lives.

**human passions:** obviously meant in the bad sense as verse 3
shows.

**the rest of the time in the flesh:** i.e. the remainder of their
earthly lives.

3. There must be a clear break in the behaviour of Christians with their pre-Christian conduct. It would however be incorrect to deduce from this that all those addressed are converts who came into the church from the pagan world and that none of them were brought up in Christian homes; the danger existed equally for those born within the church as for those who came in from outside by conversion that they might not turn away from sin. It is not a baptismal service now in progress but the expected end of all things (4:5,7, etc.) which gives the appeal its urgency. The next verse implies that they have been Christians for a long enough period for their neighbours to have observed a real change in their conduct; the writer is not therefore expecting a change at this particular moment in their behaviour, as if at baptism. The letter, written to a wide area and addressed to Christians in every stage of development, sees them all in the same danger of lapsing into conformity with the Gentile world.

**what the Gentiles like to do:** the translation obscures the strong contrast in the original between this and 'the will of God' (verse 2). Over against God's way is the pressure exerted by the vast mass of humanity compelling men to accept its degraded conception of existence (cf. the Johannine use of 'world'). A very gloomy picture of heathendom is depicted; such a view was common to Jews and Christians of the period (cf. Wis. 13–15; Rom. 1:18–32; Eph. 4:17–19).

**licentiousness, passions . . . :** an existing catalogue of vices is utilized (see on 2:1); evidence for this lies in the use of 'passions' in it to denote one group of sins amongst others whereas in verse 2 it had been used in its widest sense to denote all sins.

**licentiousness, passions:** sexual sins.

**drunkenness, revels, carousing:** sins of intemperance. Both these and the sexual sins may have followed on or accompanied festivities of a private or public nature, with secular or religious purpose; this is in keeping with the debased nature of much contemporary religious practice.

**idolatry:** refers to wrong religious practice. The word is emphasised by its position at the end of the list and because it alone is qualified with an adjective. It may appear strange to list it as one sin among others (cf. Gal. 5:20); in the description of the heathen world in Rom. 1:18–32 idolatry appears (1:23) as the origin of actual evil among men (1:24–32). It may have its position at the end of the list in 1 Peter because the other sins followed in its wake in religious festivals (cf. the association of feasting and idolatry in 1 Cor. 8:1–13; 10:14–30). It must be noted that there were many in the contemporary heathen world who mocked at idolatry and condemned indulgence in the other sins.

**lawless:** this would normally mean something contrary to the natural or the divinely prescribed order of things; on occasion it means nothing more than something which is exceedingly evil, 'abominable' (Selwyn), and this may be the sense here (cf. 1 Clement 63:2; 2 Mac. 10:34).

4. **you do not join them:** the Christians no longer rush (the word for 'join' literally means 'run together') to associate themselves with the licentious behaviour of their heathen neighbours. Since heathen religious ceremonies were part and parcel of ordinary life (e.g. all civic and national activities were bound up with them) the Christians were compelled to avoid what would have seemed to their fellows a wholly innocuous co-operation and to go much further than merely separate themselves from actual heathen worship.

**abuse:** the natural reaction of those who find co-operation suddenly ceasing. The Greek word (*blasphēmein*) means both 'slander' and 'blaspheme' and the absence of 'you' in the original permits us to adopt either meaning: probably both are intended. The heathen slander their Christian neighbours who regard this as itself blasphemy against God because they are keeping God's will. This sense of 'blaspheme' affords an easy transition to verse 5: God will judge those who blaspheme him.

5. **to him:** it is not at once clear whether this refers to God or Christ as judge. At 1:17; 2:23 God is the judge but it suits the context better here to take 'him' of Christ since he has been the real subject of all the statements from 3:18 onwards. Elsewhere in the NT he does appear as judge (Ac. 10:42; 2 Tim. 4:1; 1 Cor. 4:5).

**to judge the living and the dead:** probably a fixed liturgical or credal phrase relating to the last Judgement (Ac. 10:42; 2 Tim. 4:1; *Barnabas* 7:2; Polycarp, *Philippians* 2:1; 2 Clement 1:1; cf. Rom. 14:9). In each of the NT citations of the formula Christ appears as the judge.

**the living and the dead:** i.e. all men. The last judgement was expected shortly (4:7) and it was important to emphasise that all men would be embraced within its orbit (cf. 1 Th. 4:13–17), not only living and dead blasphemers but all who have lived and died and all who will be alive at Christ's return. Because of the fixed nature of the phrase and its meaning elsewhere, 'the dead' cannot be understood of the spiritually dead (cf. Eph. 2:1,5; Rev. 3:1; Col. 2:13); it signifies the physically dead.

6. **For:** this indicates that verse 6 gives the reason for, or basis of, the statement of verse 5 that Christ will judge all men, or possibly it may refer back to all of verses 2–5 and indicate the reason why Christ condemns unbelievers and vindicates the faithful.

**this** points forward to 'that though judged . . . God'.

**that** can be taken either in the sense 'in order that' or in the sense 'with the result that'.

**the gospel was preached:** *lit.* 'it was evangelised (gospelized).' It may be that a subject should be supplied other than the cognate 'gospel', and if so 'Christ' is the most appropriate since he has been the subject of most of the verbs since 3:18. If 'Christ' is the subject then he cannot have been the one who preached to the dead, but if we translate as in the RSV then he may have been the preacher. In either case if Christ is not the preacher then we would have expected that the preacher would be named. The tense (aorist) of 'preached' implies a definite historical event.

**the dead:** who are these? A number of answers have been given (For the history of interpretation see Dalton, *op. cit.*, pp. 42–54): (i) They are the spiritually dead. 'Dead' can be used in this way (e.g. Eph. 2:1) but this meaning is most unlikely here because the word does not have this meaning in verse 5 and because it would require a present tense and not a past in 'preached', i.e. 'the gospel is being preached to the spiritually dead'. (ii) They are the righteous dead of the OT; by their righteousness they are able to appropriate the gospel when it is preached to them in Hades and so 'live in the spirit like God'. This is again improbable because it also necessitates a change of meaning between verse 5 and verse 6 for 'dead' and because the introduction of such a reference to the righteous dead is utterly irrelevant at this point to the argument, which is the encouragement of Christians under the threat of persecution. (iii) They are Christians who have already died (cf. Selwyn, Dalton). In 1 Th. 4:13–17, where the nearness of the end presses as in 1 Peter, Paul assures his readers that the Christian dead and living believers will both participate in the full salvation of Christ's return; correspondingly the dead in our passage are believers to whom the Gospel was preached while they were alive in order that they might live for ever in the spirit like God; those living Christians who face possible death in persecution should be encouraged knowing that they too will live for ever with God. This solution implies that the preaching was done by missionaries and leaves us to take 'preached' with a personal subject, i.e., Christ, which is the more general usage of the word. This explanation is a great deal more probable than either of the preceding, yet there are serious objections to it. 'Dead' is a strange word to use without qualification of dead Christians; in the alleged parallel (1 Th. 4:13–17) Paul makes his meaning clear by writing of the 'dead in Christ' and of 'those who have fallen asleep' ('sleep' was a word used by the early Christians for the state of believers who had died). This explanation also implies a change of meaning in 'dead' between verses 5 and 6, since in verse 5 it means all the dead and not just dead believers who were once alive. (iv) The dead are all who are physically dead, and who are in this state when they hear the Gospel (cf. Beare, Knopf). If, though this is not stated, they are those who heard the Gospel at the same time as it was proclaimed to the spirits (3:19), and the aorist tense of 'preached' implies a single action rather than a continuous process, they are the dead prior to Christ's death and include both righteous and unrighteous. The Gospel is now offered to those who never had the opportunity of hearing it when alive. This creates a stronger link between verses 5 and 6: all men face judgement (verse 5) because all, even the dead, have heard the gospel (verse 6). 'Dead' means the same group of physically dead in both verses. Objections can also be made against this interpretation. Two thousand years have passed and there are now many dead who did not hear the Gospel while alive and have not heard it since their death; to this our author would probably have answered that he did not expect the world to continue for more than a few years and could not have foreseen the alleged unfairness. A much stronger objection lies with those who argue that this interpretation implies a second chance for men after they have died; elsewhere in the letter death apparently settles the fate of men (1:3f; 3:10; 4:5,18; 5:8), and the conception of a second chance would hardly encourage those who are being persecuted to resist unto death. To this it may be answered that the texts suggesting the finality of death relate to the present condition of the readers and those around them who have already heard the Gospel; since the preaching of 4:6 is envisaged as having taken place once only in the past it would not suggest to persecuted readers that they would have a second chance after death. If it is objected that by no means all the living had heard the Gospel by the time the letter was written, Rom. 15:19 may be adduced; here Paul indicates that the gospel has been 'fully preached' in certain areas, though, of course, many have not heard it. Taken all in all this fourth interpretation is preferable.

**though judged in the flesh . . . God:** we appear to have here two balanced clauses in which three contrasts are drawn, viz., judged-live, flesh-spirit, men-God, but it is difficult to maintain this fully. The second half of the contrast is reasonably clear: the final purpose, or possibly the result, of the preaching of the gospel to the dead was that they might live in the sphere of the Spirit in the presence of God or in the way in which God lives; this is what is loosely described as 'eternal life' (the word used for 'live' here is the word often used absolutely with this sense and is not the same word as in verse 2). We require to examine in more detail the first clause.

**judged:** various interpretations have been given to this word, and, in consequence, to the other words of the clause: (i) The final judgement of God (as in verse 5) when men are raised in the flesh and judged as men are (cf. Reicke, *op. cit.*, pp. 204ff). This interpretation preserves the meaning of judgement; it requires that we omit 'though', and this the Greek permits. However it requires that we take 'men' in the sense 'dead men', and it would have been easier to say this directly; it makes 'like men' mean 'as being men' which spoils the parallel with 'like God' in the balancing clause; and it destroys the contrast between 'flesh' and 'spirit', for to say that men are raised in the flesh means they appear at the last judgement in a 'fleshy' (i.e. material) existence, whereas to live 'in the spirit' does not imply a 'spiritual' (i.e. non-material) existence but life in the sphere of God's Spirit. (ii) The judgement is that which the dead suffered in death and is the judgement of God on sin (cf. Rom. 5:12; 6:23); it took place in the sphere of the flesh (cf. Dalton). This varies the meaning of 'judge' between verses 5 and 6, though in each case the judge is divine and the two occurrences of 'judge' are further apart than those of 'dead'; it reads more into flesh than in 4:2 implying that it is the place of sin, but this is an acknowledged use of the word and provides a good contrast with 'spirit'. It again loses an adequate parallel with 'like God'; it has been argued that 'like men' should be rendered as 'according to men's standards' (Selwyn) or 'in the eyes of men' (Dalton) and this does ease the parallel with 'like God'. (iii) The judgement is that which faithful Christians have experienced in the sight of men while alive, i.e., in the flesh, at the hands of their persecutors. This interpretation goes very appropriately with the understanding of 'dead' as 'Christian dead' (see above). However it involves such a radical change in the meaning of 'judge' from verse 5 (where it referred to God's judgement) that it is difficult to accept. (ii) despite its difficulties fits best to the meaning we have given to 'dead' and should be accepted: we may paraphrase it: 'that though judged at death in the sphere of the flesh according to human standards, they might live in the sphere of the Spirit as God lives'. It cannot be said however that any existing exegesis of this verse is satisfactory. If that which is here advocated is adopted then the occasion of this preaching to the dead will probably be the same as that of 3:19, i.e., Christ's descent to Hades. But we are in no position to draw any conclusion about an ultimate universal salvation.

## THE DEMANDS OF FELLOWSHIP 4:7–11

The recollection of judgement (4:5f) leads to a recollection of the eschatological situation in which the church stands; this in turn issues in a series of exhortations linked together by the theme 'love'. The individual exhortations appear in other NT writings but are unrelated and scattered; catechetical material is not then being used here directly, though the author is drawing on the church's normal instruction.

7. **The end of all things is at hand:** in common with all early Christianity the writer believes that Christ will return speedily (1:5f; 4:13,17; 5:1,10); cf. H. A. Guy, *The New Testament Doctrine of the 'Last Things'* (Oxford, 1948); J. W. Bowman, 'Eschatology of the NT' (*I.D.B.*, II, pp. 135ff). The NT writers frequently use eschatological expectation as a motive for Christian behaviour (Mt. 24:45–25:13; Mk 13:33–7; Rom. 13:11–14; Heb. 10:25; 1 Jn 2:28f) but not, as 4:7b–11 shows, to suggest an other-worldliness; what could be more mundane than hospitality! The readers may be aliens and exiles (1:1; 2:11) but they are not to abandon the ordinary duties of life. The awareness of the proximity of the end is not then used to devaluate life but to give it a new depth of meaning (cf. 1 Th. 5:1–11). We note that there

is no speculation here on the precise nearness of the end or on the signs which precede it.

**keep sane and sober for your prayers:** a disciplined life (cf. 1:13), not for the sake of discipline itself, but of their growth in fellowship with God. The succeeding verses show that our author is of anything but the view that the imminence of the end should lead to a preoccupation with religious practices. For prayer and discipline in the eschatological situation cf. Mk 14:38; 1 Th. 5:8; 2 Th. 2:2.

8. **Above all . . . love:** 'The characteristically Christian emphasis on the primacy of love' (Beare); cf. 1:22; 3:8; it is the central theme in the remainder of this paragraph.

**love covers a multitude of sins:** this appears to be a quotation of Prov. 10:12 in its Hebrew form; the LXX differs very considerably; since the latter is the text which is always quoted in our letter it is probable that the Hebrew form of Prov. 10:12 had passed into Christian usage as a detached maxim and as such is used here. It is used in the same way in Jas 5:20; 1 Clement 49:5; 2 Clement 16:4. As it stands it is capable of two meanings, depending whether we take the sins to be those (i) of the one who loves, or (ii) of the one who is loved. 2 Clement 16:4 and possibly Jas 5:20 have the sense (i); 1 Clement 49:5 is somewhat indeterminate, for if associated as it probably ought to be with the immediately succeeding clauses it refers to the sins of those loved but if interpreted by 50:5f to the sins of those who love. Thus we cannot be certain how the maxim was understood in the early church. Both lines of thought can be supported from other parts of the NT: (i) Lk. 7:47; Mt. 6:14f (cf. Sir. 17:22; Dan. 4:27); this interpretation agrees with the contemporary Jewish belief that sin is atoned for by almsgiving, the latter the equivalent of hospitality; love may then be regarded as indicating that the nature of the one who loves is open to repentance; (ii) 1 Cor. 13:4–7, which forms the best commentary on this interpretation. Neither meaning is unsuitable to the general trend of 1 Pet. 4:7–11 but the strongly social context fits (ii) better than the judgement theme fits (i); we therefore prefer (ii). The 'covering' of sin is an OT image (cf. Ps. 32:1) denoting its forgiveness by God, but this is hardly relevant here.

9. **Practise hospitality:** widely recognized as a social duty in the ancient world hospitality was emphasised especially in the early church (Rom. 12:13; 16:1f; 1 Tim. 3:2; Tit. 1:8; Heb. 13:2;

3 Jn 5–8; cf. Mt. 25:35). In view of the shortage of hotels and
restaurants visiting preachers, prophets, teachers and travellers
had to be accommodated in the homes of Church members, and
this exhortation is therefore appropriate in a circular letter like
1 Peter. But it almost certainly refers also to hospitality within the
local community for its own members; this was expressed in part
through house-churches (Rom. 16:5; 1 Cor. 16:19; Col. 4:15),
and this leads on neatly to the discussion of the church in verse
10f. It would, of course, only be the wealthier members who could
give accommodation either to congregations or to visiting
Christians.

**ungrudgingly:** hospitality can be costly and tiring, very irritating
when others trade on it (*Didache* 11–13), and perhaps dangerous
in a time of persecution.

10. **each has received a gift:** Paul expounded in depth the
conception of the gifts that all Christians have received from God
and which they are to use for the benefit of their fellow-believers
relating the idea both to the church as the body of Christ and to
his own teaching on the Spirit (Rom. 12:3–8; 1 Cor. 12); the idea
is retained here but no longer so related, nor is the varied nature
of the gifts expounded as in Paul; they are reduced in number to
two, 'speech' and 'service', though **varied** implies a greater
number. Our writer probably links up his teaching by means of the
concept 'stewards' to his doctrine of the church as a house (2:5;
4:17), for stewards were the administrative officials in households.
Like Paul he stresses that the gifts God gives are loans, not to be
treated as the Christian's own, but used for others.

**gift . . . grace:** these two words come from the same Greek root;
they imply that the gifts are a special endowment of Christians as
such and not merely inborn talents and qualities. 'Grace' is again
used somewhat objectively; see on 1:2.

11. Two types of gift are now instanced (cf. Ac. 6:1–4 for a
similar classification) and each is left so unrestricted in definition
that every gift can be understood to be coming under review.

**whoever speaks:** whether as prophet, preacher or teacher in the
worship, instruction or mission of the community, or as an
individual privately encouraging, evangelizing or rebuking
another Christian, or even a pagan.

**oracles of God:** the speaker does not give his own opinions but
as the servant of the gospel utters God's word.

**renders service:** whether as administrator or dispenser of

charity (cf. Rom. 12:7f) or as one who simply helps another in the
ordinary course of life.

**as one who renders . . . supplies:** the source of Christian
charity (love), as of preaching, is God himself; without God's help
neither can be accomplished.

**God may be glorified:** cf. 2:12.

**through Jesus Christ:** cf. 2:5; only through the reconciliation
achieved in Christ may the church offer glory to God.

**To him:** to whom? God or Christ? In favour of the former we
may argue: (i) The reference to the glorification of God in the
preceding clause links with 'glory' here; (ii) The majority of NT
doxologies are offered to God, and in particular the very similar
doxology of 5:11 is offered to him; (iii) To speak of glorifying God
'through Jesus Christ' and then to speak of glory belonging to
Christ seems odd. In favour of the latter we may argue: (i) In the
order of the words in Greek as well as in English 'Christ' is much
nearer to 'him' than is 'God': (ii) The similar doxology in Rev. 1:6
is addressed to Christ. Probably 'God' is to be preferred as the
subject of the doxology.

**Amen:** a liturgical response found at the conclusion of most
doxologies; it is Jewish in origin and signifies the assent of the
hearers (see J. Hempel, 'Amen', *I.D.B.*, I, p. 105).

Many scholars argue that this doxology ends the baptismal
discourse or liturgy (cf. pp. 21ff). However, the majority of NT
doxologies do not come at the conclusion of letters or discourses
but within the body of the material; there are only three which
come at the end, viz., Rom. 16:27 (and Rom. 16:25–7 is probably
a non-Pauline addition to the original letter); Jude 25; 2 Pet. 3:18.

## The Fiery Ordeal 4:12–19

We return to the earlier theme of persecution (1:6f; 3:13–17) and
the readers are shown the blessings which to their surprise
accompany their suffering. Selwyn (pp. 439ff) finds traditional
material here but cannot be said to have nearly as good a case as
elsewhere. On the possibility that there may be a break in the
letter between 4:11 and 4:12 see pp. 21ff; on the relationship of
the persecution of 4:12–19 to that of 1:6f; 3:13–17 see pp. 36ff.

12. **Beloved:** a new address which comes naturally after the
doxology and does not of itself imply a major break at this point;
it is used also at 2:11 where there is a change of subject matter.

**do not be surprised:** Gentile Christians, alive to their new
position as the people of God, might think it **strange** that they
should be suffering; they ought to recollect that in the OT members of the people of God suffered when they were faithful to God,
that Jesus himself suffered (cf. 2:18–25), that Peter, Paul and
many other leaders of the church had suffered, and that the
Gospel tradition contained many predictions of the suffering that
was to fall on Jesus' followers (e.g. Mt. 5:10–12; Mk 8:34; 13:9–
13; Jn 15:18–20). Suffering may be a normal part of Christian
living.

**fiery ordeal:** although under Nero many Christians were
burnt to death it is unlikely that this has occasioned the present
reference to fire; it comes instead from the biblical metaphor of
purifying and proving fire which has eschatological overtones
(cf. 1:7; Prov. 27:21; Ps. 66:10; 1 Cor. 3:13; Rev. 3:18).

**to prove you:** persecution will prove them; cf. 1:7.

13. Christians should be heartened in their present sufferings
because they will share in the glory of Christ at his return; this
future joy is not so much a reward for their present trials as an
'inherent compensation' (Beare), cf. Rom. 8:17; 2 Tim. 2:11f;
Lk. 12:8f; Mt. 10:32; Heb. 11:26. On the association of joy with
suffering, and the possibility of a primitive form here, see p. 31.

**share Christ's sufferings:** a number of interpretations of this
phrase have been given: (i) 'suffer as Christ suffered', cf. 2:20f;
Mk 8:34; Jn 15:20; but the word 'share' appears to imply much
more than the imitation of Christ. (ii) 'share mystically in the
sufferings of Christ' (cf. Col. 1:24; 2 Cor. 1:5; 4:10; Phil. 3:10);
Christians because they have been baptized into the death and
resurrection of Christ and are members of his body in their
sufferings participate in his suffering. However: (a) it is doubtful if
this is the meaning of the Pauline passages cited above (cf. Best,
*One Body in Christ*, London, 1955, pp. 130ff); (b) it is even more
doubtful if any trace of the Pauline conception of the togetherness
of Christians with Christ in his body is to be found in 1 Peter; at
2:20f; 3:17f there is only teaching about the imitation of Christ;
(c) it is difficult to fit a 'mystical' meaning to 'share' when it
re-appears in 5:1 (there rendered 'partaker'). (iii) 'share in the
Messianic woes' (cf. Selwyn, pp. 299ff; Leaney). The Messianic
woes or birthpangs denote a period of trial which the Jews
believed would take place before the arrival of the Messiah; he was
not himself to suffer in them but out of them the New Age was to

be born (Dan. 7:21ff; 12:1; Joel 2; 2 Esd. 13:16–19; 2 Baruch 25; 68; *Jubilees* 23:13ff; *Sanhedrin* 97a; cf. D. S. Russell, *The Method and Message of Jewish Apocalyptic*, London, 1964, pp. 272ff). Christians who believed that the Messiah had already come and would return again transformed this into a belief that they themselves would be involved in these birthpangs immediately prior to that return (cf. Mk 13:9ff; Rev. 7:14; 12:3ff; Jn 16:2,4,21, 22,33; 2 Th. 2:3–10). We have already indicated that this idea is present in 1 Pet. 1:5f. It suits the present context which has a strong eschatological orientation; in verse 12 'fiery ordeal' should be understood eschatologically; verse 13 envisages the survival of the readers to the appearance of Christ in glory and their eschatological joy thereat; verse 17 implies that what they suffer is part of God's plan (cf. 3:17) in the inauguration of judgement (cf. 5:10). This view is sustained by: (a) The total eschatological context of the letter in which the end is viewed as coming shortly (1:6,20; 4:5,7,17; 5:10). (b) The literal translation of our phrase is: 'share the sufferings of *the* Christ'; it is thus quite different from 1:11 where the personal sufferings of the Messiah are envisaged. Normally 'Christ' is used in the NT without the definite article; its addition here suggests that it is used as a title, i.e. 'the Messiah', and the phrase would mean: 'share the sufferings of the Messiah'. (c) The present interpretation is at least a possible understanding of the texts from Paul quoted at (ii) above (cf. Best, *ibid*); the same word is used for 'sufferings' in 2 Cor. 1:5; Phil. 3:10 as in 1 Peter, and it appears in the context of Col. 1:24. We accept (iii) as the most likely interpretation.

14. **If you are reproached ... blessed:** this recalls Mt. 5:11, to which our text is probably related; this of course does not imply that the writer of 1 Peter heard Jesus speak it.

**reproached:** a fairly general term covering everything from verbal insult to physical assault but not suggesting any idea of official action.

**for the name of Christ:** cf. Ac. 9:15f; 15:26; 21:13; the phrase does not necessarily mean that the profession of Christianity was a crime; it is written from the point of view of Christians who would view their own sufferings as 'for the name of Christ' (cf. pp. 37f).

**because the spirit ... upon you:** a further ground of consolation to them in suffering. Unfortunately it is impossible to be certain of the precise meaning of the phrase; the grammar is difficult and the text uncertain; the latter may have suffered a primitive corruption and be irrecoverable. The reading of the RSVmg which adds 'and of power' after 'glory' may be correct, but the addition of 'on their part he is evil spoken of, but on your part he is glorified' (AV) at the end of the verse is certainly incorrect.

**the spirit rests upon you:** cf. Num. 11:25; Isa. 11:2. The Spirit is promised to the Christian in time of persecution (Mk 13: 11; Mt. 10:20; Lk. 12:11f; cf. Jn 14:26; 16:7–11). Stephen was full of the Holy Spirit at his martyrdom (cf. *Martyrdom of Polycarp* 2:2).

**the spirit of glory and of God:** the literal rendering is 'the of glory and the spirit of God' and it is not clear if 'spirit' should be understood with 'of glory'. If it is taken in that way then we have here one entity described in two ways: the spirit of glory, even the spirit of God. The Spirit was an expected eschatological gift in Judaism; the Christians know his presence now. We should however perhaps understand some other word with glory, e.g. 'the presence of the glory' (Selwyn); as the Shekinah in the OT indicated God's presence in his temple and with his people, so the glory indicates his presence with them in their suffering.

15. **murderer, thief:** there is no need to see here veiled references to the accusations of cannibalism and infanticide made in the second century against Christians; the words are meant literally. Although there is no reference elsewhere in the NT to Christians who committed murder there is to those who thieve (1 Cor. 6:10; Eph. 4:28); at Corinth there was one member guilty of incest (1 Cor. 5:1–5). We should not judge the crimes of which members of the early church might be capable by the respectability of the twentieth century.

**wrongdoer:** a general word (cf. 2:12,14) which in its present context may, but need not, refer to activity contrary to the civil law.

**mischief-maker:** this word does not occur elsewhere in Greek and its meaning is uncertain. The uncertainty can be seen from the various translations which have been given to it: 'a revo-lutionary' (Moffatt), 'a busybody in other men's matters' (AV, cf. Weymouth, RV), 'a spy' (Phillips), 'one who infringes the rights others' (N.E.B.), 'an informer' (Jerusalem Bible). Unlike the first three categories it is difficult to take it as denoting a criminal. Christians whose missionary activity resulted in the splitting of families or the stirring up of riots could easily be described as 'mischief-makers' or 'busy-bodies'.

16. **if one suffers as a Christian,** i.e. worthily of a follower of Jesus who is aware that it is because he is a Christian and not a criminal that he suffers. Since not all the categories of verse 15 are criminal we are not compelled to assume that the suffering referred to here is punishment enforced by a court of law or that it involves the death penalty (cf. pp. 36ff).
**Christian:** only elsewhere in the NT at Ac. 11:26; 26:28. According to Ac. 11:26 it was first used by non-Christians to describe the followers of Christ; the latter spoke of themselves as 'brothers', 'saints', etc.; later they adopted the term 'Christian'.
**ashamed:** if the immediate prospect is execution, shame hardly seems the appropriate emotion; the word is suitable to describe a less final punishment.
**let him glorify God,** i.e. by his conduct and bearing in whatever abuse or torture he has to endure.

17. **the time has come for judgement to begin:** the writer envisages the final judgement as beginning, and this beginning is the persecution of Christians. The Messianic woes (see on verse 13) are the herald of the full and total judgement of God (cf. Mk 13:8). The 'judgement' is thus not the continuous judgement of men by God while they live but the ultimate consummation (cf. 4:7).
**to begin with the household of God:** there are many references in the prophets to judgement as falling first on the people of God (Mal. 3:1–5; Jer. 25:29; Ezek. 9:6; Isa. 10:12; Zech. 13:7–9; cf. Lk. 23:31) on the principle that those with the greatest advantage in knowing God are the most responsible for their behaviour (Amos 3:2). Though we may have difficulty at times in distinguishing between what Jesus said and its modification within the community, there is no reason to doubt that he taught that his disciples would suffer.
**the household of God:** the underlying word is the same as in 2:5 and so is the basic image.
**what will be the end of those who do not obey the gospel:** this and verse 18 are parenthetical to the writer's main purpose of encouraging his readers to stand firm amid tribulation. He is not interested in depicting the sufferings that will fall on unbelievers (contrast Rev. 6:15–17).

18. This verse is a quotation of Prov. 11:31 (LXX), where its context is non-eschatological.

**scarcely saved** does not imply doubt about the salvation of Christians, but emphasises the greatness of God's effort in saving them.

19. The main thought is resumed and summarised: the righteous though they suffer are safe with God.

**according to God's will:** cf. 2:15; 3:17. The Messianic woes are, of course, part of God's plan for the consummation of all things.

**do right:** cf. 2:15,20; 3:6,11. When translated 'do right' the Greek word used here suggests the performance of a duty in bearing suffering but it is better to take it with the more active connotation of the performance of good deeds towards others; this meaning is acceptable at its other occurrences (2:15,20; 3:6,11) and agrees with a similar phrase in 2:12 (cf. van Unnik, *N.T.S.*, I (1954) 92–110); it is compelled if we read the plural here as in **P**[72] etc. (cf. Kubo, *op. cit.*, p. 74f). If taken in this way the survival of the readers beyond their persecution is implied (i.e. death is not automatic) and it teaches that persecution is not to be faced merely in a spirit of resignation but with active goodness towards those who persecute.

**entrust:** as money is entrusted to a bank for safe-keeping (cf. Lk. 23:46; Ac. 7:59; 1 Tim. 1:18; 2 Tim. 1:12–14; 2:2). Whether the readers' sufferings are those inaugurating the arrival of the Messiah or not, they themselves need have no ultimate fear for God will take care of them.

**souls:** not a 'spiritual' part of man opposed to his body (see on 1:9,22; 2:11; cf. 2:25; 3:20) but the whole man. There is no suggestion that the body perishes in persecution and an immortal soul lives on, nor that Christians may allow persecutors to do what they wish to the body because the soul is safe.

**faithful Creator:** God is not elsewhere termed 'Creator' in the NT, though creation is always viewed as his work (cf. Ac. 4:24 etc.). Intertestamental Judaism, and especially Philo, laid much more stress on God as creator. Since he has created man he will be faithful to his own work and preserve those whom he has redeemed and who entrust themselves to him (2 Tim. 2:13; Heb. 10:23; 1 Th. 5:23f; 2 Th. 3:3; 1 Cor. 10:13).

## THE ECCLESIASTICAL CODE 5:1-5

The writer now addresses himself to two groups, elders (5:1-4)
and younger men (5:5), within the community before turning
back to the community as a whole (5:6-11). Boismard (*D.B.S.*,
VII, 1442f) points out that if we omit 5:1 and possibly 5:4 the
remainder is very similar in structure to the code of 2:13-3:7;
it in fact adds to it two elements relating to life within the
community rather than to behaviour towards those outside it.
These ecclesiastical elements we find also in other codes, cf. 1 Tim
3:1-13; 5:4-19 (see pp. 30f, 47f).

1. **the elders:** this word can indicate either the elderly, and
this may be the meaning in verse 5, or be a name for church
leaders ('presbyter' is a transliteration of the underlying Greek
word); its two meanings are related since the leaders of a community tend to be drawn from the elderly. Leaders in the Jewish
community (cf. Mk 7:3; 8:31; 11:27; 14:53; 15:1 etc.) were called
elders and the term was also in use in civil society in some areas
for leading men; the church probably borrowed the term from
Judaism. It is widely used in the NT for church officials, e.g.
Ac. 11:30; 14:23; 1 Tim. 5:17-19; Tit. 1:5; 2 Jn 1; 3 Jn 1; it is
also used in Revelation for certain heavenly beings (4:4,10;
5:5-14 etc.). Although Paul is reported in Ac. 14:23 as appointing
elders he never mentions them in his letters when he refers to
leaders in the churches (cf. Rom. 12:6-8; 1 Cor. 12:28-30;
Phil. 1:1; 1 Th. 5:12). There was no uniform nomenclature for the
leaders of the churches in the first century (cf. E. Schweizer,
*Church Order in the New Testament*, S.B.T. 32, London, 1961;
M. H. Shepherd, 'Ministry, Christian', *I.D.B.* III, pp. 386ff,
'Elder in the NT', *I.D.B.*, II, pp. 73ff). Since our author mentions
no other officials in his letter we may assume that those who
exercised pastoral and administrative oversight in the communities he addresses were, so far as he is aware, and he may not
have been aware of every local variation in title, termed 'elders'.
4:10f shows that these were not the only Christians active in the
work of the church. The elders will, of course, have received
'gifts' from 'God's varied grace' (4:10) for their office; they are
not an administrative leadership set over against a charismatic.
**fellow elder:** exclusive of 1:1; 5:12-14, this is the only verse

containing a personal reference to the writer. The present
description has been used to argue both for and against Petrine
authorship. Would Peter, who must have been aware of the
careful distinction in the church in Jerusalem between apostles
and elders (cf. Ac. 15:2,6,22f; 16:4), have classified himself as an
elder? It can be answered that since he has already described
himself as an apostle (1:1) he can now drive home his points
(5:2–3) about pastoral oversight by humbly emphasising their
relevance to himself as much as to his readers, and that if the
writing were pseudonymous its author would have chosen the
apparently higher title.

**a witness of the sufferings of Christ:** at first sight this
suggests someone who has been an eye-witness of the crucifixion
but 'witness' does not necessarily mean 'eye-witness'; it also
indicates someone who gives a testimony though he has not seen
or heard an event (Jn 1:19; Rom. 3:21; 2 Cor. 1:12; Tit. 1:13;
Rev. 2:13); in this sense the word eventually came in its use in the
church to mean 'martyr' (this is its transliteration); Peter is dead
by the time of the letter and this last meaning does not fit the
present context. If we choose the sense 'eye-witness' we can argue
that it is a necessary part of the apparatus of pseudonymity and
therefore does not imply Petrine authorship. If, as is more
probable, we choose to understand it of one who testifies to a
truth, then there is no implication that the author saw the death
of Jesus, and in 1:19; 2:21–4; 3:18; 4:1 he has already testified to
its truth and importance. It is doubtful, in any case, if Peter was a
literal eye-witness of the crucifixion. However the phrase 'the
sufferings of (the) Christ' is identical with that in 4:13 and may
be taken to refer to the Messianic woes; to these the writer has
testified in 4:12–19; this gives **so** at the beginning of our verse a
real value in linking 4:12–19 to 5:1. Within 5:1 we then have the
same movement of thought as in 4:13, viz., from the woes to the
glory.

**a partaker in the glory that is to be revealed:** the 'glory' is
already present with the sufferer in the Messianic woes (4:14).
Selwyn sees in this phrase Peter's witness to his participation in the
transfiguration (Mk 9:2–8) and argues in support of this theory:
(i) The word 'partaker' implies a reference to some kind of
concrete experience; but participation in the Messianic woes also
fulfils this condition since for our writer these would be a concrete
event, or series of events. (ii) 'partaker', if referring to future

glory, should be 'one who is about to be a partaker' (i.e. with a future tense); but if the reference was to the transfiguration we should expect a past tense, 'one who was a partaker'. (iii) The transfiguration was a revelation of the glorified Christ rather than of the resurrected Christ; but this does not mean that a reference to 'glory' will imply a reference to the transfiguration. Moreover it is only in its present form that we can argue that the transfiguration relates to the glorified Christ; the account underwent considerable development in the early church and there is no reason to assume that the stories in the gospels would have been recognized by Peter as descriptions of his actual experience. More generally we can argue against Selwyn's view that the parallel reference in 4:13 to 'glory' indicates something in which all share and that therefore the experience of 5:1 is not something exclusive to the author.

2. Verses 2f. consist of a general statement on ministry followed by three similarly formed ('not . . . but . . .') antitheses explicating it. W. Nauck, 'Probleme des frühchristlichen Amtsverständnisses', *Z.N.W.* 48 (1957) 200–220, suspects that because of this structure and of similarities of thought and wording to contemporary Jewish and slightly later Christian statements a piece of early tradition is incorporated here.

**tend the flock of God:** for the image of the flock and its shepherd see on 2:25. It is used frequently in the NT and early Christian literature to describe the ministry and its work (Jn 21:15-17; Ac. 20:28; Eph. 4:11; 1 Clement 44:3; 54:2; Ignatius, *Philadelphians* 2:1; *Romans* 9:1). The shepherds do not own the flock; they oversee God's flock and are under a chief Shepherd (5:4).

RSVmg adds the words 'exercising the oversight' after 'charge'; the additional phrase represents one Greek word from the same root as 'Guardian' in 2:25 (which see). The root is very often linked to the 'shepherd' imagery in early Christian literature and this probably accounts for its insertion here in some manuscripts. If Nauck's hypothesis is correct that we have here a piece of primitive tradition, then our author may have added it himself and those strands of the textual tradition which knew the pre-Petrine formula have excluded it. Its presence adds nothing of importance to the thought.

**not by constraint:** did leaders in the church have to be coerced to act, and, if so, why? Because of the many duties and burdens of leadership, or, more probably, because of the dangers to leaders in time of persecution? The coercion was presumably by moral persuasion leading to some form of consecration service from which the elder could not afterwards resile.

**willingly:** the RSVmg adds to this 'as God would have you'. This is grammatically difficult and its meaning uncertain; it is probably original (though not to Nauck's supposed pre-Petrine form) and was later omitted in some manuscripts because of its difficulty. (Both of the additions in the RSVmg in this verse appear in P⁷²). It adds a religious dimension to 'willingly' which might not otherwise be clear; the elder's urge to perform his ministry must not come from his own enthusiasm but from his devotion to God.

**not for shameful gain:** church leaders would certainly have to deal with money (Ac. 4:34f; 6:1–3; 11:29f; Rom. 15:25 etc.). The context suggests that the danger does not lie so much in the temptation to enrich themselves from what passed through their hands as in the desire to accept office for the attached salary; the evidence indicates that church leaders were being paid in this period (Ac. 20:33f; 1 Cor. 9:7–14; 2 Cor. 12:13–18; 1 Tim. 5:17f; Mt. 10:10b). The peril of greed is recognized elsewhere in early Christian writing (1 Tim. 3:3; Tit. 1:7; Polycarp, *Philippians* 11:1f; *Didache* 15:1).

**but eagerly:** because they were serving God and rejoice to care for his sheep.

3. **not as domineering:** to extend their power and authority is one of the greatest of temptations to those in official positions. The true ideal for the Christian leader is given in the service of Jesus as summarised in Mk 10:42–5.

**in your charge:** the meaning of the Greek word rendered 'charge' is difficult. It probably refers as in the RSV to that part of the flock ('flock' is singular, 'charge' is plural) put in the charge of each elder, or group of elders, for which he is responsible to God; it may also suggest that these 'charges' are their part in the inheritance of God (the word is from the same root as that for 'inheritance').

**examples:** the ideal of service and of readiness to suffer is best presented not by exhortation but by example; men become aware of the depths of Christ's service through the sacrificial life of his followers, especially of those in leading positions in the church (1 Cor. 10:32–11:1; Phil. 3:17; 2 Th. 3:9).

4. **chief Shepherd:** already at 2:25 Jesus has been described

as 'the Shepherd' and now that other shepherds have been introduced it is natural to describe him as 'chief' (cf. Heb. 13:20). The under shepherds are given their reward, the 'crown of glory', by the chief Shepherd. In the OT God is described as the shepherd of Israel (Ezek. 34:15; Jer. 31:10); as the title 'Lord' (see on 2:3) was transferred from God to Christ, so also was the title 'Shepherd'. The use of one image to describe both the ministry of Jesus and that of the leaders of the church shows that the pattern of their ministry is to be that of Jesus' own ministry (Mk 10:42-5).
**is manifested,** i.e., in the Parousia; the implication, which is supported by the rest of the epistle, is that Christ will appear while they are still acting as shepherds, for the end is at hand(4:7).
**unfading:** *lit.* 'made of amaranths', an unfading flower.
**crown of glory:** in the ancient world crowns were associated among other things with royalty, with supernatural beings (the nimbus), with victory in athletic contests and in war, and with rewards for service to the state; it is the last which provides the background for the image here. The crown itself is participation in the glory that is to be revealed (5:1) at the parousia.

5a. **Likewise** indicates a new item of instruction (cf. 3:1,7).
**younger, elders:** is 'elders' now used in its primary sense of 'the elderly' implying that the 'younger' are the young in years (cf. 1 Tim. 5:1f), or are the 'younger' a definite group within the community like the group of 'elders'? The latter view (cf. Spicq) is attractive because: (i) It involves no change of meaning in 'elders' between 5:1-4 and 5:5. (ii) The 'younger' were recognized at times in Hellenistic society as an organized group (cf. C. A. Forbes, *Neoi*, Philadelphia, 1933). It is however difficult to find evidence of such a group in the early church; Ac. 5:6,10 possibly indicates their existence (cf. 1 Jn 2:13f). Polycarp, *Philippians* 5:3, clearly differentiates the 'younger' from the deacons. Whichever interpretation we choose we have no idea why the injunction is inserted; since this is a circular letter and probably incorporates here part of an ecclesiastical code there can be nothing in the actual situation of the readers to call it forth. It may be no more than a general admonition to reverence age or a rebuke to the younger for their general tendency to introduce ideas and ways which seem too revolutionary to the elderly. If 'elders' denotes a church office then it is not just reverence to age but obedience to ecclesiastical authority which is demanded (cf. Reicke).

5b. The exhortation now turns from particular groups within

the community to the community as a whole.

**Clothe yourselves:** the image is that of a garment being tied on, and very possibly reflects Jn 13 where Christ, about to wash the feet of his disciples, ties on a towel to perform this humble duty.

**humility:** see on 3:8. This virtue will hold the diverse parts of the community together (cf. Phil. 2:3) and is required as much of the leaders of the church as of those who are subject to them.

**God opposes . . . humble:** quoted from Prov. 3:34 (LXX) with 'Lord', which the Christians might take to be Jesus, changed to God. It is also quoted in Jas 4:6.

## CLOSING EXHORTATION TO STEADFASTNESS
### 5:6–11

It is not clear whether this section begins here or at 'Clothe yourselves . . .' in verse 5; at that point the writer began to address the community as a whole but continued to follow the line of thought of 5:1–5a; it is only in verse 6 that a new theme, suffering and steadfastness, appears. Boismard (*Quatre Hymnes baptismales* pp. 133–63; cf. Carrington, *op. cit.*, pp. 52–4) suggests that 5:5b–9 taken alongside Jas 4:6–10 indicates the use of another baptismal hymn. In both passages Prov. 3:34 is quoted with 'God' replacing the 'Lord' of the LXX, there is an exhortation to resist the devil and a promise that God will exalt those who humble themselves before him. The wording of the alleged hymn appears to be better preserved in James. Boismard suggests that the hymn would have been used in the baptismal liturgy prior to the act of baptism, at which point later liturgies include a renunciation of the devil and his works. Unfortunately there is not enough in common between 1 Peter and James to permit a clear reconstruction of the hymn nor even to allow us to deduce with any certainty that it was baptismal. We can say that both 1 Pet. 5:5b–9 and Jas 4:6–10 are indebted to early tradition which in some form, whether as a hymn or a catechism, must have held together the ideas they share. There is no need to argue for a literary dependence of either epistle on the other.

6. **therefore,** i.e. in view of the OT text just quoted; but the direction of thought changes; in verse 5 humility was inculcated as an attitude toward others, now it is an attitude toward God.

**Humble yourselves:** for Christian humility see on 3:8. Humility is now shown to spring from a right relation to God, from an acceptance of what he ordains—and the context implies that he ordains persecution.

**the mighty hand of God:** a phrase used frequently in the OT for God's acts of deliverance, e.g. Exod. 3:19; 6:1; Dt. 9:26; this meaning for the phrase accords with the exaltation of the readers but not with the call to humble themselves. The 'hand' of God is however also used in relation to God's discipline (Job 30:21; Ps. 32:4; Ezek. 20:34f) and this meaning is appropriate to the idea of humility. The hand which sends persecution (cf. 3:17; 4:19) also sends deliverance.

**in due time:** *lit.* 'in time', and the word is the same as that used at 1:5. Used by itself it can denote 'the last time' (Mt. 8:29; 1 Cor. 4:5), and this is the meaning here. God will exalt them when the period of suffering (the Messianic woes) is over and the Messiah has appeared.

**exalt:** the contrast 'be humbled/be exalted' is found in the Gospels (Mt. 23:12; Lk. 14:11; 18:14), but since 'the sentiment is thoroughly Hebraic' (Selwyn) there is no necessary dependence on the words of Jesus. God's hand will exalt them at the appearance of Christ which is very near (cf. 1:5; 4:7,13 etc.). The exhortation is not then a general religious sentiment but is eschatologically oriented.

7. **Cast all your anxieties on him:** the clause is a quotation of Ps. 55:22 in the LXX version and in the Greek of 1 Peter depends on 'humble yourselves' (verse 6); he who accepts what God ordains will also leave the resolution of his anxieties to God. Mt. 6:25–34 (cf. Lk. 12:22–31) connects freedom from anxiety with trust in God as Father. It is not directly stated what anxieties the writer has in mind; the context of persecution supplies practical content to the saying; Lk. 21:18 provides a similar assurance and Lk. 21:14f (cf. Mt. 10:19) indicates one possible anxiety.

**he cares about you:** 'The conception of God as concerned with the afflictions of man is the peculiar treasure of Judaic and Christian faith; Greek philosophy at its highest could formulate a doctrine of His perfect goodness, but could not even imagine in Him an active concern for mankind' (Beare).

8. **Be sober, be watchful:** the advice of verse 7 might perhaps engender fatalism or suggest that little effort was needed on the part of the readers; instead they must be thoroughly

alert. The two verbs recur together at 1 Th. 5:6 and may have formed part of regular Christian instruction in respect of persecution (Selwyn) or, since 1 Thessalonians like 1 Peter is much concerned with eschatology, more probably of the attitude to be adopted when the end is expected. Separately the verbs often carry this eschatological orientation ('watch': Mt. 24:42f; 25:13; Mk 13:34–7; 1 Th. 5:10; Rev. 3:2f; 16:15; 'sober': 1 Pet. 4:7; 1:13, and possibly 2 Tim. 4:5).

**Your adversary the devil:** belief in the devil appears only in the later parts of the OT (1 Chron. 21:1; Zech. 3:1); it had entered Judaism from Persian dualism and became increasingly accepted in the two centuries before Christ. It was an attempt to explain the existence of evil (contrast 1 Chron. 21:1 with 2 Sam. 24:1); the strong monotheism of Judaism prevented the devil occupying the same independent position over against God which the evil power possessed in Zoroastrianism. Gradually in Judaism, and later in Christianity, all the evil that afflicted the people of God, whether as a group or as individuals, was attributed to the devil. Here he is regarded as responsible for the persecutions by which the church is assailed; our author has elsewhere attributed them to God's will (3:17; 4:19; 5:6), but does not discuss the difficult theological and philosophical problems that arise.

**adversary:** the derivation of the word Satan gives it a meaning similar to 'adversary', i.e. one who opposes. On the 'devil' see E. Langton, *Essentials of Demonology*, London, 1949; T. Ling, *The Significance of Satan*, London, 1961; T. H. Gaster, 'Satan', *I.D.B.*, IV, pp. 224–8.

**a roaring lion:** the image is that of the cruel beast of prey. In Judaism persecutors were often described as lions (1QH 5:5ff; 1QpNah; see also the Targums on Isa. 35:9; Jer. 4:7; 5:6; Ezek. 19:6; cf. 2 Tim. 4:17). Entry of the image into Christianity may have been assisted by its appearance in Ps. 22:13; this psalm is cited frequently in the NT in relation to the sufferings of Christ. If there is any conception in this verse of the persecuting state as diabolical this would represent a different view of the state from that of 2:13–17; this will be discussed in relation to Babylon in 5:13.

9. **Resist him:** cf. Eph. 6:11–13; Jas 4:7. This does not mean that they should oppose their persecutors but that they should be steadfast under persecution so that they do not become victims of the lion through apostasy.

**firm in your faith:** strong in their conviction that theirs is the
true faith and that their trust in God means ultimate protection
(verse 10); cf. the use of 'believe, faith' at 1:8; 1:5,7.

**the same experience of suffering is required:** this clause is
very difficult grammatically. It is perhaps better to render it
(taking the verb 'is required' as a Greek middle voice), 'knowing
how to pay the same tax (Bigg quoting Hofmann, cf. N. Turner in
Vol. III of J. H. Moulton, *Grammar of New Testament Greek*,
Edinburgh, 1963, p. 55) of suffering'. Beare, using essentially the
same construction but adopting another meaning of the verb,
suggests a rendering similar to 'knowing how to fulfil the same
religious duty in respect of suffering'. If the verb is taken as a
passive then we might translate 'knowing that the same tax of
suffering will be paid by your brotherhood'. We need to note also
that the word translated 'suffering' is a plural in the Greek (it is the
same word as in 4:13; 5:1) and in each case we can render 'of the
sufferings', i.e. of the Messianic woes. The woes have to be completed (the word rendered 'required' carries this overtone of
meaning) and this is being accomplished by Peter's readers and
by the brotherhood throughout the world (cf. Col. 1:24); when
the woes are complete the parousia will take place.

**brotherhood:** cf. 1:22; 2:17; 3:8. Isolation in persecution
intensifies its agony; assurance that others are enduring it in the
same cause consoles (cf. Phil. 1:30). In the second century the
churches began to communicate to each other the records of their
martyrs (e.g. *Martyrdom of Polycarp*).

10–11. These verses form the conclusion to the thought of the
letter (5:12–14 are personal greetings). They assure the readers
that since they have been chosen by God they will not be abandoned by him to their persecutors but preserved for eternal life
(cf. Phil. 1:6; 1 Th. 5:23f; 2 Th. 2:16f). If the devil is their
opponent they are not left to resist him by themselves but have a
greater, God, on their side.

**after you have suffered a little while:** the persecutions
cannot last long; then the Messiah will be revealed (1:6f) and
they will have come to God's eternal glory (cf. Rom. 8:18;
2 Cor. 4:17).

**the God of all grace:** in 4:10 the emphasis lay on the varied
nature of God's gifts of grace, here it is on their all-embracing
nature and this is set out in the remainder of the verse; God's
gifts are sufficient for every occasion. The grace of God is seen in

that he both calls the readers to membership in his people and will protect them until he brings them to his glory (cf. 2 Cor. 1:3ff; 12:9).

**called to his eternal glory:** cf. Rom. 8:28–30; 1 Th. 2:12; 2 Th. 2:14 (on 'called' cf. 1:15; 2:9). In contrast to the 'little while' they suffer, the time of their participation in God's glory will be eternal. The initial call is the call to the fullness of salvation, and not just a call to suffering or to be a Christian on earth. 'glory', cf. 1:11,21; 4:13f; 5:1,4.

**in Christ:** taken here closely with 'glory' it might also be taken with 'called' (cf. 1 Cor. 7:22). It is only because of God's activity in and through Christ that they can be called to be members of his people and eventually participate in his glory. On the use in 1 Peter of this Pauline phrase cf. p. 34 and notes on 3:16.

**himself:** himself, and no other; the word is emphatic.

**restore, establish and strengthen you:** the verbs testify to the care that God has for his church; it will finally be perfected, established in all the glory it should have, and the ground which had been shaken by persecution once again steadied beneath the feet of its members. It is possible that a fourth verb 'and settle' should be added as in RSVmg after 'strengthen'; its addition or omission does not affect the general sense.

11. Another doxology similar to 4:11 but omitting the reference to glory. The emphasis that is thereby produced on God's power, **dominion,** is appropriate since it is through his power that the Christians will be preserved in persecution.

**Amen:** see on 4:11.


## FINAL GREETINGS 5:12–14

As in the letters of Paul we conclude with personal greetings and good wishes. Paul, who in some instances at any rate, dictated his letters to a secretary, normally added the last sentences in his own hand (1 Cor. 16:21; Gal. 6:11; Col. 4:18; 2 Th. 3:17). If Peter dictated the present letter to Silvanus or left Silvanus to compose it, he may have added these verses on his own, but we would have expected him to indicate it. If the letter is non-Petrine then the personal references are part of the apparatus of pseudonymity. (On the authorship see pp. 49ff).

12. **By Silvanus:** the Greek is ambiguous and could mean:

(i) Silvanus is to carry the letter to the churches; (ii) it was dictated to him; or (iii) he composed it under Peter's general instruction. Of course Silvanus might both have had some share in the writing and also been the bearer of the letter. Beare doubts if one person would have been expected to carry the letter to all the churches. On Silvanus see pp. 55ff.

**a faithful brother:** the simple description 'brother' does not preclude Silvanus from being a person of importance (cf. 2 Cor. 1:1; 2:13; Eph. 6:21). For 'brother' see on 1:22.

**as I regard him:** this does not imply that others have doubted the ability of Silvanus but emphasises Peter's confidence in his fidelity.

**briefly:** a polite formula, frequent in letters (cf. Heb. 13:22). 1 Peter is in any case brief in comparison to the importance of its subject matter.

**exhorting:** much of the letter has been taken up with 'exhortation'. This was a type of writing well-known in the early church. 'exhorting' does not govern 'that this is . . .' but is taken up by 'stand fast in it'.

**declaring that:** the author confirms the testimony that he has given throughout to the grace of God. 'exhorting and declaring' together give an excellent summary of the purpose of the letter (cf. pp. 13f).

**this is the true grace of God,** i.e. what has been declared throughout the whole letter, cf. 1:3-12; 2:4-10; 3:13-4:7a; and especially 5:10 where we saw that it included the call of God and his ultimate preservation of those whom he called.

**stand fast in it:** persecution threatens; let them cleave to God's redeeming might.

13. **She who is at Babylon, who is likewise chosen:** *lit.,* 'the fellow-elect one (feminine gender) in Babylon'; this must refer either to a female person or to something personified as a female person. If it is an actual person she can only be Peter's wife (cf. 1 Cor. 9:5), but it is a strange way to introduce her; we would expect 'with me' rather than 'in Babylon'; she would hardly have been so well-known over so wide an area that such a vague reference would identify her; moreover the 'fellow' of 'fellow-elect' implies 'fellow-elect' with the readers and not with the writer. The great majority of commentators correctly assume that we have a personification and that the church in Babylon is intended. In Greek the word for church is feminine and the

church is often portrayed as a female person, the bride of Christ (e.g. Eph. 5:22-33; Rev. 19:7f; 21:2f; 22:17). We find the same personalisation of the church at 2 Jn 1,13. If it is objected that it is strange to find the greetings of a church and of a person (Mark) set alongside one another, then it should be noted that we have the same in 1 Cor. 16:19-20.

**chosen:** see on 1:2.

**Babylon:** is the name symbolic or real? There were two Babylons, one by the Euphrates and one in Egypt, but there is no tradition associating Peter with either. If then we take it as symbolical it may denote either a real place or an idea. If the latter, it would denote the place of exile which Babylon had been in the OT, for this epistle is concerned with Christians as exiles (1:1f; 2:11f). However both writer and readers are exiles in this sense and there is nothing especially significant in saying that 'Peter' was writing from exile: so used the term is inappropriate as a symbol for the place of writing. If we take it to signify a real place we find support for this in contemporary and later Judaism which used Babylon as a code name for Rome (2 Baruch 11:1f; 67:7; 2 Esd. 3:1f,28; *Sibylline Oracles* 5:143,157ff; it also appears in the Rabbinic literature). The Christian church also used it in its apocalyptic literature (Rev. 14:8; 16:19-18:24). Moreover Christian tradition from an early age associated Peter with Rome (see p. 65), where it was believed that he suffered martyrdom in the Neronic persecutions. We conclude that Babylon indicates Rome here. The OT prophets depicted Babylon as a place of great wealth, tyranny, idolatry and vice, standing under God's judgement; this is the way in which Rome is pictured in Revelation. It also fits the situation of our letter, for judgement is just about to break (4:7,12-19 etc.). But is there a clash here with 2:13-17 where obedience to Roman authority is taught? We may note: (i) 2:13-17 incorporates traditional Christian teaching, deriving from a time when Rome was looked on as a protector; Rome, understood as Babylon, represents a new view; in such cases the traditional often continues alongside the new without the conflict being observed. (ii) To say that Rome stands under judgement as Babylon did does not of itself imply that Rome ought to be disobeyed; it is God who will bring the judgement and not man; until that time man must accept the present order of the world. (iii) In the Pastorals Paul is depicted as, or actually is, the prisoner of the Romans, yet he evinces the same attitude to Rome which we find in 2:13–17 (cf. 1 Tim. 2:1–3; Tit. 3:1–3); if the Pastorals are post-Pauline then they come from a period in which Paul with many other Christians was known to have died at the hands of Rome. In the same way in 1 Clement 59–61 we have the attitude of 2:13–17; yet the author is very much aware of the Neronic persecutions. (iv) Any other attitude than that of 2:13–17 would have been almost impossible; rebellion would have been completely crushed. (v) Members of small sects who see all government as diabolical are normally very law-abiding.

Recently C. H. Hunzinger, 'Babylon als Deckname für Rom und die Datierung des 1 Petrusbriefes' in *Gottes Wort und Gottesland* (ed. H. Reventlow) Göttingen, 1965, pp. 65–77, has asked why and when the Jews came to describe Rome as Babylon. He points out that the description only appears in Jewish tradition after 70 A.D., i.e. after the destruction of the Temple. Prior to 70 A.D. other names (e.g. Edom) were in use to describe Rome. Babylon was introduced therefore after 70 A.D. to indicate Rome as destroyer of the Temple, for Babylon had been responsible for the destruction of the first Temple. In Christian literature with the possible exception of 1 Peter all its appearances (e.g. in Revelation) are post 70 A.D. Since it is unlikely that the Jews borrowed the usage from Christians this suggests that 1 Peter, or at least 5:12–14, must come from the period after the fall of Jerusalem. On Babylon see K. G. Kuhn, *T.D.N.T.*, I, pp. 514–7; P. S. Minear, *I.D.B.*, I, p. 338.

**my son Mark:** a real person but not a real son is meant (cf. the relationship of Paul and Timothy in 1 Cor. 4:17); John Mark is intended. He came from a Jerusalem family (Ac. 12:12), was a relative of Barnabas (Col. 4:10), a companion of Paul and Barnabas in missionary work (Ac. 13:4–13), then, after Paul refused to take him again, a companion of Barnabas alone (Ac. 15:37–9); he appears to have been reconciled to Paul later (Col. 4:10; Phm. 24; 2 Tim. 4:11). A strong tradition going back to Papias (see Eusebius, *Ecclesiastical History*, III, 39:15) says that he was Peter's 'interpreter' (the precise meaning of the word is uncertain) in the authorship of the second gospel. His is thus a suitable name to appear in a work emanating from a Petrine school.

14. **the kiss of love:** Paul refers to the 'holy kiss' (Rom. 16:16; 1 Cor. 16:20; 2 Cor. 13:12; 1 Th. 5:26). By the middle of the second century the kiss had a regular place in the eucharistic

liturgy (cf. Justin Martyr, *Apology*, I, 65:2). Since in those letters in which it is mentioned it appears in the final greetings it may have been given in the Christian assembly after the reading of letters received from Christian leaders. In any case it is essentially a sign of fellowship and its use may not have been restricted to the liturgy.

**Peace to all of you:** the Pauline letters normally conclude with a similar benediction, with 'grace' replacing 'peace', but Paul does have similar prayers with 'peace' (Rom. 15:33; Eph. 6:23; 1 Th. 5:23; 2 Th. 3:16; cf. 3 Jn 15). Our writer may have chosen 'peace' here because he has just used 'grace' in verse 12. It is peculiarly appropriate to a situation of outward turmoil and persecution. For its meaning see notes on 1:2.

**that are in Christ:** the early church does not appear to have used the term 'Christian' regularly: we find it first on the lips of outsiders (Ac. 11:26; 26:28). The present phrase, which Paul made popular, implies the same as Christian but is more profound since it includes the concept of personal fellowship with Christ.

# INDEX

# INDEX

EREX

EX

Shepherd, M.H., 69, 167
shepherds, 123, 169–71
*Sibylline Oracles*, 178
Sidebottom, E.M., 44
Silas, Silvanus, 20, 49, 55–9, 61, 176f
Sinope, 15f
sin, sins, 86, 96f, 110f, 120–3, 137f,
    147, 151–4, 157f, 159
slaves, 17, 47f, 116–23
Snaith, N., 87, 142
sobriety, 84f, 159, 173f
Soden, H. von, 58, 78
soul, 80, 92, 110f, 142f, 166
Spicq, C., 171
Spirit of God, 48, 71f, 81–3, 101f, 103f,
    109, 111, 125f, 139–41, 157, 163f
spirit, human, 125f, 129, 139, 142f
spirits, the, 139–46, 149, 150, 156
Stacey, W.D., 111, 139
state, the, 33, 36–42, 47f, 112–16, 174,
    178f
Stibbs, see Walls
Stoicism, 17, 94f, 98
stone, cornerstone, 53, 100–2, 106f
Streeter, B.H., 20, 22, 64
style of letter, 26f, 49
subjection, submission, 113, 117, 124,
    126f, 148f
Suetonius, 111
suffering, 22, 36–42, 54, 78, 81, 83f,
    118–23, 131–5, 137, 150–2, 162–6
    172–6
sufferings of Christ, see Christ
    see also Messianic woes

### T

Tacitus, 41f, 111
Targums, 107f, 174
Taylor, V., 74, 90, 122
temple, 101–4
Tertullian, 124
*Testament of Solomon*, 106
*Testaments of the Twelve Patriarchs*, 102,
    112, 125, 143, 145, 149
thanksgiving, 73
1 & 2 Thessalonians, 32, 35, 42, 55f,
    129f, 156, 173f
Thornton, T.C.G., 23

Toynbee, J.M.C., 65
traditional material, 22, 24f, 26f, 27,
    28–36, 43, 47–9, 50, 52, 56, 57,
    60, 91f, 94, 100, 105f, 120, 129f,
    135–9, 149, 158–61, 169f, 172
Trajan, 16, 18, 39–42, 44f, 63
transfiguration, see Christ
Trinity, the, 72, 74
truth, 93
Turner, N., 175
typology, 147

### U

unity of 1 Peter, 20–8
Unnik, W.C. van, 42, 45, 112, 119,
    166

### V

Vaux, R. de, 90
Vermes, G., 102, 130
Vespasian, 42
victory of Christ, 135–50

### W

Walls, A.F. and Stibbs, A.M., 39, 51f,
    53f, 61f, 151
Wand, J.W.C., 17, 53f, 77, 132, 134,
    151
Weidinger, K., 31
Weiss, J., 18
Whiteley, D.E.H., 90
Williams, C.S.C., 18, 62
Windisch, H., 20, 73, 120, 122, 135
wives, 47f, 123–8
woes, Messianic, see Messianic woes
Wohlenberg, 83
word of God, the, 75, 94–6, 98, 99,
    124f, 160
wrong-doers, 111f, 118, 131, 164

### Y

younger, the, 167–71

### Z

Zahn, 50, 55
Zealots, 33, 113, 132
Zerwick, 132
Zion, 106